Acclaim for Alma Guillermoprieto's

Dancing with Cuba

"A pleasure to read, full of humanity, sly humor, curiosity and knowledge." —Katha Pollitt, *The New York Times Book Review*

"Written with the deftness that has made Guillermoprieto's dispatches in *The New Yorker* some of the best writing on Latin America, *Dancing with Cuba* makes a significant contribution to the in-depth understanding of contemporary Cuba."
—*The Miami Herald*

"Few dancers write memoirs, and so the world of dance remains an elegant mystery to many of us. . . . This is a tale, then, of artists and poets, dancers and architects—bewildered, always in conflict, trying to keep alive standards which they knew were essential, but which were also suspect, not to say dangerous." —Doris Lessing, *The New York Observer*

"An honest memoir filled with the struggles most young people wrestle with: love, identity and idealism." —*USA Today*

"The memoir's greatest strength is its ability to infect the reader with the feverish, hopeful and heartbreaking sense of the early days of the revolution." —*Elle*

"Guillermoprieto . . . is a sensualist and a dramatist in prose. . . . *Dancing with Cuba* seethes with confusion, passion, and anger." —*The Village Voice*

"As much a pleasure as an astonishment." —*Harper's*

"Excellent. . . . Guillermoprieto writes so well."   —*Newsday*

"Guillermoprieto brings out the flavor of the time . . . insightful."   —*Street Weekly* (Miami)

"[*Dancing with Cuba*] is a loose mix of half-memories, reporting and musings on the place and meaning of art. . . . The mix works for some of the same reasons Guillermoprieto had such difficulty in Cuba—the sophisticated, intelligent singularity of her voice, her insistence on recognizing life's grays and her sly wit."   —*Associated Press*

"A bittersweet page-turner."   —*Dance Teacher* magazine

"[*Dancing with Cuba*] is elegantly written and captures both the spirit and rhythms of Cuba during a period of dramatic change and political upheaval."   —*Tucson Citizen*

"A vivid memoir."   —*The Wall Street Journal*

"In recalling and reconstructing those days, [Guillermoprieto] has given us a convincing portrait of a young woman torn between her sympathy for those in need and her desire to do nothing except her art, between her conviction that the Castroites were trying to do good and her revulsion at their rhetoric, their methods and their very selves."
                                   —*The Washington Post Book World*

Alma Guillermoprieto

Dancing with Cuba

Alma Guillermoprieto writes frequently for *The New Yorker* (where the first chapter of this book appeared in 2002) and *The New York Review of Books*. She is the author of *Looking for History*, *The Heart That Bleeds*, and *Samba*, and she was named a MacArthur Fellow in 1995. Raised in Mexico and the United States, she now makes her home in Mexico City.

Dancing with Cuba

Dancing with Cuba

A MEMOIR OF THE REVOLUTION

Alma Guillermoprieto

TRANSLATED FROM THE SPANISH
BY ESTHER ALLEN

VINTAGE BOOKS
A DIVISION OF RANDOM HOUSE, INC.
NEW YORK

The Library of Congress has cataloged the Pantheon edition as follows:
Guillermoprieto, Alma.
Dancing with Cuba: a memoir of the revolution / Alma Guillermoprieto.
p. cm.
1. Cuba—Description and travel. 2. Cuba—History—1959–.
3. Guillermoprieto, Alma, 1949– —Travel—Cuba. I. Title.
FI765.3.G85 2004
972.9I06'4—dc2I
2003044200

Vintage ISBN: 0-375-72581-4

Pa' que bailen los muchachos

Contents

Dancing with Cuba

Prologue: After Havana

More than three decades ago I spent six months teaching modern dance in Cuba. From that experience I've retained only my fragmented memories and a few concrete souvenirs that help me prove to myself, when I have doubts, that I really did go on that journey that so thoroughly unraveled my life.

Among the shards that survive is a box made of tropical wood inlaid with silver thread: the word *vuelve* (come back) has been clumsily engraved with a knife or nail inside the lid. Next, a spiral notebook: in the few pages of it that are left, I find notes from a teachers' meeting, a few other reflections, and the originals of the letters I wrote to my students at the end of the course. Those letters were of no use to me at all when it came to reconstructing my stay in Cuba: I couldn't match the students in my memory with the names that appear in the notebook; nor, to my embarrassment, was I able to read all the way through any of the letters, written by the inept young woman I once was.

For evidence that my time at the dance school of the Escuelas Nacionales de Arte wasn't as disastrous for those kids as it ended up being for me, I have to turn to the little wooden box, which the administrative staff gave me on the last day of class, and to another little box made of white cardboard—the kind a rosary would come in—that was my gift from the students. The day before, in farewell, I had given them two boxes of chocolates, an exceptional luxury to which only we foreigners were granted access, thanks to a special ration card that authorized us to make such exotic purchases in a special store. When one of the students saw the chocolates, she instructed the others never to eat them but to keep them in eternal memory of me. Twenty-four hours later I was extraordinarily relieved to see that they had disappeared down to the last sweet. In their place the students gave me the white box: inside was a kind of crude puppet made with thread and the foil used to wrap the chocolates. A few years ago I discovered that although the box was still in its place, along with another of that era's luxuries—the cotton in which the doll was wrapped—I had lost an essential component of the gift: the lid, on which the students had written their names in tiny letters.

With nothing to go on but this fistful of tatters, it would be absurd to claim that the following pages are a reliable historical account of the events that took place in my life during those six months. Yet this is not a novel. It is a faithful transcription of my memories, some of them hazy, others riddled with holes left by the passage of the years, others patched up by time and the filters of experience and distance, and still others, no doubt, completely invented by the stubborn narrator we all have within us, who wants things to be the way they sound best to us now, and not the way they were.

I must suppose that all the dialogue here is invented, though it seems to me to have been dictated from some intact corner of memory. The letters are reconstructions. As far as possible, I've tried to protect the potential victims of my memory by changing names and assembling composite characters, notably in the case of Eduardo the guerrilla and his successors, but in the case of the historical figures and the school staff, this made no sense. Elfriede Mahler, Lorna Burdsall, Teresa González, and Mario Hidalgo (as well as Roque Dalton, Oscar Lewis, and the legendary and now deceased Manuel Piñeiro) are who they are. I deeply regret that Elfriede is no longer alive to defend herself from what in all certainty are the many injustices my animosity continues to inflict on her.

ONE

New York

One autumn day in 1969, before the start of the advanced class at the Merce Cunningham dance studio, Merce came over to me and said that there were two opportunities for teaching modern dance that he thought might interest me. One was in Caracas, with a group of dancers who were only just forming their own company, and the other was in Havana, where there was a government-funded school dedicated to modern dance.

My life in dance had been routine and predictable until then, if not exactly normal. In Mexico, my native country, I joined a modern dance company at the age of twelve. At sixteen I left my father's home and traveled to New York to live with my mother, who had moved here following her separation from my father. I kept on dancing. At first I took classes at the Martha Graham studio. In the world of modern dance the brilliant, temperamental Martha was the most revered choreographer. Starting in the 1930s, she had revolutionized not only dance but theater as well; her use of sets and costumes turned on its head every standard notion of what can be done and communicated on a stage. Her quest for a body language that reflected the deepest inner conflicts, and the way she used gestures and movements to stage great myths, centering them on the internal universe of a single woman—Medea, Joan of Arc, Eve, all of them ultimately Martha herself in any case—brought her admirers and disciples from all the arts. She was, moreover, the first creator of modern dance to devise a truly universal dance technique out of the movements she developed in her choreography. I had studied Graham technique in Mexico, and one of my reasons for moving to New York had been to train directly at the source, at Martha's studio on East Sixty-third Street.

By that time, in the mid-1960s, Martha was very old and more or less pickled in alcohol. She put in rare appearances at her own studio, interrupting even a class that one of her best dancers was teaching to hurl philosophical exhortations and wounding comments at us, mocking our lack of passion and our flabby muscles. One of my most terrifying memories is of a mute hiatus during a class when all of us stood frozen in some pose Martha had demanded while she moved through the room, pinching this dancer in a rage, giving that one a tongue-lashing. Pain was necessary for dance, she always said, and I think at that stage in her life she wanted to contribute to our training by guaranteeing that we would suffer. After a couple of years of this I felt the need for a less orthodox and oppressive atmosphere and switched to the Cunningham studio, partly because I admired Merce's work with all my heart and partly because, after Martha's, Merce's studio was the best known.

Elegant, alert, and unfailingly courteous, Merce Cunningham was an established artist at the forefront of the Manhattan avant-garde. Modern dance has always been an art of the few, and there are not many choreographers who, like Merce, can afford the luxury of a standing company, and fewer still who have a studio where they and their company can earn money and create a pool of future dancers by offering daily classes. Even so, the studio and the classes barely enabled Merce and his company members to get by. His audience was devoted but small, and during performances one sometimes heard boos and hisses from baffled spectators who hadn't imagined, when they purchased their tickets, that the dancers would not go *en pointe* and that the accompaniment would be not tuneful music but a series of sounds generally produced at random, either on traditional instruments like John Cage's delightful "prepared piano" or, more often, by means of electronic gadgets. That was the case in *Winterbranch,* a rather long dance with no stage light that was performed throughout to a very loud metallic screech—hard even for the dancers to take.

Friend, collaborator, and source of inspiration to artists like Jasper Johns and Robert Rauschenberg, lifelong companion and creative partner of the composer John Cage, Merce, always an innovator, always evolving, was respected even by his detractors for the clean harmony of his work, for the simple, lucid logic of the technique taught at his studio, and for the modest, unassuming way he had one day taken his leave of Martha's company, where he had been a principal dancer. Without any rhetorical fuss he left behind the obsession with passion and narrative that was characteristic of Martha and her disciples; the use of dramaturgy as the connecting thread of choreography; and rhythmic music that guided the dancers' movements like a tambourine leading a trained bear in a circus. Instead, he chose to pursue the meandering paths of abstraction, chance, and Zen philosophy. Yet his avant-garde experiments never interfered with the technical perfection and extraordinary refinement of his choreography. In his own way he was a classicist.

Those of us who left Martha's studio for Merce's were attracted by that Apollonian temperament, which demanded concentration and intensity but rejected drama. It was mainly women who came to his little studio on Third Avenue at Thirty-third Street to take beginning, intermediate, and advanced classes, and quite a few of us were in flight from Martha. Merce's courteous distance came as cool salve on a burn, though it too had its price. Merce sometimes taught a beginners' class that started at six P.M. He didn't say much but would correct the students very patiently, and several of the more advanced dancers, including some who were already members of the company, would take the six o'clock class in the hope that Merce would at least cast a glance at them. All of us saw him as a flame flickering in a dark chapel. We spoke his name as if it were written entirely in capital letters, and we laid siege to him with our eyes. In return, he almost never said a word to any of us.

The fleeting heyday of American dance was just beginning, and most of us who were to be found in the modern dance studios then, with who knows what tangle of secret dreams inside us, had to work as secretaries or waitresses (I was the latter) in order to pay for classes and our own spartan expenses. This meant that we came to class already tired. Merce's studio was a bare cave that stank of sweat and often lacked heat on the coldest winter days. Our motley layers of sweaters and sweatpants couldn't protect us from the cold. The concrete floor was covered with shabby black linoleum, and before class we would wrap tape around our feet in an effort to close up the alarming cracks that appeared on our bare soles as we spun across that adhesive surface. After class we rinsed off the sweat as best we could at the sink in the studio's tiny bathroom, then went home on the subway, sprawled in the seats to give our rebellious muscles some relief. All of this took its toll on our bodies, but we had no money for massages or therapies. As it was, David Vaughan, the brisk but softhearted Englishman who took our money at the front desk—and who is to this day the company's resident historian—more often than not gave us a stern look and a class ticket on credit. We went on ridiculous diets: a friend asked me privately one afternoon, with a blush, whether I thought constipation could have a significant effect on your weight; she'd been feeding on lettuce and broccoli for a week, had been constipated for five days, and had weighed herself on five scales but hadn't lost a pound on any of them. Generally, by about age thirty-five, dancers no longer have healthy feet or knees or much elasticity left in their tendons, ligaments, and joints. We were eighteen, twenty, twenty-five years old, and we were the oldest young people in the world: our time was already running out.

Men were so scarce in this world that choreographers fought over them even if their feet were as flat as pancakes and their shoulders looked as if they'd been left dangling from a hook at birth. They strolled into class with a self-sufficient air, while we women were fervent and eternal supplicants, forever hoping against hope, suicidal gamblers who—despite the mirror's daily confirmation that our insteps were too low, our hips too wide, our legs too short, our arms too long, and our backs too stiff— would nevertheless go off to class in search of the miracle that would fulfill all our desires. *Look at me, say I'm beautiful, say I'm for you. Choose me. Let me dance in your company.*

When Merce didn't teach the beginners' class himself, he was replaced by one of the younger members of his company. The intermediate class was passed around among more established members of the company, and when they were on tour, it was taught by other dancers, most of whom had performed with Merce at some point. Though the intermediate class seemed to hold little interest for him and he rarely taught it, on his way up to his small apartment over the dance studio he used to pause in the doorway for a few moments, one shoulder lightly resting against the frame, his long arms folded neatly against his torso, his long legs together, and his curly head—heavy and canine—tilted attentively to one side, watching us. I would watch him too out of the corner of my eye, and I liked to think that he was sending me some correction with his gaze, which I caught in midflight and obeyed. I liked even more to think that he was aware that I did.

It was after one of those classes that he approached me for the first time. Merce, then fifty years old, employed certain well-worn theatrical tricks that nevertheless worked their full effect on us. One consisted of deploying his immense courtesy to convey the impression that you were doing him a favor by listening to him; another was to speak so softly that you were forced to concentrate completely on his words. That afternoon he leaned toward me to murmur that if I agreed and it was convenient, I might want to start taking the advanced class (which he almost invariably taught himself). That encounter, which can't have lasted more than thirty seconds, was one of the heart-stopping moments of my life.

It would never have occurred to me that there might be anything better in life than dance. I suffered because it was my destiny to suffer: I was plagued, among other things, by crippling shyness, by a sense that I was superfluous in the world, by a feeling that my face and body were unacceptable, by insomnia, loneliness, and severe anxiety attacks that often kept me even from going to class. But I had no complaints at all about my life, which, seen from this distance, truly was marvelous.

My comrades in enchantment and I stood in line for three

whole nights, one after the other, to buy cheap tickets for the standing-room section of the Metropolitan Opera House. (Someone always brought coffee and cookies for everyone in the line, and the spirit of solidarity was absolute.) For three nights running we watched Rudolf Nureyev and Margot Fonteyn perform Kenneth MacMillan's *Romeo and Juliet*. We watched all three performances standing up but at the back of the orchestra section, at much closer range than we could otherwise have afforded. The memory of Nureyev falling to his knees in ecstasy to cover Fonteyn's skirt with kisses still takes my breath away. The Martha Graham company was at the height of its glory. In 1965, during a three-week season at the Mark Hellinger Theatre, we took in the entire repertory of that monstrous genius (again, standing behind the last row in the orchestra section). During those three weeks our state of exaltation was so great that we managed only with difficulty to eat or speak.

My romance with Merce began the following year. Several of us went to a performance in a small auditorium at Hunter College, and the sight of such pure, limpid dance, so free of sentimental baggage that it seemed to be performed by a flock of subtle, iridescent birds, convinced me immediately that I was in the presence of a true revolutionary. It wasn't long before I left Martha's studio.

New York City offered us much more than dance. We watched Japanese and Italian movies at the Thalia and alternative films at midnight at the Waverly or the Bleecker Street Cinema. We learned that if we arrived at the New York State Theater after the first intermission, the ushers would let us in to watch the rest of the New York City Ballet's program free, and thus we became familiar with a good part of George Balanchine's repertory. At the Apollo Theater we saw Wilson Pickett and James Brown; at the Fillmore East, Jefferson Airplane and Janis Joplin. We had a friend who worked as an usher and helped us sneak into Carnegie Hall, and we put together expert picnics in Central Park while waiting in line for free tickets to the performances there.

One day we heard that the revolution was in Brooklyn, and we went to the Academy of Music—again, we stood in line all afternoon, this time waiting for half-price tickets—to see the leg-

endary Living Theatre, back in New York after a long exile in
Europe. The actors took their clothes off and crawled naked all
over the audience, which struck us as thrilling in the extreme.
It was the period when the traditional divisions were beginning
to blur between classical and modern dance, dance and the martial arts, dance and theater, improvisation and performance. Joe
Chaikin and Jean-Claude van Itallie, Robert Wilson, and the actors at the Performing Garage were inventing revolutionary theatrical forms, and we were inventing a new form of dance.

I say "we" because though I was neither a choreographer nor a
famous, outstanding, or even promising dancer, I too was part of
this avant-garde, dancing here and there with choreographers
who were getting their start. There was Margaret Jenkins, for
example, a dancer who taught Merce's intermediate class when
the company was on tour, and who was starting to create her own
choreography: she'd book a performance at a theater in Queens
or in a Staten Island gym and then ask several of us who took her
class to rehearse with her. I believe that she paid us five dollars a
week for the rehearsals and thirty dollars for the performance.
But I would have paid for the chance to perform, especially when
it came to the experiments concocted by Elaine Shipman, one of
my best friends, who was clearly destined for the opposite of
stardom.

Elaine earned her living as an artist's model and was so beautiful that just looking at her filled me with delight. She had elegantly sculpted cheekbones, skin the color of black coffee. She
also had the flattest, most inflexible feet I've ever seen, and a
little belly—as if she were three months pregnant—that never
went away. Long before it became fashionable, she refused to
straighten her hair and wore it in an Afro cut close to the skull;
artifice simply wasn't her style. Every other dancer in the world,
including me, learned to dance by imitation: when we saw our
first dance teacher walking with toes like newly sharpened pencils, with legs stretched stiffly and heels turned out, we understood immediately that this was a superior mode of locomotion,
and sought to do likewise. Elaine's temperament resisted this
kind of subjugation, to the point that she had to struggle to
learn the movement sequences in any choreography but her own.

Year after year she has remained incapable of self-betrayal or attempting anything that looks the least bit fake. Her childhood dance teachers were descended from Isadora Duncan's school of movement, and she retains that arcadian, lyrical, spontaneous, and organic vision of dance. We took the same classes and stood in line together to see Martha's company perform, and she was the person I most enjoyed playing at being soignée with. We would array ourselves to what we thought was devastatingly elegant effect in velvets and plumes acquired in Lower East Side flea markets, then perch at the bar of the Russian Tea Room and order one silk stockings each, which we consumed in ladylike sips, both to keep from getting drunk and to stretch out the evening. We carried precisely enough cash for the drink, the tip, and the subway fare home.

Shy and defenseless as she was, Elaine managed to find a sponsor in Baltimore and another one in Newport for her "events." (The word *happening* was vulgar.) Our "company"—there were four or eight of us, depending on the day of the week—performed in an avant-garde gallery in the depths of a gloomy postindustrial area that was not yet SoHo. We also danced on the rusty rails of an old train yard in Baltimore, before an audience of perhaps twenty people. With Elaine's best friend Harry Sheppard, who remained her artistic partner until he died of AIDS, we made a movie. I can't remember much about my role, except that Elaine dressed me in a very beautiful full-length white dressing gown, and I had to appear and disappear from a tree. To this day, Elaine's work very much resembles her, it seems to me; it remains so natural that one can't help being charmed, and it is filled with startling moments of evocative power.

One evening in Merce's dressing room another of my friends, Graciela Figueroa, mentioned that she had started rehearsing with an odd woman who had a funny name—Twyla Tharp—and she was seriously considering reaching the conclusion that the woman was a genius. That was how Graciela talked; she was the only woman friend I had who read Søren Kierkegaard and

Theodor Adorno, and for years, against all logic, I was convinced that Julio Cortázar had based the character of La Maga in his novel *Hopscotch* on her. She was from Uruguay, penniless, and eternally harried by visa problems; though Merce's studio was accredited by the Immigration and Naturalization Service to authorize temporary student visas, they could be renewed only three or four times. And there wasn't a dancer in the world— except for defectors from the Kirov or the Bolshoi—who could get a green card. I had a resident visa and no problems with the government thanks to my mother, who was Guatemalan by birth but had taken U.S. citizenship long ago.

Graciela's accent, when she spoke English, was like Elaine's feet—absolutely resistant to civilization. *Chessss,* she would say, meaning "yes," and the word *unbelievable,* which she often used, came out of her mouth in about seventeen syllables. She also shared Elaine's unruly quality—a kind of gorgeous awkwardness in the way she moved—but in her case it was joined with great strength, astonishing speed, and enormous daring. It's possible that no other woman has ever leaped as high on a stage as she did. I, for one, have never seen anyone do so.

Yes, said Graciela, this Twyla woman was on the strange side, something new. A bit of a drill sergeant, but her work was very interesting: she didn't use music or even electronic accompaniment, like Merce, but total silence. At rehearsals the dancers used tennis shoes rather than ballet slippers or bare feet, and they struggled with movements that seemed improvised and *completely casual*—Graciela drove home the consonants of *completely* with a hammer and stretched *casual* out into four syllables— but in fact were diabolically hard. Twyla had suggested to Graciela—and here Graciela neighed like a colt—that she take ballet classes.

I never had the opportunity to see one of Twyla Tharp's events from the audience. Not long after Graciela started working with her, she told me that Twyla was putting together a large open-air piece called *Medley,* with sixty dancers (*sixty dancers!*—instantly I took the measure of her ambition and her madness), and it might not be a bad idea for me to audition. Two weeks later I started rehearsing with Twyla.

At eight o'clock on a balmy summer morning a breath of mist rises from the grass of Central Park's Great Lawn and drifts above it for a few fleeting minutes. It's only the evaporation of the previous night's dew, a flimsy, transparent veil that vanishes in the first breeze, but if you are fortunate enough to be dancing on that meadow at that hour, it serves to reinforce the feeling that you are floating. Perhaps the police horses that are taken out for a run then share this sensation, and so do the members of a football team who, in the distance, seem to be swimming in invisible water as they go through their complicated drills. For me, those bright mornings when we rehearsed *Medley* were the first irrefutable proof that being alive was worth it.

We rehearsed three times a week. I would emerge from the subway a little early and wait for the other dancers at the entrance to the park. Then the whole cluster of us would make our way to the heart of the park: the immense expanse of green meadow marked off at one end by a toy lake and the tower of a small pseudomedieval castle. In the evenings a Shakespeare play was performed in a modest amphitheater at the foot of the castle as part of the festival that Joseph Papp was making into a beloved summer ritual.

Twyla didn't have the slightest interest in hearing the same applause every night from that stage; nor did she covet the theater's dressing rooms, orchestra pit, and wooden bleachers that could hold almost two thousand spectators. If I interpret her thought correctly, she wanted her dancers to move across the meadow like an element of nature; she dreamed that the spectators would stand and walk among the dancers as if strolling through an orchard. She also wanted the dancers' movements to be "natural," and though there was an obvious contradiction between this aesthetic ambition and her technical demands, she meant that she was seeking an antiformal language of movement that, in following the trail blazed by Merce, would be unpredictable in its sequences and devoid of "theatrical" structure. She had decided that the work would begin in late afternoon and culminate during the slow summer sunset, with a section of

movements performed not merely in slow motion but at the pace
of a leaf unfolding or the sun sinking, so that our bodies would
imperceptibly reach a point of stasis just as the night's first stars
were appearing.

In the early sunlight and the grassy scent of morning, surrounded by a dense green wall of trees, isolated from the noise
of Central Park West and Fifth Avenue, whose tall buildings
framed the meadow, I felt as if my breathing were forming stan-
zas, the verses of a long hymn of thanks to Twyla, the park, the
sun. Out of the corner of my eye I saw equestrians trotting past
and football players hurling themselves through the air, and I
liked to think that all of us—the horses and their riders, the ath-
letes, and the dancers—were caught up in the delight of sharing
this marvelous, improbable New York moment.

"That was awful," Twyla would say, with no smile of complicity but no impatience or rage, either. "Let's try it again."
Twyla's efficiency was almost cartoonish. She arrived at rehearsals
promptly, with a list of things to do during the session; she never
wasted time improvising but brought whole minutes of movement already worked out and memorized. She delegated tasks
immediately—"Sara, you rehearse the adagio group. Sheela, go
back over section three"—and before the session was over she
gave everyone instructions for the following day's rehearsal. Just
as Graciela had said, there was something almost military about
her, but her talent for movement was so prodigious and she was
so smart, intense, and strange that five minutes into the first
rehearsal she had amazed and won me over.

Twyla had the compact body of an Olympic gymnast and, like
a gymnast, seemed capable of changing course halfway through a
leap, suddenly ricocheting off thin air in the opposite direction.
She danced as competitively as an athlete and with the same terrifying efficiency that she brought to our rehearsals. She didn't
draw out her movements, seeking some hidden sensuality or languor in the spaces between them, but she did prolong to a maximum the end of an off-center arabesque, just to see how long she
could maintain that impossible position. She had a perverse way
of showing off her technical prowess. For example, she would do
a double pirouette while revolving her arms behind her like the

blades of a windmill and then immediately, without the slightest pause to leave room for applause or a sigh of wonder, slide into another equally difficult step, a leap that landed as a roll on the ground, say, and then go from there into another spin, as if to let it be known that she was after something far more exalted than our mere admiration. Her style of dancing was deadpan—but that was also her style when she wasn't moving. In her round face, with dark, round eyes, her mouth was a thin line whose ends barely turned upward to signify a smile. Her laugh was a quick bark. At the end of rehearsal she dismissed us with a "Thanks, everyone" as she looked through her daybook for her next task. She wasn't *simpática,* but she was irresistible.

Twyla's great achievements, perhaps, still lay in the future, when she became the pampered choreographer of the American Ballet Theater and conceived legendary solos for Baryshnikov and the duets she danced with him, but I've never heard anyone speak of the works of her more established phase with the same mixture of respect, astonishment, and gratitude that *Medley* evoked in its audience and its dancers. And in the intimate, devout atmosphere of that first company, Twyla forged her own dance language, an idiosyncratic mix of Fred Astaire, George Balanchine, and street cool that break-dancers and ballet choreographers alike have now assimilated so thoroughly that we see it as spontaneous and natural.

Not even her obsessive efficiency can explain how Twyla managed to keep up her nonstop creative output. Whenever she created a dance, she had to imagine, invent, polish, and memorize the whole work. She had to rehearse her own movements and work separately with each member of what she had begun to call the "core company" and with the rest of us. She had to train for at least an hour. On top of that she had to find financing for the project, obtain permits from the city and the Parks Department, design a program, and do publicity. Above all, Twyla was constantly on the lookout for studios or large, cheap spaces where we could rehearse in the afternoons. Dance nomads, we went from space to space, a different one each week, some of them so shabby that Merce's studio seemed almost luxurious by contrast.

Wearing the same tennis shoes we used for morning rehearsals in the park and the miscellaneous assortment of ragged T-shirts, worn-out leotards, and mismatched socks that became the fashion around that time, we felt divine. It was in the 1960s that decency and modesty lost all connotations of elegance, and outlandishness, self-revelation, and fanatical sincerity were eroticized: *I'm poor, make something of it,* said our clothes, and dressed in them we prepared to learn to dance in a language I called Twylish.

We learned the adagio the same way she had composed it: first the leg movements, a long series of figures—linked, broken up, knotted, and tied together again—that were sketched out with the feet. Then we worked on the second part, for torso and arms. Both halves were horrendously complicated and difficult; they offered neither rhythmic support nor logical continuity. A work of classical ballet is relatively easy to memorize because all the steps have a name and the rhythms are well known—eight-four, two-four, two-three, slow, fast, or waltzed. Even Merce held on to the practice of dividing a phrase of movement into counts "Five-two-three, turn-two-three, seven-two-three, glide-two-three, and *again!*-two-three. . . ." But Twyla, during that stage of her evolution as a choreographer, had decided to abolish rhythm. And the movements we had to learn, with their apparently arbitrary sequence full of dynamic breaks and the insolent, pop style that their very design demanded, were like nothing anyone had ever seen. Memorizing one of her pieces turned out to be like trying to learn a madman's monologue—disjointed words whose secret keys we gradually found. During those early rehearsals we could all be heard talking to ourselves: "Big step right, shift to the other leg—One! Two! Jump! And now turn and a hip thrust, head to the floor and— oops—*en dehors,* the *soutenu* is *en dehors*! Where did my arm go?"

It took us about two weeks to barely learn the two phrases of the adagio that lasted, at most, a couple of minutes. At that point Twyla told us, without a blink, that we could now join the two parts—that is, perform the leg and arm adagios together. It was like playing Ping-Pong and reciting *The Rime of the Ancient Mariner* at the same time, and some never got the hang of it.

To save time, Twyla had the core company dancers rehearse

the chunks of choreography she had designed specifically with them in mind—solos, they might have been called in a less revolutionary time—with the background dancers who performed those same movements simultaneously. In addition to Graciela, the core at that time included Rose Marie Wright, Sheela Raj, and Sara Rudner.

Rose Marie, the youngest of the group, was very tall, endlessly generous, and patient as a teacher, and when she danced, she was as fresh and glowing as her name. She was the only core member who had trained entirely as a classical ballet dancer. Sheela, who was even smaller than Twyla, had enormous liquid eyes and olive skin and was perfect. Her nose was perfect, her toes were perfect, her shoulder blades were perfect. The carriage of her arms, her *developpé,* and her *relevé* were all perfect. Slender, agile, quick, and sinuous, she learned Twyla's impossible phrases on the first try and by the end of the rehearsal had already made them her own. One day she cut off the heavy jet-black braid that hung down to her waist. I believe it was an attempt to make herself uglier, because such an excess of beauty was starting to strike all of us as in questionable taste. But all she managed to do was unveil the perfection of the nape of her neck and worsen her effect on men, who gazed after her sadly wherever she went. Like Graciela, she was haunted by the specter of *la migra;* the agents of the Immigration and Naturalization Service insisted that for the good of the United States of America two of the most promising dancers in the country had to be sent back to wherever they came from.

When Twyla put her various core dancers in charge of different sections of the rehearsal, I always prayed that I would be working with Sara Rudner. The core company was perfectly egalitarian—everyone was a soloist and had to meet the same technical challenges—but we all knew that even though the title didn't exist, Sara was the principal dancer. She had the beauty of a Russian icon of the Virgin Mary, every movement of her body sketched a perfect line, as if she herself were a pencil, and she danced with remarkable spiritual intensity (without Twyla's ostentation or Graciela's dramatic emphasis, yet with a total passion for movement). But it wasn't only that: Sara, calm, warm-hearted, laughing, was for me the emotional center of the group. It never occurred to me to try to dance the way she did, but if I'd been given the chance to trade lives with someone else, I would have wanted to be born again as Sara Rudner.

Sara was living with her boyfriend and therefore led a separate life, but she sometimes came along on our outings. One day Graciela arrived full of news about a place she had found in Chinatown that, for ninety-nine cents, served an enormous platter of noodles cooked with all kinds of vegetables and bits of meat. "I swear it to you! A *lot* of chicken. And meat! It is unbelievable!" she exclaimed. We were always hungry, but New York City's cheap ethnic restaurants were one of the reasons we felt privileged within our poverty. Graciela's discovery seemed so exceptional that we had to go try it out, and even Sara went with us.

It was a strange period in our lives: none of the rest of us had boyfriends. I was still sharing an apartment with my mother, because with the money I earned as a waitress I couldn't have aspired to anything better than a small, sordid space like the one that Sheela and Graciela shared in the East Village. And I'd never had a boyfriend—only a few forlorn beddings.

Elaine went from one brief disaster to another, with lengthy recovery periods in between. Graciela lived through a series of agitated experiences that, since she was Graciela, went far beyond the mere problem of male-female relations and became philosophical inquiries, repostulations of the very nature of love that always left her drained and bewildered.

Our closest male friends were gay, and to our frustration we endlessly confirmed that without exception they were more loyal, more fun, freer, and more imaginative than the handful of heterosexual males who inhabited our world. With our gay friends we held parties, danced, and went out. Sometimes Sheela would make curry. Sometimes I made *mole*. Elaine, who loved make-believe, would organize tea parties for Harry Sheppard and me. She would set the table with little embroidered napkins (in an unmatched assortment of patterns) and flowery porcelain cups (all chipped), then present us with a platter of tender ears of corn, barely roasted, along with a bowl of melted butter to dip them in. And we ate like wild boars.

No one ever asked me then, and I don't know if I myself understood that I had a life that was not only extraordinary but *real*—the kind of life that doesn't happen by accident but is put together only slowly and with effort.

Twyla continued to work with the core company after *Medley,* and I went on dancing with her too because she always needed more people—six or twelve women she used as a kind of corps de ballet. I remember in particular a performance at the Wadsworth Athenaeum, in Hartford. While the core company performed the dance piece that had been commissioned by the Athenaeum, the rest of us presented a retrospective of Twyla's early choreography in the museum auditorium. That performance allowed me to reconstruct in my own body the origins of her work, which had begun five or six years earlier (and included dances as inscrutable as *Tank Dive,* in which a dancer, alone on the stage, holds for two minutes the ninety-degree angle of a diver preparing to plunge). At the Metropolitan Museum of Art we performed *Dancing in the Streets of London and Paris, Continued in Stockholm and Sometimes Madrid,* and this event received more attention from the press than *Medley* had. About fifteen dancers performed it. I didn't think this new piece was as original in its movements or as atmospherically evocative as the performance in Central Park, but I remember with gratitude and astonishment the rehearsals held in the museum after hours. It was a deliciously clandestine pleasure to practice our movements (or "tasks" or "activities," as we representatives of the avant-garde said then) in the empty space of the Spanish patio and on the great stairway at the museum's entrance. One night I couldn't resist the temptation and lightly ran my hand over a medieval tapestry.

———

It was during this period that Merce, feet joined and head tilted, mentioned to me one afternoon after the advanced class that there was the possibility of an offer to go abroad and teach dance.

Someone else might have felt as if she'd just been handed a bouquet of flowers: *Merce had noticed me!* I felt as if a bucket of boiling, freezing water had been dumped over my head. Merce had walked over not to say "I want you to dance with me" but "There's a gig a thousand miles away that might interest you." When I tallied up my achievements since coming to New York to dance, Merce's proposal seemed to me evidence of my failure. I was nineteen when he invited me into the advanced class, and I thought a door was opening onto the best future I could have dreamed of. Now I was twenty, which in dance-world time is a very different age, and no one had ever said to me "When you move, it enraptures my soul, dance forever." Like any young woman who aspires to be a dancer, I had no interest in being mediocre. I wanted to be used in the best possible way; I was convinced that I had great things to do onstage, that I harbored a dramatic presence of enormous force and projection. Nevertheless, I now came to the realization that I was accumulating more impediments than achievements. After so many years of training it was time for me to be something more than just a capable performer, but I was painfully conscious of my intrinsic physical limitations: my flat feet, my lack of "turnout"—the rotation of the femur in the hollow of the pelvis, which allows the knees and feet to point completely outward, like those of an iguana. I was never going to achieve technical virtuosity; that was a fact.

I haven't mentioned that I was also severely myopic; I'd never been able to get used to contact lenses, and in those days optical surgery was an experimental technique used primarily in the Soviet Union. Every morning when I woke up, the first thing I did was grope for the thick glasses that had first been prescribed for me when I was six. I felt hopelessly lost without them. Onstage, blind and exposed before the audience, I became a frightened, gray animal. I was panicked at not being able to see and equally panicked at being seen. The performance in Hartford, during which I had to appear onstage wearing only a flesh-colored maillot and the famous tennis shoes, had been a torture I would not be able to endure again. I felt that each one of the defects I took stock of every day in front of the mirror—the hips, legs, shoulders—was now exposed as if I were a side of beef hanging in the window of a butcher shop. I learned that I was a coward.

I had another carefully guarded secret. Ever since as a little girl I had chosen modern dance, I had never wanted to be just a dancer: I had always wanted to be like Martha Graham. I wanted to use my body to invent a brutal, mythical theatrical art that would be completely new. When, around the time I turned twenty, I first saw Robert Wilson's productions, I was choked with desolate, senseless rage: Wilson had ransacked my brain and stolen my ideas! His works were the same ones I had dreamed of, literally, in dreams so intense that when I woke up I wrote them all down, complete with indications for the lighting. Watching Twyla at work, so pitiless, so obsessive, I knew that I possessed no such capacity to move mountains, to sweep budgets, bureaucracies, and the lives of those around me along in my path in order to make my dreams real. I didn't dare ask even Elaine and Harry, who were more like family to me than my real family, if they wanted to rehearse with me.

All these years later I have no way of knowing how harsh or confused my evaluation of myself was at the age of twenty. I do know that when Merce suggested I go and teach classes in a distant country, my usual state of anxiety and depression only worsened; I felt that everything—Merce's rejection, my own solitude—was conspiring to drive me away from all I had ever dreamed of.

Even Manhattan, the magical realm of my adventures, suddenly began to seem like an island under siege. A thief had looted the apartment I shared with my mother. Graciela and Sheela's apartment was also robbed. (Graciela later recognized the thief on a bus.) A woman I knew was raped. Someone broke in to rob Graciela and Sheela yet again. We were used to theft and violence, which were as much a part of everyday life as the plague of cockroaches that were the native fauna of New York City kitchens; but I sometimes felt great fear, and though I didn't dislike the hippies who thronged the streets of the Village, East and West, their world could be squalid. One afternoon I went to a neighborhood clinic in search of a prescription for something to help me shake a lingering cough. In the waiting room I sat next to a girl who was covered with sores and was hallucinating under the effect of some psychedelic. In the low tide of early morning, as I walked to the Village cafeteria where I worked, I would have to sidestep the victims of heroin, the era's drug. Since the cafeteria was at one of the busiest corners in the Village, many young artists would ask permission to put their posters in the windows, announcing local performances and exhibits. With increasing frequency we were also asked to post flyers bearing the photograph of some teenage-boy or barely-adolescent-girl runaway, the proletariat of the new hippie nation. Sometimes parents came in, flyer in hand, to ask if we recognized their children, and their anguish was painful. But I understood and admired the young nomads, even when they ended up lying on a street corner, coughing and covered with sores. I too had an urgent need to separate from my mother.

From Merce I'd received offers that I took as a rejection: Caracas or Havana. From Twyla, I'd had no more than her habitual indifference, but the friendship that bound me to the members of the company made me clutch at one last straw. I talked to Sara. "I don't know. I don't know what to tell you," she said. "Talk to Twyla."

One afternoon after rehearsal, my heart in my throat, I lingered in the studio until the others had left. Twyla was putting her practice clothes away in her tote bag, ready to go. I told her I'd been offered a position teaching dance in Cuba. What should I do? Busy with a shoelace, she lifted her eyes for a moment. "If I were you, I'd take it," she said. "You're not going to get anywhere hanging around here."

I didn't even think about the possibility of going to Venezuela, maybe because I knew absolutely nothing about the country. But I did know something about my other option. When I started dancing at the age of twelve in Mexico, the modern dance company I joined had just returned from a tour of Cuba. The dancers often spoke nostalgically of their journey to that island, recently conquered by the Revolution, and I hadn't forgotten their descriptions of Havana: the full moon shimmering on the ocean as they strolled along the Malecón, the tempestuous romance between one of the women and a bus driver, the rumba . . .

I didn't understand what my fellow dancers said about Fidel and the Revolution, but those stories too were full of emotion and romance. Revolutionary Cuba and Fidel Castro had always been able to count on support from both the Mexican government—which saw in the defense of Cuba the defense of the principles of sovereignty and nonintervention—and the country's antigovernment intellectuals. This may seem contradictory, but there was a logical explanation: in the nineteenth century Mexico lost more than half of its territory in a war waged against it by the United States, and ever since then anyone who plays David to our powerful neighbor's Goliath will always be admired. In its lone standoff against the full might of our arrogant neighbor, Fidel's Cuba embodied the most just of all causes. Generally speaking, revolutionary leftism is part of a long tradition among Mexican artists, and I took it for granted that the Cuban Revolution was on the side of good, and the U.S. government on the side of evil.

And yet I was living in New York and had never felt the slightest desire to go to Cuba or the slightest flicker of curiosity about the place. Politics played a very small role in my life. I was horrified by the little I knew about racism and the Vietnam War, and I wept over the students who were massacred in my country in 1968: it would have been almost impossible to be alive at that time, in that city and that milieu, and not feel the same. But I didn't have a TV, and I think it wasn't until several years later that I first watched a television news show in New York. I didn't even read the newspaper, except for the arts section and Craig Claiborne's recipes—whenever my mother happened to rescue the *Times* from the office where she worked as a secretary and bring it home. At subway newsstands while I waited for the next train, I followed the front-page news about the hunt for Che Guevara in anguish, but I never gave much thought to the purpose of his struggle and his life as a revolutionary. Instead, what shocked me was the image of a starving hero hunted down across mountains and arid precipices by a pack of ravenous human predators.

My political attitude toward the world I lived in, if I had one at all, was, I believe, a mixture of sincere elements of antiauthoritarianism, anticlericalism, horror of torture, revulsion at social inequality, defense of animals, terror of any type of violence, and distrust of anything related to big business, especially advertising. To me, this was the attitude of a revolutionary, as I felt I was in art. But my deepest conviction, so deep I would never have been able to articulate it, was perfectly elitist: I had no doubt that we artists were the highest form of human life. That conviction justified my existence.

Merce himself was only the intermediary in the matter of the Cuban dance school. When I told him I'd decided to apply for the position, he said that the school's director, who was in New York looking for teachers, had dropped by the studio to ask whether he could recommend anyone, and he simply happened to think of me. If I was interested, I could give her a call. Her name was Elfriede Mahler. "You'll form your own opinion of her, I'm sure," Merce told me, with the closest thing to a smile of complicity that a gentleman can give. "But it could turn out to be interesting."

Over the phone Elfriede agreed to come to dinner at my house with her husband, Harold—I think I remember the name correctly—the following weekend.

A North American woman with unkempt gray hair and a constricted smile that did nothing to hide her ill humor walked glumly into my house-proud mother's living room. Despite her Valkyrian name, Elfriede Mahler was neither German nor imposing. Nothing in her bearing gave any indication that she had ever been a dancer, and there wasn't a glimmer of charm in her personality. From the moment she said hello, she spoke as if she were on the defensive, with a permanent edge of anger to her voice, as if she were expecting someone to tell her that what she'd just said was stupid. She must have been about fifty, like

Merce, but she looked much older. We quickly learned that she and Harold, a journalist in his sixties and a longtime Communist Party militant, had arrived in Cuba at the beginning of the Revolution. The couple were now back in the United States—for the first time in many years, I believe—to see their families, buy a few things, and above all, look for teachers for the dance school.

Elfriede was the director of Cuba's National School of Dance, which was one section of the National Schools of Art, or Escuelas Nacionales de Arte (ENA), inaugurated in 1964. The school had the full support of the Cuban government, Elfriede said that night, which meant that it was housed in lovely, spacious installations, with not just one or two but four dance studios, all immense. The students entered the school at the age of twelve and at sixteen chose to specialize in either modern or Afro-Cuban dance. On the verdant grounds of the school, which was located on the outskirts of Havana, far from the city's noise and tumult, they were provided with a highly nutritious diet and a rigorous academic education. The class now about to graduate was the school's first, she explained, and therefore it was far less homogenous than those that came after it; it included students as old as twenty-two, and their technical level was quite uneven. Elfriede seemed aware of her own limitations as a dancer and teacher. She told my mother and me that she and another modern dancer, also from the United States, were the only two teachers. They urgently needed to revitalize their program and open up new horizons to the students, especially those who were about to graduate.

All of us made an effort, but the evening did not sparkle. Elfriede and Harold forked away indifferently at the dinner my mother had spent the whole afternoon cooking, and she in turn reacted with a certain lack of enthusiasm to the revolutionary slogans her guests were continually proffering. Denouncing the hardships that the U.S. economic embargo had caused Cuba, the two of them gave as an example the fact that there were no electrical appliances in most homes. My mother, who paid close attention to matters of food and comfort, wondered aloud about the difficulties of living without a refrigerator in the monstrous Cuban heat.

"Oh, not at all!" Harold shot back, sputtering soup onto his threadbare tie in his eagerness to clear the Revolution of any taint. "Luckily, Cuba has such a splendid climate that refrigeration really isn't necessary."

Poor Harold! That sentence alone sufficed to make me categorize him forever as a perfect imbecile. And it's certainly true that he had just made a statement of enormous stupidity. But it's also true that I understood nothing about love, and that Harold was in love—heart, body, and soul—with his Revolution.

Poor Elfriede! She and I would have gotten along better if we'd each followed the dictates of our hearts. For the fact is, she didn't care for me any more than I cared for her. But she was desperate: it wasn't easy to convince any dancer of more or less adequate skill to give up her classes and her eternal illusions in New York City and go live on a Communist island surrounded by sharks and economic embargoes. She'd found a dance student in Chicago who seemed interested in teaching dance to the first-year students, but hadn't yet finalized an agreement with her. She'd also asked an established New York City dance teacher to give an intensive one-month course the following summer, but that teacher too was undecided. Now she had to give up on the idea of finding a kindred spirit for the position that was most important to her, because in all New York I was the only candidate for the job of full-time teacher for the older students.

Poor me! I was about to condemn myself to working in intimate quarters with a woman who already struck me as unbearable. If I'd been just a little more tolerant, if I hadn't considered her lack of charm and grooming to be a mortal sin, I could have acknowledged at least some merits in my future supervisor: Her determination and optimism were admirable. And her courage as well, for it now occurs to me that she was certainly violating one of the many laws that forbid citizens of the United States to have any contact with Cuba, and by returning to her native country she was risking sanctions, fines, and perhaps even jail for collaborating with the enemy.

The humility with which she accepted her own limitations was undeniable, as was her willingness to recruit a teacher of Cunningham technique. In all Latin America at that moment there was not a single dance group that would have thought for one instant of straying from the road paved by Martha Graham. Nevertheless, Elfriede had decided to break through her school's isolation, looking for someone not from the companies of Paul Taylor or Anna Sokolow or Alvin Ailey—artists less scandalously avant-garde—but from Merce himself. It would have been fair to grant her at least that much.

Of course, if I'd been a bit more tolerant with myself, I wouldn't have accepted, out of unrequited love, a job in Cuba that I didn't want.

If I agreed, Elfriede said after dinner, she could offer me a one-year contract, with my plane ticket, travel expenses, and lodging all covered, and a salary of $250 a month, paid of course in Cuban pesos, which couldn't be exchanged for dollars but were very good pesos all the same. She turned to me with her very best screwed-on smile and a barely disguised pleading in her glittery little eyes. I said yes, I would accept, and the pleading became relief, but not warmth.

Despite our mutual distrust, we came quickly to a satisfactory agreement: in exchange for a salary, a plane ticket, and travel expenses, I would give two classes a day for a year—one to the group that was about to graduate, the other to the fourth-year students. I would teach Cunningham technique two days a week and Graham technique the other three. This was the best and most important arrangement Elfriede and I managed to come up with: it struck both of us as a good idea to offer the students a range of possibilities rather than a single approach to dance, and it also seemed wise to give priority to Martha, whose technique was and is undoubtedly the most established, coherent, and original in modern dance.

A few days later Elfriede left New York, and I seem to recall that we worked things out so as not to have to see each other again. She told me over the phone that as soon as she was back in Cuba she would begin the application process for my visa and work permit. The Cuban Mission to the United Nations, which had offices on Fifth Avenue, would notify me as soon as my entry to Cuba was authorized. The visa would be sent with all due haste to the Cuban Embassy in Mexico, and after picking it up there, I would take a direct flight to Havana. With any luck I could be starting the job at the beginning of the new year.

My friends reacted to the news with curiosity and excitement, and my mother worried: she didn't much care for the idea of socialism, and Fidel Castro's beard and general demeanor did not impress her favorably. Elaine thought the idea of traveling to an unknown land was fantastic. I suspect that Graciela thought I might be making a mistake to abandon my exploration of dance in New York, but she didn't want to meddle.

I couldn't tell anyone how disconsolate the idea of the trip made me because I would have had to confess to failures and disillusionments that filled me with shame. When I thought of Cuba, Manhattan seemed newly joyous and full of possibilities, and the pitfalls in my path looked minor. But as soon as I thought of canceling the trip and staying in New York, the future darkened once more. Whom would I dance with, if not Twyla? And how long could I go on accepting the role of third choice? I tried to boost my spirits by telling myself that it was good to leave home and put myself to the test; it would be a voyage of discovery on the legendary island of the Revolution, and I would come back a veteran teacher, ready to earn a living by giving classes. Above all, I repeated to myself that I was leaving New York only for a year, and that everything would be exactly the same when I came back. The only difference would be that in a year I would have stopped suffering over Twyla and could begin to dream again and move in new directions. I could pick up my life as before, cook *mole* for my friends as before, return to my classes as before. My world would be just the same, and I would be, too.

TWO

Cubanacán

I landed in Havana on May 1, 1970, four months late. My visa hadn't come through until mid-March, and when I arrived in Mexico to pick it up, there was another unexpected delay: my stubborn cough, the product of weeks of rehearsal with Twyla in an unheated studio, turned into bronchial pneumonia. I'd been convalescing in Mexico City for a month when on the spur of the moment I decided to catch the next flight to Cuba. By chance there was a seat for me. The thought that it might be wise to notify someone in Havana of my arrival never crossed my mind.

A dancer friend who was well acquainted with Cuba had helped me pack for the trip. The multiple effects of the economic embargo that the United States began imposing on Cuba's revolutionary government in 1960 were terrible, she said: there wasn't much to eat, though no one went hungry, and there was nothing to buy in the stores. Following her instructions, I packed light clothes for the hot climate and all the shoes and sandals I could manage: when my shoes wore out, there would be no way to buy new ones. Many books, because books would be scarce (but I had to choose them carefully, or the *compañeros* from the Ministry of the Interior who would go through everything at customs might take them for subversive materials). I took one small luxury—a bottle of expensive perfume whose purchase I tried to keep secret even from myself—and another, larger extravagance: an early-model portable tape deck. This technological innovation, which weighed about seven pounds and was operated by a row of clumsy pianolike keys on one end, ate up most of my savings. I packed Bach, Mozart, and some jazz cassettes, as well as the Beatles' *Rubber Soul* and the latest Aretha

Franklin and Creedence Clearwater Revival. My adviser had warned me that anything having to do with rock and roll or rhythm and blues was banned in Cuba, but I didn't believe it: how could anyone possibly want to censor "Respect"?

For my friend's Cuban friends and the people I would meet, I brought an entire suitcase full of gifts: tins of Australian butter, powdered milk, chocolate bars, boxes of Danish cookies. ("Whatever has lots of calories," said my friend, pushing the cart up and down the supermarket aisles.) We bought bars of soap, plastic combs and mirrors, and a shopping bag full of sanitary napkins and tampons that I never gave away because they became my greatest treasure. I spent my last dollars on transistor batteries, notebooks, pens, and a book that risked being considered subversive, but that Galo, my friend's best friend on the island, was longing to read: *Cuba, est-il socialiste?* At least the accusatory question was in French. As this inverse image of Cuban deprivation piled up in my room, I was moved: my stay on the island would be a rite of purification, a baptism by fire. I began reading Che:

> It is at this sort of moment that great decisions are made: this type of struggle gives us the opportunity to become revolutionaries, the highest rank of the human species, but it also allows us to graduate into men. Those who find themselves unable to achieve one of these two stages will have to say so, and give up the fight.

In the end, the stockpile I accumulated in preparation for my new ascetic life was worthy of a wartime hoarder. The customs official in Havana's José Martí Airport stared in astonishment at the cornucopia of packages and bundles that spilled out of my suitcases, while I counted the secret rivulets of sweat trickling down my spine and thighs.

The room was empty by then, all the other passengers had left, and the poor man was hopelessly bewildered. Why hadn't anyone come to pick me up? Where was my *responsable*? Who had authorized me to board the plane? And this book—whom was it for? Fortunately Cuba maintained friendly relations with Australia, but why did I want all this butter? As for the tape recorder, well, he was very sorry, but it was staying with him. One by one he removed newspaper-wrapped bundles from a wicker trunk and unwrapped them, and one by one yet another pair of shoes or sandals, new or used, appeared, until seventeen pairs were heaped on the table. He piled up the chocolates, the cassettes with their illegal music, the cookies. Three hours had gone by and the afternoon was drawing to a close, but the heat was still stifling.

Eying the customs official, I calculated my losses. Was I going to spend a year without music, perhaps without shoes, maybe without books? Had I lost the chocolates, too? I could think of no explanation other than the truth for my assorted luggage, but I couldn't find a way of putting it that would make all my bundles and my presence logical and unobjectionable to the customs man. Obviously I had committed a series of grave errors, and was ashamed. So many things I was trying to bring in, so many privileges I wanted to ensure for myself in advance, when the right thing to do here was to share in the general deprivation. I said nothing.

The official squinted at me one more time. He took one long last look at my visa. It was in order. Under the category of "foreign technician," I was authorized to reside in Cuba for one year, teaching classes. My destination was the Escuela Nacional de Danza at the Escuelas Nacionales de Arte in Cubanacán. He sighed.

"Take it all away, *chica*. I don't know what to do with you."

"The tape recorder, too?"

"Everything."

"The tapes?"

"Everything, I said. I don't want to look at you anymore!"

Stunned by triumph, I dragged my trunks and suitcases to the airport waiting room, where my spirits collapsed once more. It was deserted. There was neither an information booth nor a place to change money nor anything that looked like a taxi stand. The only furniture was a row of metal chairs in a corner. The last flight had arrived, the airport was closing, and on top of everything else it was International Workers' Day, a sacred holiday of the Revolution. A policewoman stuck her head out the door of an office, questioned me closely, and upon learning that I had landed in Cuba *por la libre*—on my own—scolded me for my lack of discipline and respect for the Revolution.

Finally, grudgingly, she pointed to a graying man who was waiting outside the airport next to a jalopy—the last taxi of the day. The trip to Cubanacán, he informed me, would cost one peso. Looking through my wallet, I showed him one of the ten one-dollar bills I was carrying—the entirety of my capital—and asked if he could change it for me.

"What are you doing, *chica*! Don't you know you can get in trouble for that? Put that away!"

In Mexico I'd been warned that the dollar was illegal currency in Cuba, but not that the minimum penalty for incitement to trafficking in dollars was several years in jail.

It took considerable effort to convince the taxi driver that I was lost without him, but since this was true, he finally agreed to take me to the Escuelas Nacionales de Arte. There, I promised him, we would find someone to pay him for the trip in Cuban pesos. We loaded my small mountain of bundles into the car, which seemed to sigh from the deepest depths of its long-suffering shock absorbers, and we were on our way.

The rural landscape we drove through on the roughly ten-mile trip from the airport to Cubanacán was a panorama of solitudes. Coming from Mexico, where rosaries of villages are strung along the roads leading into the capital city, and where the word *village* immediately brings to mind the sounds of bells, firecrackers, and blaring radios, I thought the deserted expanses of sugarcane field we were driving through, colored by the last light of the day, looked like the landscape of another planet. From time to time a pickup truck rattled past, loaded with campesinos on their way home. Here and there a housing project rose, startlingly incongruous in these agricultural surroundings. And the horizon was repeatedly interrupted by a steeplechase of billboards that exalted not Coca-Cola or Burma-Shave but the

Revolution: *¡Diez millones!* (Ten million!) *¡A cumplir!* (Let's get the job done!) And then a series, one word per billboard:

¡COMANDANTE

EN

JEFE:

ORDENE!

COMMANDER-IN-CHIEF: COMMAND!

At times we were accompanied by a cyclist, pedaling along at the same speed as the taxi's weary engine. Sometimes another car, decrepit and patient as a mule, calmly passed us by. Our car, also like a mule, suddenly came to a stop. The taxi driver, who'd been steering along in total silence, muttered something, got out, lifted the hood, spent a few minutes investigating the situation, and then, peering in through the window, asked for the loan of one of the bobby pins I was wearing in my hair. He did something to the motor with it, and we started up again and continued on our way, still in silence.

The thing I remember most clearly about our arrival in Cubanacán is that after a flustered turn or two around the school until I stumbled on someone who could pay the taxi driver, by which time night had already fallen, he got out, again lifted the hood, and presented me with the bobby pin. When I told him he could keep it, he rewarded me with the only smile of our brief time together. Otherwise, my sole distinct memory is of the warm embrace of a very surprised woman who introduced herself as the school's Communist Party delegate. It was her turn to be on duty this holiday evening, and when I explained who I was and how I'd arrived, she gave me an effusive and scandalized welcome. She must have been the one who paid the taxi and took me to a bedroom in the dormitory reserved for special guests. Perhaps she found me a snack as well. I recall an impression of dampness, frustrating darkness, and the muted background roar of the jungle. The mosquitoes were an invisible army. My room's lone lightbulb gave off a sad, faint light. As soon as I was alone, I felt as if I were about to collapse from the anguish closing in on me from under my skin: *What am I doing here? What have I done, what have I done, what have I done?* From the moment I got off the plane I'd felt as if I were wearing a corset that was squeezing me tighter and tighter, and by then it was no longer allowing me to breathe. I learned that when a character in a novel paces around a room in circles, it isn't simply a literary affectation: I discovered myself, at some hour of the night, doing precisely that, incapable of sitting down. I remember the dampness of the sheets when I finally did get into bed.

In the very early morning I woke suddenly from a monstrous nightmare: blood was flowing from the wicker trunk, and when I got up to investigate, I found not shoes but heads, bloody severed heads, lying in the newspaper wrappings. Awake now and with the light on, I verified that one of the bundles in the trunk was indeed moving. I opened it. A gigantic cockroach flittered clumsily into my face and fell back, dragging its wings among the folds of paper and trying to turn over. Other cockroaches pitched and turned in their newspaper nest.

Again I was the protagonist of a scene out of a dime novel: when a group from the school came to my room that morning to take me to breakfast, they found me burning with fever. I went straight to the hospital.

The doctor on duty in the Carlos J. Finlay military hospital was muscular, dark-skinned, and mustachioed. He examined me in a cubicle that must once have been a closet in the old and elegant hospital building. After the Revolution a much larger population had access to medical care, and the hospital now had to make use of every inch of space. Despite the close quarters, the room had everything that was necessary: gleaming medical instruments, an examination table covered with an equally dazzling white sheet, thermometers, and Baumanometers.

A robust black nurse cheerfully came and went. Her buttocks jiggled like playful little animals, and laughter spurted out of her on any pretext, as if the little animals were tickling her. She and the doctor were reeling through one version of the conversation I would hear repeated to the point of delirium throughout the following months: she'd had to stay on duty at the Committee for the Defense of the Revolution all night because X hadn't shown up, and she was going to arrange for Y to stand in for her next night duty so she'd have time to pick up a crate or bag of rations from an aunt of hers who was keeping it for her because Z's ration of rice was more than he needed since A had been mobilized for the sugarcane harvest. For the first time since my arrival I felt like smiling.

With a final pat on my back, the doctor said that, apart from the inflamed colon that was my chronic affliction, and the episode of fever and bouts of coughing that were undoubtedly the aftermath of an improperly treated infection, my health was flawless. It would be better, though, if I stayed in the hospital a couple of days longer so I could start getting rid of that stubborn cough. He didn't change his mind when I insisted I was used to coughing and it was hardly worth my taking up a hospital bed.

"But *muchacha*! How can you think we'd let you leave in the state you're in! We're here to serve the Revolution, and as an *Internacionalista* you deserve the best of care!"

This was disturbing. I was no Internationalist; I was just a dancer. I thought I should at least have the decency to tell him I had a good job and urgently needed to start working.

"None of that, *chica,* none of that! The *Internacionalistas* aren't just those who risk their lives with guns in hand! We Revolutionaries know to be grateful for every effort: those who stand up to the police in the entrails of the Empire and risk their lives to protest the Butcher Nixon and his genocidal war are fighting, too—and I'm sure you've done that. And now you've come here to share in our hardships, to offer us the best of your experience and show us your solidarity. Don't give me that sad face, *muchacha*! How can you think that the best of our Revolution won't be for you!"

I went back to my room with the doctor's exclamation points and capital letters shooting after me like a rain of arrows and buried myself in bed as if to hide. In Mexico my bronchial pneumonia had been treated by the friend of a friend, who happened to be a doctor. In New York too I was used to depending on charitable doctors or neighborhood clinics. In Havana, however, I'd just had the first complete medical examination of my life, including X rays, tests, and three days in the hospital. And it wasn't going to cost me a cent. Or rather, I'd just been informed that this care was being given in exchange for a certain conduct, a stance toward the world that bespoke my bravery and social commitment. But I held none of that currency. I'd never participated in a demonstration against the Vietnam War, I'd never stood up to the Butcher Nixon: it had never occurred to me that I had a moral obligation to protest against injustice. I'd never once imagined that I belonged to a wider community than that of my friends and fellow dancers.

At the same time I felt threatened by the force of something I wouldn't have been able to call rhetoric. Through my mother's influence I was, from early childhood, as voracious and indiscriminate a reader as she was, a reader of novels—or *consumer,* I should say, given the urgency with which I devoured every novel that fell into my hands—and of every other kind of printed text as well. And far more than the twists and turns of plot, what held me rapt was the use of language. From Dr. Seuss to Vladimir Nabokov to Jorge Luis Borges, I appreciated and remembered any word whose impact on another made a phrase come to life. "*¡Viejas, jijas del demonio!*" (Old crones, spawn of the devil!), Juan Rulfo had Lucas Lucatero say in the very first line of a story, and I remembered. "Nurse that tooth," said Humbert Humbert when his nymphet's mother offered him the choice between a cozy drink with her and retiring to bed with an aching molar, and I wanted to applaud the brilliance that could compress so many emotions into just three words. The uncertain grace of Beatriz Viterbo's movements in Borges's "The Aleph," so precisely reflected in the stumbling syllables of her name; the "*¡Viban los compañeros!*" (Long lib the comrades!) that, in his funeral hymns for the Spanish Republic, César Vallejo had the dying Pedro Rojas write, "with a 'b' for the buzzard in his entrails"; the delicious irony and grace with which Nancy Mitford's protagonists described the varieties of tedium, and the care with which they differentiated between those who called paper to be used for letters "writing paper" and the parvenus who said "note paper"; the "green lightning" of Ramón López Velarde's parrots; and Octavio Paz's "green, glacial rage." I treasured words and carried them with me.

I also took great care with my own writing in the letters I sent to my friends in Mexico, which were full of words and phrases painstakingly selected according to context, each one examined with care to establish its precise degree of brilliance or dark density. In fact, after dance, the pleasure of language occupied a paramount place in the list of things that mattered to me. But this new, exhortatory way of speaking that the doctor had used and that resonated through the hospital was different, and from the first it left me uncomfortable and perplexed: Humanity, Solidarity, Internationalism, Revolution, Imperialism, Sacrifice. These were sledgehammer words, of such enormous weight that I couldn't help paying attention to them, and they seemed to invite careful reflection. But I also experienced them as crushing words, without nuances or secrets. Already in my first conversation with Elfriede and her husband those kinds of words had annoyed me, because in their mouths they sounded artificial and forced. But the doctor had used them in a perfectly natural way. There were other phrases, written in the newspapers posted on a designated section of wall on every floor of the hospital, whose meaning I could not fathom. What, for example, did "alienation of labor" mean? and "Onward to the ten million!"? And why did these phrases carry so much weight in the kindly doctor's mind that he didn't need to ask me who I was or where I came from? The phrases had already given him the answer. What was I doing here? In what country, on what planet so different from my own, had I just landed?

"*Chica,* you look sad, but you'd better liven up soon!" said the woman in the bed next to mine. "Just think! There's only two weeks and a day to go until the ten million, and when we get there, we're going to have the biggest party this country has ever seen!"

Ten million what? Ten million tons of sugarcane that had to be harvested in order to overcome the imperialist blockade and begin building a socialist nation in earnest. "Because thanks to the Revolution we have schools and good nutrition and the kind of medical care only white folks could enjoy before, you know? But the Yankees create a lot of suffering for us with their embargo, if you want to know the truth. We never manage to make much headway with the economy, and that's why Fidel said we have to make this all-out effort. And you know we're with Fidel; whatever he says, we do. *'¡Hasta la victoria siempre!'* "—Onward to victory forever!

Again, I heard the exhortatory turns of speech that made me feel small, incompetent, and at the same time, skeptical. What *was* this funny way of speaking?

"But it hasn't been easy," my neighbor was saying. "There hasn't been a letup in fourteen months. I'm here in the hospital because I had some kind of collapse—I was just too tired, I couldn't breathe, I had all these pains in my body—something terrible. So one of my cousins—he's in the military—found a bed here for me, in what is the very best hospital, you may have noticed. But I've *done* my part for the *zafra:* I didn't take a single day off for over a year. Because Fidel said it: *'Los diez millones van!'* "—The ten million are a sure bet!

The slogans and exhortations I heard those first days, the chaos of everyday life, the deprivation and exhaustion, were all related to the enormous effort of the sugarcane harvest.

At the beginning of 1966 the government had launched what is still today the most ambitious modernization plan ever implemented in Cuba—and perhaps in the entire hemisphere—the Zafra de los Diez Millones, or Ten Million Ton Harvest. From that moment on, the island was catapulted into an increasingly heroic effort to achieve a harvest of ten million tons of sugar in 1970—almost three million tons more than the all-time capitalist record, and about double the average harvests during the first ten years of the Revolution. According to Fidel's calculations, a ten-million-ton harvest would allow the Revolution to settle its debts to the Soviet Union and generate a surplus. With that precious margin of profit, the Revolution would be able to finance its own development and would free itself from what was becoming an alarming dependence on Soviet aid.

Fidel was to announce this great victory on July 26, 1970, the anniversary of the Revolution. In preparation, the whole island was dressed up in the slogans I saw all over the walls of the hospital. The words had to be repeated, chorused, and shouted, and thus fatigue would be overcome, faith renewed, and spirits raised. When Brigade 2506 invaded the island at Playa Girón, when the atomic blast that would wipe Havana and perhaps all other cities off the face of the earth was expected from one moment to the next, slogans hadn't been necessary: in truly critical situations they're superfluous. But now the effort was slow and blind. Workers didn't take vacations but went to the fields to cut cane. The cheerful nurse didn't go home to bed but stayed on for an extra night shift in place of the fellow worker sent off to the cane fields. And all this was happening not after years of abundance but after many years of privation. People couldn't even think about the consequences of the failure of so massive an effort. They preferred to repeat slogans.

It's easy to see all this now. At the time, contemplating my fate from between the hospital's crisp sheets, I struggled to understand how the size of a harvest could be a matter of historic interest. Even the word *zafra,* as the annual sugarcane harvest is called, was one of the many in the newspapers posted on the wall whose meaning escaped me. For though my stock of words was rich, I had to acknowledge that it wasn't very strong on terms related to the wide world of construction, agriculture, manufacturing, or any subject beyond the realm of Art.

I found a refuge from insistent Cuban reality on an abandoned terrace at the end of the hall. An unceasing joyous hubbub surrounded the other bed in my room; my fellow patient's relatives were numerous and highly expressive. They spoke among themselves and with their sick family member at top volume— about their work shifts, their rations, their mobilizations, their nephews and nieces—and they spoke to me too, inquiring after my health with a generosity that grew even more intense when my roommate told them I was Mexican. *"¡México!"* they shouted, and immediately joined in a chorus of praise for my country: its

movie stars, its *ranchera* music, its oft-reiterated solidarity with
Cuba, and the heroic negative with which it had replied to imperialist pressures to break off relations with the country of the
Revolution. I sank all the deeper into a shame I couldn't fully
understand, much less explain. What had I done to deserve such
praise? Seeking a little quiet that first afternoon, I pushed open
the door at the end of the hallway and saw that it led onto a
terrace. Beyond a low, wide parapet, the street was visible,
two floors below. The terrace was shaded by a marvelous tree
whose dense foliage concealed an infinity of flowers, yellow on
some stems, lilac-colored on others: a *majagua*. The parapet was
wide enough to lie down on—there seemed to be no end to my
exhaustion—and I spent many hours in the shade of that miraculous tree, contemplating the movement of its branches and trying to impose calm and order on my thoughts.

I thought, among other things, about Adrian, whom I'd met
a few weeks before leaving New York, and about Jorge, who
often came to visit at the house in Mexico where I was recovering
from bronchial pneumonia and who'd promised to write me in
Havana. Overwhelmed by loneliness as I was, the one thing I
didn't think about was an issue that, until the moment I boarded
the plane, had seemed urgent: deciding which of the two ro-
mances threatened less pain. I thought about both of them and
wished with all my soul that some god of communication would
take pity and bring me in one rush all the letters each had promised. In fact, I would have settled for a single letter—even a post-
card, a small chain of words to reconnect me to my world and the
person who was rapidly becoming a stranger: myself.

After many hours of sleep, I felt better. Lying in the shade
of the *majagua* (all the nurses' pleas that I forgo my excursions
to the terrace were to no avail), I told myself that the time had
come to decide whether I was staying or beating a retreat to New
York before I wasted any more of anyone's time. Once I'd put
it to myself like that, it was obvious that I was not going back. I
wasn't ready to accept another defeat. What was more, I thought,
my spirits already a bit higher, I hadn't even seen the school yet.

The next day a nurse came to the terrace and said, not without some relief at seeing the last of me, that I should go back to my room and pack my things. Elfriede Mahler—or Elfrida as everyone in Cuba called her, and as I will also from now on—and Lorna Burdsall, the dance school's assistant director, were waiting downstairs.

The open faces of the youngsters who would be my students immediately disarmed me when I finally met them the following morning. They'd been sitting on the studio floor chatting, but the moment they saw me come in, they stood up and formed ranks, military style. During the silence that followed we scrutinized each other avidly. I was expecting them to have the ordinary misgivings any student feels when faced with a new teacher, or at least the same misgivings I felt about them, or simply the reserve that cloaks the gaze of any pedestrian in Mexico City. But the students who gazed back at me were smiling with curiosity and eagerness. Some were teenagers of sixteen, and a few were my age or a little older, but as I looked into their eyes, they all seemed several lifetimes younger than I was. For months I'd been waiting in terror for the moment I would meet them, and during long, sleepless nights I'd asked myself again and again how I would keep them from noticing my fear, my inexperience, the inadequacy of my skills. But after that first glance my primary impulse was to protect them.

When I saw the rags they wore for practice clothes, I was ashamed to have spent so much money on perfume and sandals. At Elfrida's suggestion, I'd taken up a collection of old tights and leotards among my classmates in New York, but they hadn't come up with much: dance clothes are expensive, and no one ever has too many of them. Certainly the bag I'd managed to fill didn't contain enough to replace this motley assortment of faded, ripped, and drooping leotards, made of the crudest fabric, all of them too short in the legs and too big in the shoulders, or the opposite. The almost military greeting the students had given me, their rags and tatters, the extraordinary variation in their skin tones and physiques, and their air of earnest enthusiasm gave them, to my mind, the look of a small army of irregulars, just back from a skirmish that had left several of them in a bad way but ready and willing nevertheless to go forth into the next battle.

As Elfrida was introducing them to me one by one, I took a closer look at their bodies, which would be the raw material of our work together. They didn't have what I was used to thinking of as dancers' bodies, but they were a unique and beautiful collection of people. One chocolate-colored girl had legs so long they seemed to emerge from beneath her rib cage. She was named Carmen, in homage to Cuba's most popular Virgin. Only one student—Roberto—was taller and blacker than she was, but he didn't have the same stiff look. The long muscles sculpted across his body suggested backbreaking physical labor, and indeed I later learned that he had been brought up in a family of stevedores and was used to hard work. Another girl, Antonia, was very serious, with porcelain skin and straight blond hair, not very tall but with long bones. There was a boy—José—with cinnamon-colored skin and classical proportions, and next to him a boy of medium height with a long torso, broad shoulders, and the pronounced facial features of a Spaniard. His name was Manolo, the classic name for a son of Spaniards, which indeed he was. Isabel, a girl with the profile of a cameo, also looked very Spanish and had something in her expression that bespoke great efficiency. Then came a girl named Pilar who was very overweight, with hair black as ink and skin white as paper, and finally a mulatto boy who struck me as the most beautiful of them all. He was named Orlando, and though he didn't look it, he was the group's youngest member, barely sixteen years old.

José, he of the cinnamon-colored skin, broke the rapt contemplation in which all of us were absorbed. At a signal from Elfrida, he made a short welcome speech. I don't remember exactly how I responded, but I know I was awkward: it didn't occur to me to express my joy at being in Cuba or to thank Elfrida Mahler for having brought me, but I did ask the students not to form a line from now on when they saw me come in. Elfrida's smile tightened a notch.

I had decided that in order to give them and (above all) me a greater feeling of security, we would begin by covering the terrain that was most familiar to us all: for this first class, we would work on Graham technique. I imagine I spoke to them about what I thought they could find in the technique, with its long and inventive series of codified exercises, all based on the vital movement of the diaphragm as it takes in and expels air. I suppose I must have told them something about myself and how I spent several years learning Graham technique, first in Mexico, then in New York. I don't know if I told them that the class we were about to embark on was the first I'd ever taught in my life. At last, because there was no other way to postpone the beginning, we began.

The first mass of the morning must give priests the same transcendent satisfaction that we dancers feel at the start of the day's class: the teacher arrives, stands before the dancers, looks them over to make sure they're ready, gives a brief nod, and then with an "And . . . one!" gives the opening count. At that moment the world falls into place. The sun rises each day, the earth rotates on its axis, the herds graze in the meadows, and we do the breathings in four counts—first without the head lift and then with, four times on each side, followed by the breathing with a spiral in the torso on three counts, twice; adding the head tilt sideways, back, and up, twice; and then the leg extensions, four times with the right leg—twice without the arms and twice with—and four counts to change to the other side. Nondancers may think it could drive someone crazy to do exactly the same exercises every day of his or her entire life, but during the years I spent as a dancer, this repetition seemed as inevitable, comforting, and natural as breathing, and never more so than on the morning when, having crossed continents, seas, and cultural abysses to reach that dance studio, I found myself again repeating the movements of the Graham canon with a group of students who put every ounce of their devotion into each new exertion. It was as if the entire studio had suddenly been flooded with light. I felt that there was no reason to be afraid in this space: the students and I would always have things to learn and share here.

The class itself was sweeping me along: Martha's floor sequence is as codified as the section of a ballet class known as the barre. As the class proceeds, the teacher chooses between this and that exercise of the canon, but fortunately for all beginning teachers, there's no need to invent anything. The movements already exist, and so does the sequence in which they must be presented. Seated on the floor with our legs crossed, we expanded and contracted our torsos, then added flexings and extensions of leg and arm to the contractions. Here, I told the students, you have to try to make your legs barely skim the surface, as if they were floating, instead of dragging them heavily across the floorboards. With the class under way, I began the process of memorizing the students' bodies. Orlando, the one I found particularly beautiful, looked as if he were built from wooden planks, though his feet were flexible and pointed well. Pilar, the heavy girl, was completely elastic and had the best sense of rhythm in the group. Carmen, with her long, supple legs, was obviously the one who had the best chance of becoming a dancer, but she had almost no strength. Seated on the floor, without muscles in her belly or back to hold her up, she looked like a marionette about to flop over. In general, all of them were surprisingly weak in the torso. Except for Manolo and Roberto, with their proletarian musculatures, all of them had flaccid abdomens.

The students, meanwhile, were examining me in turn. I was taking great care to perform the exercises well, not because I feared their critical scrutiny but because it was clear that whatever I did would be law to them from that day forward. If, while talking about the next exercise, I crossed one leg over the other, all of them immediately crossed their legs, too. If I gave a last little flourish to the movement at the end of a phrase, Antonia and Carmen imitated it exactly. Fifteen minutes after the class had begun we were all dripping with sweat. It required no vanity on my part to realize at a glance that Elfrida and Lorna hadn't been the most satisfying role models; nor did it take much modesty for me to understand that I wasn't earning the admiration of my new students: they'd yielded it to me in advance, for among the many things they lacked were teachers they could admire. Seeing them so enthusiastic and voracious, I wished I could be Mary Hinkson or Yuriko Kimura for them—two dancers in

mpany I particularly admired—and decided that if
as hard as I could that I was Mary or Yuriko, some-
r spirit and beautiful technique would show through
nents.

The floorwork ended, and we rose from the sitting position in
order to continue with the center section. The great strength
that the floorwork gives to the abdomen and inner thigh muscles
imparts an almost karatelike force to Graham dancers' movements and allows them to move through space with an inim-
itable elastic flow. But once my students were on their feet, their
lack of strength made them move spasmodically, as if they were
mainly struggling not to fall down. Rather than seek the roots of
each movement within their own bodies, they merely tried to
imitate the positions. It made me laugh to hear myself calling
out the same exhortations my friends and I had so often gig-
glingly mimicked as we were leaving Martha's studio. "From the
vagina, girls! Movement is born in the gut!" Martha would shout,
pounding her fist against her belly as if she were stabbing herself.
I tried to express the same idea with a bit less drama.

Finally, we reached the diagonal section. Here the dancer
moves across the floor from one corner of the studio to another
with a combination of steps and leaps that are more freely invented and more personally executed—the part all of us like
most. For those who are already members of a dance company,
this is an opportunity to dance without the tensions and restrictions of the stage. For those who haven't yet had the chance to
appear onstage, the diagonal is where they can move with the
greatest breadth and expression, like real dancers. For the whole
class, it's the moment to risk everything. Here the students
proved to me that they had dancers' hearts. They threw themselves into the movement, fearless and exalted, arms beating the
air, leaping with all their might, their faces filled with emotion.
A dancer can have all the technique in the world, but she will
always be boring to watch if she has nothing to say. My new students didn't have much in the way of technical prowess, but they
made me want to go on watching them a long time. They finished the class exhausted, and so did I.

After class Elfrida and Lorna accompanied me to the school

dining room, and I was finally able to see part of the Escuelas Nacionales de Arte.

The school was about eight miles from the center of Havana in a suburb once known as Marianao. It was a luxurious neighborhood with serpentine streets and immense gardens, rechristened with the indigenous name Cubanacán after the Revolution: the students either called the school Cubanacán or referred to it by its initials as the ENA. The ENA facilities were on the grounds of the former Country Club, which, along with the neighboring Havana Yacht Club, was a prime symbol of the "sugarocracy": the complacent, racist, corrupt, and—as even the names of the two clubs indicated—hopelessly colonized Cuban bourgeoisie.

There is a relatively unfamiliar photo of Fidel and Che, probably taken on the very day they came up with the idea of creating a vast school to educate the artistic youth of the entire hemisphere or even, with any luck, all that part of the planet then beginning to be known as the third world. The photo shows the two heroes of the Revolution pretending with great amusement to play golf. In fact, they were taking symbolic possession, in the name of the people, of the Country Club, of its vast English lawns surrounded by the *manigua,* the jungly Cuban flora; of its turquoise swimming pool; and especially of its resplendent main building, full of marble, chandeliers, and mirrors in the finest neocolonial California-Caribbean style. It isn't clear whether Fidel himself made the decision not to demolish the main building, when he gave orders to dismantle the rest of the club in order to turn it into a great breeding ground for the arts, or if it was simply that here, as in the rest of Cuba, the economic imperative required that buildings that were in themselves representations of the class enemy be preserved. In any case, when the school was built, each of the arts—theater, dance, ballet, music, and plastic arts—was given an independent complex of buildings, with its own classrooms and studios. But the school's administrative offices were located in the marmoreal salons of the old Country Club building. Anyone who came to the school had to pass through its wedding-cake portal and spacious lobby. Viewed as a work of architecture, the structure was a poor imitation of alien glories, yet in the period I knew it, it was beautiful, because the labor of Revolution was turning out to be very harsh, and after years of privation and constant scarcity the former home of the Country Club had become, even for those who had never enjoyed any of its luxuries, nostalgia incarnate, a ghost-building of by-gone splendor and ostentation, a magical world in a bubble.

The ENA dining room was located in that central building. To get there from the dance school, you had to cross what on that first night had seemed to me to be a jungle. And indeed, for someone emerging from the urban labyrinths of Mexico City and New York, it *was* a jungle: plants with leaves the size of umbrellas, ferns as big as trees, vines that fell to the river from the upper branches of a ceiba tree, and—in contrast to the supposed pastoral glade of Central Park—not a single building to be seen. But in fact, the other schools were only a stone's throw away, and students from those other schools soon began appearing on the path to the dining room. They eyed me with great curiosity: it wasn't every day that a stranger came to the ENA, let alone one who was soaked with sweat from head to toe.

The walk down the little path through the foliage seemed eternal. I'd been working for hours and desperately needed to eat. After three days of living on rice and bland soup in the hospital—an invalid's diet, I thought—I was ready to devour anything that was set in front of me. After what Elfrida had told me about the excellence of the students' nutrition, I was already seeing myself sitting down to a robust loin of pork accompanied by a mountain of fried plantains, and maybe rice with black beans, and a platter of tropical fruit to finish the meal. With embarrassment, I realized I was having to gulp back the saliva that was flooding my mouth. At some point Elfrida had remarked that, in order to avoid any shameful displays on some future international tour, the students at the ENA learned the very finest table manners, and that recollection worried me. I was awkward with a knife and fork, and I'd virtually never had a glass of wine: I hoped I wouldn't be the one to offer a shameful display in front of the students. But now I was quickening my steps to reach the dining room, which I imagined to be full of mirrors, chandeliers, crystal, and porcelain and chilled by a roaring air conditioner. I

wanted glasses or whole barrelfuls of any liquid I could get. I was
hot, thirsty, dying of hunger, and very tired.

What Elfrida had undoubtedly meant when she praised the
school's food was that there was no lack of it. When we reached
the dining room, which had neither tablecloths nor crystal gob-
lets nor air-conditioning, the students let us pass directly to the
front of a line that ended at what must have been the main
kitchen of the Country Club restaurant. Lorna managed to find
some tin trays that didn't have too many dents and held mine
out to the *compañero* in charge of food: a thin, wiry graying man
with a heavy three-day stubble who dished up the meals from
behind an immense counter. Thirty years later I still remember
his resolutely unsmiling face. He stepped over to a stove where a
few cold pots sat and placed a slice of hard green tomato in one of
the tray's small compartments. In another he put a slice of boiled
plantain. Then in one of the two larger compartments he served a
gigantic helping of rice and, next to it, a ladleful of the same
bland vegetable soup I'd eaten in the hospital—which, I now
learned, was made from chickpeas, with a few flecks of potato
and carrot and a large amount of onion. In the final small com-
partment he placed something dark, hard, and bouncy: gelatin
dessert.

"Con huevo," Elfrida told him: with egg. Those of us from the
dance school were entitled to an extra portion of protein, in addition to a glass of milk at breakfast and dinner and a glass of
yogurt at midmorning. The man fried an egg in a pot of oil he
had on the fire and placed the egg on top of the pile of rice.
Finally, on his own initiative, he picked up a clean spoon, dipped
it into the immense cauldron where he'd just fried the egg, and
dumped the boiling oil on the rice. Unsmiling, he handed the
tray back to me.

For a moment I was five years old again; the mountain of
starch, grease, and gruel that faced me was more than I could
bear, and my mouth and throat filled with tears. But it was ridiculous to weep over this lunch—which, I immediately understood, was far from the worst that the school had to offer. As I
picked out the driest grains from the oil-soaked rice, a consoling

thought came to me. I'd been promised a salary, and I began making plans. Surely I could eat very well in the restaurants of Havana; at least there would be fish from the sea that surrounded us, and tropical fruit, and the famous ice cream of Coppelia, which Elfrida had already told me about. As soon as they paid me, I decided, I'd go into Havana every afternoon and spend my income on ice cream and stupendous meals.

"When will they put back the mirrors?" I asked Elfrida toward the end of lunch, during which, as I learned more about the school and its routines, our conversation had gone quite smoothly. Now Elfrida raised her eyes with the unexpected flash of rage that would eventually become all too familiar. "Never," she declared, as if she were swearing an oath. I was confused. What did she mean, never? And why all the aggression?

We were talking about the mirrors that normally cover at least one and preferably three of the walls of any dance studio. When I noticed their absence that morning, I took it for granted that ours were the kind mounted on frames with wheels, which are used in many places where funds are scarce, and that they'd been broken, or been sent out for renovation, and hadn't come back in time. I supposed all that almost without thinking about it; the idea of a dance class without mirrors was inconceivable: a writer can read his text, a painter can examine his painting, a pianist can listen to the notes, but a dancer has no way of examining her work except in a mirror, because she herself is her own medium and instrument. The mirror is the most valuable tool a dancer has—even more important, perhaps, than the best teacher. From the teacher's voice alone one can, in theory, understand the correction "lengthen the leg from the inner part of the thigh, not from the knee"; but when that same teacher grabs your leg with one hand, pats the knee, and strokes or pinches the muscle that is to be worked while holding your back straight with the other hand, then, having achieved the desired effect, exclaims "Look!" and raises your eyes to the mirror, you can almost feel a kind of gear that links gaze, body, and memory clicking into place. The mirror is also a great help during adolescence, when someone can point out how ridiculous you look wearing the moony expression of Galina Ulanova in *Swan Lake* while executing an ordinary plié. Later, it helps you compare different dramatic effects, or contrasts of line, and maintain them.

The mirror also poses certain dangers, the greatest, of course, being its ability to destroy the self-esteem of the many would-be dancers whose bodies are something less than perfect. But Elfrida understood so little about dance that she thought mirrors were a symbol of vanity and of the decadence reflected in every tarnished looking glass in an ornate frame that survived on the walls of the old Country Club. *"¡Somos revolucionarios!"* she declared with a defiant thrust of the chin—We're revolutionaries! There would never be mirrors in the dance studios of Cubanacán.

Elfrida and Lorna offered to take me for a drive after lunch, but I told them I'd rather stay at the school and rest. They must have thought I was avoiding their company, and while that was true, I was also avid for a walk around the school to get my bearings and take stock of the world that would be mine from that moment on. From my room in the guest house I set out once more across creeks and through jungle, and in the small courtyard that was the heart of the dance school I stopped to examine its strange architecture. More than a school, I decided, the series of round studios with their communicating paths seemed like an African village. I changed my mind immediately: floating over each of the structures was not a thatched roof but a ribbed vault that gave the complex a fragmented yet majestic air, as if it were a great pagan temple or the lunar observatory of some past or future civilization. Who had built it? The sun shone with benevolent warmth, boughs swayed in the cool afternoon breeze. Everything was immaculate; not so much as a fallen leaf lay on the courtyard's brick floor. Pots of impatiens gave a cheerful greeting at the foot of the columns that lined the serpentine walkway. No one was there; the students were at their academic classes, and all the adults had left. I was grateful for the silence.

I reviewed the situation. My students were undoubtedly on the positive side of the balance sheet; I was enchanted with each one's unique beauty and with their intensity, with the clamorous, gesticulating way they spoke and the questions they asked when class was over: What is Martha's studio like? Is it true that an artist's life in New York is very hard? What do you think of my instep? But it was all too clear that their training had been almost criminally deficient—Elfrida herself had warned me of that from the beginning—and I had no idea how to cure them of all their bad habits: how to make them stop working their legs from the lower front part of the thigh, for example, and start using their abdominals instead of letting the back do all the work. I felt that my entire stock of knowledge had been used up that morning. And that was all there was to the positive side.

Among many other worrisome issues, there was, for example, the problem of music. There was no piano in the studio; nor was there musical accompaniment of any kind for the class. An old-fashioned record player could be pressed into service, but a class with recorded music is even worse than a class with rhythmic clapping; both teacher and students become puppets. The students were used to having their exercises counted out with clapping or a small drum, but that, it seemed to me, was why their movements had so little nuance, especially since they were at the age when most dancers have to learn to relinquish the excess of nuance that is called affectation.

Then there was the school staff. At lunch I'd met Teresa, the director of the folklore program, and of them all she was the one person to whom I took an enormous and immediate liking. Hilda, the school secretary and party delegate, I had met that first night when she welcomed me and paid the taxi. She was cheerful, straightforward, and hardworking. There was also Nancy, a woman of about twenty-five whom Elfrida had ultimately managed to recruit in Chicago. She'd arrived at the school about a month before I did and was in charge of the second- and third-level classes—children of twelve to fourteen. I thought she was nice, down-to-earth, and very *gringa*.

Finally there was Lorna Burdsall, the assistant director. Now, in memory, I understand her better. She too had gone to Cuba from New York City, where she'd been trained as a dancer and studied liberal arts at Barnard College. What had brought her to the island was her devotion to a college classmate who had become the man of her life: a big redheaded Cuban who, once back home, had planted a bomb or two in Havana before going to the Sierra Maestra to join up with Fidel's guerrilla troops. When Lorna married Manuel Piñeiro, he and the Revolution were young and rebellious. Ten years later she found herself married to one of the regime's most powerful and entrenched figures: Piñeiro was in charge of Fidel's personal security and that of all the operatives involved in the international struggle. He was the director of the legendary Departamento Américas, charged with exporting the Revolution and promoting the creation of guerrilla groups throughout Latin America. In theory, Piñeiro took his orders from the Central Committee of the Communist Party, but in fact he answered only to Fidel.

When I met him a few weeks later, I hadn't yet realized that Manuel Piñeiro was something more than Mr. Burdsall. Lorna was blond, still young, and attractive, though my snobbery kept me from seeing her as such. (I generally found very little merit in dance people who did not know how to dance.) She never spoke of her husband and seemed almost embarrassed by the perky red Jeep she parked every morning next to Elfrida's Soviet hulk. I imagine she must have had a hard time convincing her husband—who, apart from being officially responsible for the Revolution's paranoia, was the target of all kinds of hatred and attacks and lived and probably slept surrounded by his most trusted men—that she didn't need a bodyguard. Lorna went about on her own, and I never saw her use her status to achieve greater power at the school. Nor did I ever notice that the many small privileges I was able to enjoy during my stay in Cuba—the pleasant room I was given in Havana's best hospital, to begin with—were unquestionably due to Lorna's discreet intercession.

That first day the only thing I knew about Lorna was that she was yet another of the people in charge of the Escuela Nacional de Danza who understood very little about dance. Who, for example, had determined the layout of the classrooms? I crossed the courtyard and went back inside the largest of the three circular structures that were the vital center of the school. Each of these brick constructions sheltered only an indispensable reception area and then, down two steps, an enormous dance studio with a wooden floor. Each was crowned with its respective brick vault.

Between the vault and the walls some open brick latticework allowed a glimpse of the sky and served as ventilation. Visually, the result was extremely beautiful, but the acoustics were a disaster. Every clap of the hands populated the space with echoes; every phrase from the teacher generated ghosts. Nevertheless, you had to shout in order to be heard by someone on the other side of the immense space.

No music, disastrous acoustics, poorly fed students, no idea of how to conduct the next day's class . . . and Elfrida. I'd already seen the defensive, defiant glitter in her eyes, the inexplicable rage, and I hadn't even managed to launch the fundamental battle for mirrors. Would my entire future on this island be no more than one long confrontation with the woman who had hired me? The long discipline of dance had given me a habit of obedience, and as a Mexican I was always respectful of hierarchies, but just seeing her standing on her chubby legs, listening to her badly accented Spanish and the tight-lipped tone in which she said "we" to mean "you"—"we're going to work very hard for the new teacher, aren't we?"—provoked in me an uncontrollable rebellion. How could I stop it? How would I gain her trust when I was opposed to everything she seemed to believe in? There was no one I could ask for advice. I looked for support from some of that morning's memories and sensations: the contact of my bare feet with the smooth wooden floor polished by a thousand earlier footfalls; the laughing embrace we all fell into at the end of the class. But the anxiety and fear that had been hovering since the moment I landed came back and hit me all at once now, as if the air had been suddenly forced from my lungs.

THREE

Havana

The fears that troubled my dreams were dispersed by a clean, clear morning, perfumed by the smell of the jungle and riotous with the sound of a thousand and one birds, each rehearsing its own repertory of whistles, cheeps, and warbles. I arrived at the studio in high spirits, but even so, the next class, the introduction to Cunningham technique, did not go well. We were attempting to understand a practitioner of the avant-garde who performed onstage in the same spirit in which he exercised the discipline of meditation. For the students it was like trying to travel to Neptune. The more time I spent explaining, the more distracted they looked and the colder our muscles grew. Angry with myself for not having prepared a better class, I caught a glimpse of Elfrida and Lorna, sitting like statues in the viewing area, watching me, and suddenly I was sure that Elfrida deliberately modeled her conduct on Queen Elizabeth of England, the current one: she had the same little smile carved into the corners of her lips that Her Majesty always dons before she goes out.

". . . So that's why, in Cunningham technique, there isn't really a sequence of exercises that we'll always repeat," I heard myself saying, and got tangled into an even worse knot. There *was* a sequence, but it would vary, because art, in Merce's view, has to resemble nature, and nothing in nature is ever the same. So there must be varying approaches to the leg warm-ups . . . Pilar tugged up the sleeve of her leotard, then pushed it back down; Manolo was counting the muscles on his diaphragm with his fingers. Suddenly I couldn't remember if it was better to start off with the ankle warm-ups or with the pliés. We needed music. The small drum I was using to mark the tempo sounded as if it were beating a dirge for the death of time. The class ended at ten, and it was a relief to see that the hands of a small clock on loan from Elfrida had finally dragged themselves to that goal.

"Where so fast, *compañera*?" Teresa, the folk dance teacher, asked when I passed the door of her studio, burning with shame. "We're waiting for you in here. Did you forget that we promised to show you our work today?" Teresa was about thirty, white, with delicate, pretty features. The more terrible what she had to say was, the more she smiled. "I lost a lung because of tuberculosis," she'd told me the previous afternoon, her lips forming a gentle, mischievous curve. "Now I'll never be able to dance again," and the smile illuminated her face like sunlight breaking through an overcast sky.

"Come in, *niña*," she said now. "Unless you're not interested. It looks like the main thing on your mind right now is lunch, not Cuban folk dance. Does anyone have a piece of candy left over?" There were no volunteers, so she groped through her shoulder bag, took out a handkerchief tied in several knots, and extracted one of the pieces of candy she saved every day from the midmorning snack to take home to her husband.

Teresa González, or Tere, had spent nearly ten years isolating and dismantling the fundamental elements of Afro-Cuban dance. Her technical concerns clashed with my concept of what folk dance, and particularly Afro-Cuban folk dance, should be. I wanted it to be spontaneous, primitive, and if possible, a little bit orgiastic. Tere, however, felt great disdain for the showbiz of Cuban native dancing. When they graduated, the students who wanted to could join the Conjunto Folklórico Nacional, but Tere held out the hope, she said, that the technique they learned from her, those letters of the body's alphabet, would also be used by future dancers and choreographers as the basis for a new kind of dance: modern, yes, but fundamentally Cuban.

Some muscular jet-black men were sitting in front of what in Mexican rumba movies were always known as *tumbadoras*. In fact, they were the Batá, the three sacred drums—the Okónkolo, the Itótele, and the Iyá—Tere whispered to me as she settled down beside me. Hooking one sandaled foot behind the other ankle and modestly tugging down her short flowered skirt, she introduced me to the musicians. The one with the beret was

named Lázaro, the one with the little straw hat Teófilo, and the
oldest one, Jesús Pérez, was the most renowned Cuban *tocador* in
half a century and the last man who knew how to "make the
leather talk" like the Yoruba masters of old in Africa. In general,
the *tocadores* were dockworkers, Tere noted, and not professional
musicians. Commissioned by the ENA, these three *tocadores* were
collaborating as informants about the musical and dance traditions of the Cuban people. The *toque* that began at that moment
was an invocation of Yemayá, the Yoruba goddess of the oceans.
Nieves Fresneda, a tall, angular old woman, also an informant,
would show us the siren goddess's steps.

Nieves wore a circular skirt made of blue cotton that rippled
out through the air around her, its four or five ruffles edged in
white embroidery. She still had her blue jeans on underneath,
and she wore a bandanna tied around her head and a shirt with
the sleeves rolled up, as if we'd interrupted her while she was
mopping the floor. Dragging her rubber flip-flops in time to the
beat, she moved forward until she was facing the drums, which
were emitting a complex rhythm, interweaving the deep, reso-
nant tones of the Iyá, the softer and more pronounced beats of
the Itótele, and the sounds of the female drum, the Okónkolo.

At first her movements were regular and precise: her bony
arms sliced through the air like scissors while she marked out the
same rhythm as the middle drum with her feet, swaying softly,
her face severe. But just as the *tocadores* began to mingle their
voices in harmonies that were somewhere between Tibetan and
feline, a gigantic wave seemed to swell through her solar plexus:
crouching toward the floor as if a subterranean force had gripped
her by the ankles, she began undulating her torso, moving her
arms as if they were made of water, and shaking the blue skirt in
ever broader waves until she herself had become a sea.

My trance was broken by a sudden change in the rhythm—
faster, more jangly. Tere, addressing the room at large, announced
that the *tocadores* would now tell the *pataki,* or story, of the
terrible duel between Oggún, deity of the forest and of metals,
and Changó, lord of thunder and of war. "They're singing in
the Yoruba language," she informed me. At that moment I saw
Roberto advancing from one corner of the studio and José from

the other, my awkward, beautiful students, now transformed into gods. Roberto, his face overshadowed with fury, closed in on his adversary as if he were vengeance itself, with implacable steps that leveled mountains and toppled massive ceiba trees. José, arrogant and unsuspecting, made the earth tremble with his footsteps. His pelvis, more alert and alive than his face, was at the center of each of his movements, as if his whole being were a phallus.

Changó is a mischievous, womanizing deity, Tere murmured in my ear. His colors are red and white, and he is the preferred divinity of Cuban men. In combat, the folk dance teacher explained, Changó throws lightning bolts whose force emanates from his genitals, but in the end he is defeated by Oggún's great sword. As the drums beat louder, Roberto knocked down Changó-José and stepped over his vanquished body, and now it was the thunder god's turn to run and crawl from the fury of the taciturn god of trees. According to the legend, Tere explained, Changó had even been forced to disguise himself as a woman in order to escape. That was why, in the syncretism that allowed Cuba's mainly Yoruban slaves to keep their gods clandestinely alive, a female saint was worshiped during the Catholic mass: in the beatific person of Santa Bárbara, who in the iconography of Catholicism wears red and white and carries a sword, they were in fact worshiping Changó.

Unable to pay much attention to Tere's words, I watched a gigantic Changó shake his head and puff out his cheeks in rage; I watched Oggún, the Annihilator, brandish the serpent of his sword, and I trembled lest the immense sweep of his gestures knock me over. With the exception of Merce, Nureyev, Paul Taylor, and Martha's principal male dancer, Bertram Ross, I now concluded, all the other male dancers I'd ever seen were a pack of skinny fops. No wonder I didn't tire of looking at those two boys during class: they might not have my technique, but they had another one, and in the performance I had just seen, they were true artists.

The rhythm changed once more, and the other students appeared dancing a *rumba de cajón,* or box rumba (the first and most

primitive type of rumba, Tere explained, danced by the dockworkers of Havana to the sparse accompaniment of a wooden box
and a couple of spoons to mark the beat). Isabel, the girl with
the cameo face, was a superb *rumbera*. But my eyes were still
imprinted with the image of Roberto and José.

The next day, when my class was over, I stopped at the thresh-
old of Tere's studio to watch the final minutes of hers. The students were crossing the floor on the diagonal in great strides,
waggling their heads as Changó does in one of his movements,
lifting the advancing leg high, knee bent, foot flexed at every
step, then lunging forward into a deep plié. Advancing alongside them was Nancy, the teacher from Chicago. She was taking
the folklore class with her own third-year students, and she'd
already told me with a laugh that though she felt ridiculous, she
was learning a lot and enjoying herself. Watching her, I thought
that no one in the world had ever looked like more of a washed-
out *gringa* than she did, vaguely sketching octopuslike gestures
among all those wildly alive young *rumberos*. I decided I'd rather
die than give in to my enormous yearning to try out those movements for myself, and consoled myself by listening carefully and
trying to decipher a single two-four among the dizzying swell of
rhythms that flooded the room. When Tere left the studio afterward, I peppered her with questions. So, then: Each god has his
own rhythm, songs, *patakí*, and steps? And does each god have
an equivalent Christian saint? And this religion no longer exists?
Not quite, Tere answered. That was why it was important to
record and document it. But on that particular point I noticed
she was a bit uneasy.

There is a very famous line by the revolutionary *trovador* Carlos Puebla—"*¡Se acabó la diversión! ¡Llegó el Comandante y mandó a
parar!*" (The fun is over! The Comandante arrived and ordered it
to stop!)—and a joke that made it all the way to Mexico, in
which Fidel, exasperated with his people's perennially lubricious
ways, shouts an order from the head of a demonstration: "*¡Que se
acabe la rumba!*" (No more rumba!) Joyfully adoring their Comandante en Jefe, as ever, the people obediently sing out the
order: *¡Que se acabe la rumba!* [That sounds good.] *¡Que se acabe la*

rumba! [One more time.] *¡Que se acabe la rumba . . . Aé!* And with
that everyone starts sashaying down the avenue to the rhythm of
Fidel's exhortation, now irredeemably transformed into a conga.

I remembered that joke as I listened to Tere now, trying to figure out from her gestures and the gaze that she kept fixed on the
ground whether the shame I could see in her evasions and suddenly confused explanations was due to the fact that Fidel did
not know how to dance ("They say not even one step. He just
doesn't like to and—well, what can we do?"), or whether it was
because she was trying to explain to me that Fidel—and Che too,
of course—didn't want revolutionaries to waste their time dancing. ("I understand that we're not here to have fun. And of course
everyone has their own ideas about culture, and he has his, which
don't include popular dance. But the Revolution has always unconditionally supported this project, and that's the truth.")

"Have you ever had the chance to see Fidel up close?" I wanted
to know. "He's incredibly handsome, isn't he? Didn't he come to
the opening ceremony of the school?"

"No. He has more important things to do." Tere smiled. "You
have to understand, sometimes our leaders really don't get it
when it comes to their own Cuban culture, but that's because
they're still seeing Afro-Cuban music the way they used to when
they were fighting Batista and Yankee decadence, and even music
had become prostituted. *¡Compañera!*" In Cuba anyone about
to deliver a theoretical pronouncement always began by saying
"*¡Compañera!*" or "*¡Caballero!*" with great emphasis. "What happened here wasn't a Marxist-Leninist revolution, I swear, but a
gigantic national uprising against Yankee domination. I always
say that Fidel is the son of José Martí, not Lenin! Why else do
you think that every year he gives his speech to mark the anniversary of the Revolution at the foot of the statue of Martí?"

The explanation continued on the way to the dining room.
"You have to understand that in Batista's time, a mafioso, Meyer
Lansky, stuck his nose in here and succeeded in transforming
Cuba into a Yankee whorehouse. And all the boys who went up
to the Sierra Maestra with Fidel always believed that the rumba
and prostitution were the same thing. And, well, there's something to that. You know Hollywood sold an image of Cuba as the

place of pleasure and sex. Any Yankee who ever came here was a Yankee in search of the exotic, and you know that when they say 'Oh, very exotic,' the only thing they're thinking about is how to maneuver some juicy mulatta into the horizontal." Tere's explanation of the Mafia penetration of Batista's Cuba differed in one essential way from the accounts I would later read: she treated the cultural legacy of those years with respect. "It's true," she acknowledged, "that the rumba and the *son* have a lot to do with whorehouses, the same way jazz was born in the New Orleans brothels. And both are music played by blacks. Here in Cuba, among the leaders of the Revolution and the intellectuals, there's just as much racism as there was before among *la gente decente*— because they're all *decente,* if you want to know the truth. Or most of them, at least. Nice boys from good families, all of them. So our music and dance have been marginalized a little, because there are a lot of people at the highest levels of leadership—and I don't like saying so—who are ashamed of everything Cuban and think our culture is decadent. But that's just for the present. Because already, for the very generation we're educating right now in this school, for example, the music has other roots. And the leaders who are being born now will have a different mentality tomorrow."

"And Celia Cruz?" I asked.

"Celia Cruz left because she wanted to and no one stopped her," Tere answered curtly, and I thought it prudent not to insist. But the fact was that Celia Cruz, Cachao, and Pérez Prado, the greatest glories of Afro-Cuban music, had opted for exile.

"We have singers here who are much better, a thousand times better, than Celia Cruz, you hear me?" said Tere, as if she'd listened in on my thoughts. "And no one suffers one bit if she or anyone else goes to Miami. All they are over there is *gusanos.* Here on this island we have an inexhaustible supply of musicians, composers, and singers. Look at Beny Moré, the greatest of them all; he chose to die here."

But there's never been anyone else like Celia, I thought, and kept it to myself.

In time I would learn that in Cuba blacks are all too often *negritos* or *un negro* or *el negro aquel*. And that Tere was right about

Fidel's mistrust of all things "African," though that mistrust was often mingled with and compounded by his militant condemnation of all organized religion. In the wake of the anti-Castro invasion at the Bay of Pigs, Fidel made a speech in which he proclaimed the socialist vocation of the Cuban Revolution. After that all public religious ceremonies were prohibited, and a discreet but relentless persecution of religion began. It was directed primarily against Catholicism and its priests, but also against that other *cosa de negros,* Santería: the syncretic Afro-Cuban religion whose rhythms and legends formed the basis for the apprenticeship of Teresa González's students in Cubanacán. That was why Tere answered so evasively when I asked if Santería still existed, and that was why the Yemayá I saw, Nieves Fresneda, and the masterful *tocadores* like Jesús Pérez were called informants, as if they were mere anthropological specimens and not fervent believers.

I'd exchanged only a few words with the informants at the very beginning of the class. But it occurred to me that the best accompaniment for my class—the greatest privilege, really— would be the rhythm of the Afro-Cuban drums. I asked Tere if she thought the *tocadores* would want to work with the modern dance classes as well. She gave me a sidelong glance. "Well, give it a try! But it's not going to be easy. These people aren't easily led: if you want to pick up the beat from them, go right ahead. But if what you want is for them to follow you . . ." She shrugged.

It was not, as I initially feared, a question of machismo or hostility to modern dance. In fact, the *tocadores,* taciturn men who rarely smiled, readily accepted the proposal: perhaps they were interested in being seen as musicians rather than informants. In any case, one morning Lázaro, Teófilo, and Jesús arrived punctually at my studio with their arsenal of percussion instruments and set everything up to play. I asked them for a four-four beat, and we were all plunged into the deepest perplexity. Neither they nor I had the slightest knowledge of music theory, and I didn't know how to keep time with the *clave de son*—the "one-two-three, one-two" that is the basis of all Afro-Cuban music—which can coincide but not necessarily synchronize with a traditional European four-four. We tried for a long time; the *tocadores* ended up beating four counts four times on the largest drum, they grew visibly bored, and the rhythm felt to the students and me like a series of nails being hammered into a coffin. The students, who did know something about music, tried to explain what was needed to the *tocadores,* but there was no way. Tere intervened with no better results. At the end of the class I asked for a simple waltz time—"one-two-three, one-two-three, one-two-three"—and to their own astonishment the musicians could not even stay on the beat. They would start out counting with their lips and marking each "three" with their heads, and by the seventh or eighth measure they were lost. It was precisely what happened to me when I tried to decipher the *clave de son* in the *toques* to Yemayá. The mystery intrigued us and made us all laugh; it taught us something about the difference between what's learned with the head and what's assimilated through the body, and by the third class we were all fascinated by our failure.

We gave up on the experiment, but not before I'd brought the tape player, a technological innovation that even Lorna was unacquainted with, to the studio and recorded five minutes of a drum session. When I had asked the *tocadores* if they'd ever made a record I could listen to, they gave me a strange look. Just as the dance students didn't know what they looked like, Lázaro, Teófilo, and Jesús, probably the best percussionists in Havana, had no idea what they sounded like. I recorded the beginning of a *toque de santo,* rewound the cassette under the tense, expectant gaze of the musicians, and pressed play. We heard a flat, distant, tinny jumble of sounds. Seeing the musicians' sad surprise and disappointment, I stopped the tape. They took their instruments permanently back to the folk dance studio, with its wide latticework windows that looked out on the jungle. And I went on clapping my hands and using a little drum every morning in the modern dance studio and pacing around in circles every afternoon as I tried to reach a better understanding of how to structure a class and how to dance without music.

"I thought you were never going to call me," said Galo. "So I came to get you." It was the end of my first week in Cubanacán. I'd rejected Lorna's invitation to go to the beach with her children and was facing an empty weekend when I received a message in my dorm room that a visitor was waiting for me in the lobby of the administrative building. My Mexican friend's best friend, a man of medium stature, about thirty-five years old, with an amused gaze and a dancer's body, examined me from head to toe. I wished he weren't gay. "Well! Let's go for a drive," he declared, once his inspection was complete. "Want to?" I wanted to. It was true I would never have called him—I was too shy to make a phone call to a stranger—but now I felt like throwing myself into his arms in relief.

I ran back to my room for the gifts our mutual friend had sent. Galo's companion, a slender young man with glasses and a serious face, helped me load the stack of boxes into the car. With Pablo at the wheel, we drove off to tour the fragile, vaporous elegance of the Cuban capital.

"This is a city that never loses its refinement, you'll see," Galo said. "From the slums of Santos Suárez to the crumbling buildings of Old Havana, it's always elegant," he added with some fervor. "But today we'll focus on the neighborhood of Vedado." With its alluring name—meaning "forbidden"—its gardens overflowing with vines and its houses whose spacious porticoes were sustained by delicate columns, Vedado was the symbol par excellence of the capital's glory and of its ruin. From the beginning of the twentieth century it had been at the forefront of every trend: its collection of delicate but emphatically modern art nouveau houses and its compact art deco apartment buildings, each covered with designs and bas-reliefs as if it were a little sculpture rather than a large dwelling, were all jewels of twentieth-century avant-garde architecture.

We strolled down the sidewalks in the shade of spreading trees. The functional names of the streets—L and 14, 27 and G—contrasted with their extravagant reality. Here and there we glimpsed a turn-of-the-century mansion, protected by wrought-iron gates, covered with vines as if bedecked in lace, half hidden by the mango, *majagua,* and *almendro* trees in its ample gardens, and gradually falling apart without losing any of its panache, as if time itself had congealed around it to protect its beauty. This was nothing like the crude, exotic, movieland Havana I'd imagined until now. How could a revolution—by definition abrupt and radical—have emerged from this city of subtleties and the decadent filigree of light and shadow that filtered always through its vegetation?

"Now I see the movie you have in your head," Galo mocked, when he heard my exclamations of astonishment. "Big black men walking through the streets holding machetes, all the women wearing fruit-and-feather hats, and instead of TV antennas, coconut trees!"

We took a quick detour to admire that monument to the splendor of tropical tourism, the Hotel Nacional. Built by foreigners who came to Havana to bring their dreams to life, it bore a great resemblance to my own dreams, and as soon as I saw it, I wanted to stay in one of its shuttered rooms, which I imagined furnished with rattan rocking chairs and ceiling fans. "Don't even think about it," Pablo disappointed me. "It's primarily reserved for Soviets."

We continued along Línea, the main avenue that marks one of the borders of Vedado, until we reached Rampa, a broad, bustling street that starts at the city's most dynamic modern crossroads. Along the way Galo and Pablo played tour guide: this graceless modern building was the Hotel Habana Libre, once known as the Havana Hilton; here is Eloy's Bar; this building is the headquarters of Prensa Latina, the Cuban press agency; this is the Yara Cinema. The steep incline of Rampa ended at the Malecón, the oceanfront boulevard that runs along Cuba's northern border. As they crashed against the breakwater, the huge waves of high tide were drenching sidewalks, cars, and unwary pedestrians. Sea spray, ocean—and ninety miles away the United States, with its atomic arsenal, its hatred, and its implacable will to destroy the Revolution.

"Are we that close, Galo? Ninety miles isn't far, is it? Could you get there swimming?"

"You try it." Galo was continually astonished by the kinds of questions I asked, but we Manhattanites don't know how to measure distances bigger than city blocks.

"What's on the other side?"

"Cayo Hueso"—Key West—"and the theater where José Martí gave his final patriotic speech before embarking for Cuba. And a significant percentage of this country's population."

My relief at being in such congenial company made me voluble. I'd spent a week trying to hide the truth about myself: not only was I not a revolutionary, I was also ignorant. Now, with Galo and Pablo, I felt no need to pretend—maybe because it would have been useless to try to deceive Galo's ironic, observant gaze, or maybe because Pablo's presence was so gentle and companionable—and I fired off all the questions I'd been accumulating. What was Fidel like? Why wasn't the Plaza de la Revolución in the center of the city, like the Zócalo in Mexico? Why was there a ten-million-ton harvest? Why didn't Che stay in Cuba? How did the Vietnam War begin? Why was the official newspaper, *Granma,* so boring?

"Because it's run by fools," Galo answered. "Look, here's the university. That stairway there is where Fidel stood when he led the great student march of 1952. That's when he first started making a name for himself, not long before the attack on the Moncada barracks."

Galo was one of those people who don't fit comfortably into any category, which made life complicated for him and for the Revolution. He had once been a dancer but had evolved toward the theater, where his interest in physical movement isolated him from a vanguard occupied primarily by artists like the tragic diva Raquel Revuelta. While he was passionate about Cuba, Galo had a critical temperament, and his youthful travels had made him cosmopolitan. His critical spirit distanced him from other defenders of the Revolution who, while undoubtedly less passionate, were also more unconditional than he was. Galo was homosexual, intellectual, and revolutionary. ("Of course, I could have been born black as well," he consoled himself.) Galo's boyfriend, Pablo, had the face of a very young boy, but he had a degree in statistics and a fairly high-level post in the Junta Central de Planificación, the hugely important Juceplan, or Central Planning Committee. That afternoon we were driving a little Soviet car that Pablo had been authorized to use as a kind of medal of honor.

Galo's situation was less solvent: he gave classes here and there and was a part-time consultant to a theater department, but he had plenty of time left over to read, which he did voraciously. In fact, the only thing that made him exclaim with pleasure when he opened the boxes of gifts in the car was the French book with the dicey title that our friend had sent him: *Cuba, est-il socialiste?* by René Dumont. "This is an important man: he's a Maoist agronomist and a graduate of the Sorbonne—very well trained. He worked here at the beginning of the Revolution . . . Let's see what he has to say. I think what we're doing with agriculture in this country is creating one motherfucker of a bureaucracy. This is a country where you spit a *fruta bomba* seed on the sidewalk, and before you can say *diez millones* there's a plant three feet high in its place—and yet months go by when you can't get your hands on—forget *fruta bomba,* not even an orange or a mango— not even yuca, *carajo!*"

I didn't know what *fruta bomba* was, or what the Moncada barracks were, or what an agronomist, much less a Maoist agronomist, did, but I had no time to ask any questions because we'd just parked the little car on a stifling, narrow street full of noisy tenements that smelled like garbanzo soup, and we were now strolling around a corner to find before us, in the rosy light of afternoon, Old Havana's cathedral plaza.

It was like a small theater, cozy and intimate, with the same air of expectancy that an empty stage has when the curtain has just gone up but the dancers haven't yet appeared. Bordered on all four sides by stone buildings centuries old, the plaza was nevertheless completely free of the monumental impact that colonial sites in my own country have. We were in the capital city of an island in the sea, and the pale, porous stone that the buildings were made of was no more than petrified coral, floating in the eyes like sea foam. The plaza's warm magical atmosphere was also enhanced by the modest scale of its buildings and the way the tropics continually insinuated themselves into its façade of Iberian solemnity. The graceful cathedral, for example, was adorned by a frontispiece whose curving forms mimicked the skirts of a flirtatious girl. At the palace of the Marqueses de Aguas Claras, behind a forest of columns and vines, we could glimpse swinging doors and folding screens made of colored glass—the traditional *mamparas*—and windows that were topped with half-circles of the same glass, called *medios puntos,* all daubing their cheery reflections on the stone floors.

"Later we'll have Boris explain *mamparas* and *medios puntos* for you," said Galo. "They're his great passion." Who was Boris? "A friend we're about to introduce you to. He and Carlos must be waiting for us already. Let's go."

On the way back to Vedado, I let out a howl of frustration.

"What's wrong?"

"It's just that I forgot my money, and I wanted to invite all of you out to dinner in some magnificent restaurant."

Galo and Pablo laughed so hard that Pablo had to pull over, take his glasses off, and wipe away the tears. "Magnificent restaurant!" they repeated, and doubled over with laughter once more. I didn't get it. Galo bent toward me from the backseat, took my head between his hands, and gave me a sonorous kiss. "I promise you that someday we'll all have dinner in a magnificent restaurant. But right now all we can offer you is dessert, and even that is a lot."

Once more we parked at L and 23, the corner of modernity. Across the street from the Habana Libre was the park that was home to the ice cream emporium Coppelia, whose glories the students and even Elfrida had sung. We went in and immediately confronted a long line; Galo and Pablo checked through it until they found, about fifty feet away from the ice cream counter, Boris and his friend Carlos.

"There you are. When did you get here?"

"About two hours ago. The line's not so bad today."

Then Pablo told them about my generous invitation to dine, and this time I got the joke: if you had to wait two hours in line to get an ice cream, how long would you have to wait for dinner in a restaurant?

"A whole day," Carlos answered, without laughing. "And they won't give you the reservation for that same day. They say that now, to get a table at El Conejito or the 1830 you have to start waiting the night before."

Why? Why all the lines? Why the scarcity? Why the absurdity of a country surrounded by the sea without so much as a sardine to eat? Why couldn't you invite someone out to eat without including an eight-hour wait on line in your plans?

"It's because we're at war," said Pablo. "The United States has us under siege. Surrounded!"

"They've got us by the small hairs," said Boris, making a precise illustrative gesture with both hands. He shared with the majority of his compatriots an inexhaustible lewdness.

Pablo, however, was serious. He didn't talk much, except when he set out to explain some detail of the national economy, and he always adopted a learned air when he was talking about numbers. As he was now. "At Juceplan, there's no economic project that isn't sabotaged in some way by the Yankee blockade. It doesn't just make it harder to acquire raw material: many of our most serious production bottlenecks are caused by the lack of spare parts. Because, suppose we manage to get around the embargo by going to Europe and Latin America, buying urban transport from the British, for example, as we've been doing with the Leyland corporation, which sold us all the *guaguas*—buses—you see in Havana now. But even then, in order to really modernize the sugar industry in the face of the embargo, we'd have to start over from scratch! On the production side alone, in order to be efficient we'd have to buy and build a whole new sugar mill for every old American sugar mill we have, before we could ever begin to increase capacity. And what else could we do with no access to replacement parts or new parts or up-to-date equipment? The entire modern sugar industry was built by the Yankees."

He took a deep breath. "So there you have it: we have to channel all our resources and all our production into this harvest, and if we don't come out ahead this time, we're going to have real problems. And under such terrible conditions, with all these difficulties, there's nothing left for the population. The United ates wants to destroy us, and with the embargo they're almost succeeding."

"Of course we're doing our share, too," Galo put in.

The conversation moved at the same leisurely rhythm as the line. To almost anyone coming from the capitalist world, very little seemed to happen in Cuba. Only about a dozen films premiered each year, if that many, including the mortifying offerings of Soviet socialist realism. For weeks on end the front page of *Granma* would announce everything except the news (THE DELEGATION FROM THE BA'ATH PARTY OF SYRIA LEAVES FOR HOME AFTER A WEEK-LONG VISIT TO CUBA), while many things were happening that the public was never informed of (SERIOUS DIFFICULTIES IN REACHING TEN MILLION TONS). Consumerism, which in the United States tried to convince us all that we would achieve sexual splendor by switching to a new brand of deodorant, did not exist.

Neither was there much change in the daily life of the population: few foreigners came; few Cubans managed—or perhaps even tried—to get an exit visa, and it wasn't easy to obtain a permit to move to another city or even to a new apartment. Rarely were there any new neighbors. There was a prevailing sense of immobility, and since nothing ever seemed to happen, the hours abounded. Living suspended in time like the Vedado's old mansions often exasperated me, but at other times—such as that afternoon at Coppelia—it left me spellbound. Conversation, a way of sharing time that in New York was ruled by the imperative of maximum speed and concision, was, here in Cuba, a baroque art. Standing in line, Galo and Pablo ramblingly narrated to Carlos and Boris, in minute detail, the ride we'd just taken, adorning each stage of the journey with its little dose of exaggeration, sting, and humor, and there was still plenty of time left over for me to give a detailed account of my first week in Cubanacán. Chatting like this was delicious.

"What flavor do you want?"

Of the forty flavors posted, only four or five were available, and none of them particularly tickled my fancy, but the rum raisin turned out to be memorable.

"If we go to a restaurant, will they have everything on the menu?"

"Lately I've heard they have lobster, frogs' legs, and rabbit," answered Carlos, who seemed to be connected to some permanent secret transmission about anything having to do with standing in line and food supplies.

Pablo: "And *masitas de puerco?*"

"No. There's no pork."

Me: "And fruit?"

"There's never any fruit. But, *¡ven acá!* Tell us about how Elfrida Mahler found you."

The four of them left me at the door of Cubanacán, having first carefully shown me where the bus stopped and where I would need to change buses for Galo's house, "because there isn't always going to be enough gas for us to come and pick you up." We all hugged, but the afternoon's splendor was already beginning to darken, as if the black stain that eats away at the full moon had appeared. I was afraid of being left alone; I'd never been as alone as I was in Cuba. And I was also consumed by the most urgent and difficult question of all, the one that came up every time I heard a Cuban talk about the Revolution—*their* Revolution. It was a question I couldn't ask, because it filled me with shame: Why were all of them, from Galo and Carlos to the folk dance teacher Teresa González and even Nancy, the teacher from Chicago, so perfectly in harmony with the Revolution, and why was I so sure I was only pretending every time I tried to feel the same way? What would I have to do to become as interested in politics as they were?

That Monday, sitting on the floor during the *merienda* of yogurt and a couple of pieces of candy that was distributed at mid-morning, I tried again to arouse the students' enthusiasm for the Cunningham technique, which we'd be tackling again the next day. I explained a little more about Merce's work and the type of avant-garde dance I was interested in watching and performing in New York. But even the vocabulary was problematic.

"Here *vanguardia* is anything that has to do with the party," Roberto-Oggún clarified.

"Over there it's something that breaks with convention, isn't it?" interrupted Antonia, who was the daughter of artists. "Something that people may not understand but that can open up new directions in art."

"But if people don't understand, then what's the use?" Roberto wanted to know. "For example: When you and your friend do those performances you were telling us about, and it's not even a theater, just a street, and you haven't done anything to publicize the event, and the musician is just improvising anything at all on whatever instrument he wants, and you haven't even rehearsed with him beforehand, and you two are doing what you call 'movement sequences,' which doesn't really sound like dance—who is that for?"

"Well, it's for us," I answered. "And for those who can or want to enjoy it just because, by some accident of destiny, they happened to walk past us at that moment in that place, while we were engaged in that particular activity."

"No," said Isabel, a very serious expression on her cameo face. "I don't think that would ever interest me. It would be like dancing locked up in a closet! For what? It isn't that I'm interested in the Soviets' socialist realism"—Isabel pronounced the word with distaste—"or that I want to dance *Sylphides* like Alicia and her crew and hear everyone applaud and say 'How lovely you look!' But I think my ideal as an artist is to enter into communion with the public, to embody something—a mystery or an emotion—that's inside all of us, to transcend myself."

"But the other thing is even more moving," I said. "Experimentation, the true risk and freedom of creation."

"No, I don't think so," said José-Changó, who was listening at a distance as he stretched his leg at the barre. "But it's hard to have an opinion about something you've never seen. Why don't you perform one of Merce's choreographies for us, so we can understand what his work is like?"

I answered that I didn't know any of them by heart, and that furthermore I'd have to obtain Merce's authorization and he would have to be willing to let me use the work for free.

"Explain that one more time: He sells his work as if it were a piece of merchandise? He's paid by the item for his artistic time?"

The one thing I understood fully in the ensuing clamor was that I was completely undermining Merce's prestige. What was more, I myself didn't know much about performance rights and royalties, except that in Martha's case, she had strictly prohibited any staging of her work by any company but her own—a thing that struck me as entirely reasonable—and that Martha, but perhaps not Merce, insisted that any course in Graham technique could be taught only with her authorization and in exchange for some form of payment, even symbolic, made to her studio— a demand the students and I were brazenly violating. I decided to change the subject.

"But then what *do* you want to dance?"

"That's precisely it, Alma," Orlando cut in. For some time he'd been lying on his back with his legs raised and opened out into a V, trying to lengthen the tendons in his inner thighs, which were very tight, but now, with a bound, he was crouching on his feet. "You've just put your finger on it. The way things are, there's not much choice. Look: the only modern dance company in the whole country is the Conjunto. Is this entire class going to join? That's absurd: there's no room!" Never before had Orlando, the most beautiful of my students, said so many words at once, but now he was speaking urgently about a concern that was obviously not new. "And where, then, are the students who graduate next year going to go? What's more, the Conjunto always dances the same thing! Eduardo Rivero has two good choreographies to his name, and that's it. I don't want to grow old dancing *Suite Yoruba.*"

"I like the Conjunto," said Carmen, who had a lot of flexibility in her hips but not in her back and was seated with her feet in second position, struggling to touch her chin to the floor. I knew why she liked the Conjunto, whose rehearsals I'd already gone to see. She was made for the role of the fire-woman in *Okantomí,* a sensational duet that was the anchor of the company's repertory. I suspected that Carmen, who was less intellectually curious than the others, wouldn't mind growing old to the nightly ovation of an enamored public.

My pupils' earnest questions were actually alarming confessions: they knew almost nothing about the profession they had chosen to pursue. There were no dances they could watch on a stage, and no dances they could perform, and they had a ravening hunger, a *physical* hunger, for material. But Orlando was right. There was no way that all the students coming out of the ENA dance school could join the Conjunto, and furthermore, its repertory really wasn't very interesting. But where else could they go?

"Why, to the Folklórico, of course," said Antonia sarcastically, and José and Isabel laughed with her.

"What's wrong with the Folklórico?" Pilar, the chubby girl with jet-black hair, who was effortlessly doing a sideways split, then settling her navel, chest, and chin on the floor, asked indignantly.

"There's nothing *wrong* with it, no one said that," answered Roberto. "But think about it: if I'm breaking my back taking four hours of classes every day, learning this technique and that technique and this theory and that one—for four whole years!— just to end up dancing the same role of Oggún that every last folk dance group in every last trade union in this country performs—though I'll have a better costume, of course, a real machete, authentic choreography, and all that, but every night for the rest of my life performing the dance of Oggún, which I learned ages ago—then I don't know what I'm doing here."

"But the working conditions are good, and they go on tour outside the country," Pilar insisted.

"Oh right, very good conditions, *chica,* absolutely." Now it was Roberto's turn to be indignant. "Have you ever set foot in their rehearsal studio? Our studios are better. And have you ever gone to the Ballet Nacional building? Have you seen those studios? If Alicia wants a marble toilet, she gets one. And the first-class practice clothes they get? And the kind of food they eat?"

José: "The truth is that the Folklórico people are almost as forsaken as the modern dancers. The only dancers with any privileges in this country are Alicia's. They live the good life."

Orlando leaped into the center of the following silence, speaking rapidly and addressing only me, as if he were afraid the others would interrupt him. "Alma, I want to study ballet," he confessed to everyone's astonishment. "Don't get me wrong: I don't want to dance *Giselle* or *Swan Lake*—that doesn't interest me. It's just that they dance better than we do! They have better technique. Okay, all right," he raised his voice to be heard over the others' protestations. "We have a modern technique and they don't know a thing about that, but they move faster, leap farther, have higher extensions. I want to be able to lift my leg higher, too. That's not so bad, is it?"

Of course it wasn't, I told him. What was more, I was thinking of going the following week to the headquarters of the Ballet Nacional in Vedado to introduce myself to Alicia Alonso and ask permission to train with her company, because I couldn't go on for much longer without taking class. Why didn't we go together?

"But that's not really allowed," said Antonia.

It was the first opportunity I had to use a word I'd just learned: *contradicción.* This was a *contradicción* within the Revolution. Alicia Alonso was a marvelous dancer and organizational dynamo who had accepted an invitation extended by Fulgencio Batista to return to her native country and found a classical ballet company. When the Revolution came, she decided to stay on, and the Revolution adopted her as its standard-bearer. In ten years she had formed a top-notch company of dancers with their own performing style. This was admirable. Nevertheless, it was also true that classical ballet was the most extraordinary aesthetic achievement of Czarist Russia, though the Soviet Union's stubby bureaucrats had never given much thought to that origin when they came to power. Even I knew that in the USSR not a hint of modern or abstract dance, or any other dangerously avant-garde artistic movement, was permitted in the theaters. But in seventy years there hadn't been a single diplomatic delegation to the Soviet Union that wasn't invited to spend an evening in the Bolshoi Theater watching *Swan Lake* or *The Fountain of Bakhchisaray*.

Following the Russian example, Cuba's cultural leaders were

entirely unstinting in their financial and moral support for Alicia's company, while providing very few resources to the Conjunto Folklórico Nacional, which had the potential to be hugely popular, but with a repertory taken almost entirely from black culture. And at the same time, in Cubanacán, the leadership of the modern dance school, the most marginal and impoverished of all the nation's dance institutions—but perhaps the most fervently revolutionary—had taken up an already outmoded quarrel from the creators of the new dance in the United States and transplanted it to Cuba, decreeing that ballet was a decadent, bourgeois art and denouncing as a traitor anyone who tried to sneak into Alicia's studio in order to decipher the mysteries of a pirouette.

Poor kids, I thought. Not even I was that alone.

Then the miracle that everyone had warned me could not happen happened. "Be prepared for long delays in receiving your mail," Lorna took care to inform me. "Sometimes it takes as long as six months, though normally the delay is no more than eight weeks or so. It's because the people in intelligence have to go through everything, and they're understaffed. Occasionally"—and here she gave a quick laugh, as if asking for forgiveness—"they delete some things. Especially in the letters you send." Nevertheless, when I went by the school's reception desk one morning, ten days after my arrival, Hilda smilingly held out an envelope from New York. A letter from Adrian. He'd put it in the mail the day after we said good-bye to each other, about six weeks earlier.

Come back, the letter said. And since he didn't know anything about the people in intelligence, it said many other things, which I would never have wanted anyone but me to read for any reason.

I had met Adrian about a month before I left New York, during a training course for sales personnel in the shoe department at Macy's. The work paid a little more than waitressing, and I badly needed to save money for my trip. Adrian, more expert than

I, planned to take the five-day course and fail it, which would give him an automatic right to take it again. After the second course he would give up, thus obtaining, with a minimum of effort, ten days' pay that would allow him ten days off in which to write poems. Selling shoes was a horrible, exhausting business, he warned me when we exchanged a few words during the first day's coffee break, and he was right. I lasted exactly five days at it, and I think I held out that long only because I liked the idea of running into Adrian now and again, though I would never have admitted that. He was so disconcerting, it took me a long time to figure out that he attracted me. He was on the verge of being marvelously handsome, but he wasn't. He had a very beautiful body, but his bearing was ungainly. His enormous green eyes bulged out a little, his slightly whiny voice emerged from a mouth with a lazy downturn, and in general the expression on his face didn't give much indication of intelligence. That was why I let him approach me: I hadn't noticed—he kept his head low when he spoke—that at moments a light flickered in his gaze that allowed a glimpse of the hunter deep inside him.

He was ten years older than me. He was a Jew, born in Poland, and almost his whole family was exterminated in Auschwitz. The only one to escape was his mother, a very poor woman who managed to cross the border with him and take refuge in Belgium. When the Nazi troops reached Belgium, she managed to find one ticket aboard a freighter, leaving Adrian in hiding with a peasant family. She landed in New York, where she made a meager living as a cleaning lady, and was finally able to send for her son when he was seven years old. Adrian finished out his childhood on the Lower East Side of Manhattan and eventually earned a degree in mathematics.

When I met him, he was primarily interested in poetry and Buddhism. He also spent many hours a week practicing *kempo,* a martial art. He didn't much like the city. He had lived for long periods in the cold and inhospitable north of New England, near the Canadian border, but when I met him he had just returned from two years in Puerto Rico, which he left either because he broke up with the Puerto Rican woman he was living with or because he couldn't find a good martial arts studio to practice *kempo* in: I never really knew. He spoke quite a bit of Spanish, read a lot, spent hours every day working on his poems. He wrote only sonnets and lived in absolute poverty.

I have no idea what we talked about when we met at lunch hour in the employee cafeteria, he coming from his second training course, and I from an exhausting morning spent racing through eternal rows of shelves in search of six pairs in size seven and a half, then running back with the stack of boxes to place them at the feet of a woman who was obviously a size nine. Conversation with Adrian was so strange that I could never anticipate what he would say, or reconstruct his logic afterward. I do know that it was an implacable logic, like that of a very small child or a retarded person, and he would throw out passing observations that, in their simplicity, would have made the Buddhist monks he so admired laugh. He made me laugh, too (though it always took me a couple of seconds to figure out if he was joking), and then he left me thinking. I was also thrown off by his absolute lack of gentlemanliness or gallantry. He didn't wait for me to arrive with my sandwich before he began eating his (which he brought with him to work, so as not to have to pay a little more in the cafeteria), and he never opened a door for me. He never treated me to a cup of coffee. (In general, like many people who have lost everything, he was exaggeratedly careful with his money.) But he did come to find me in the shoe department one afternoon and insisted I go outside with him that very minute.

A solar eclipse was beginning, the only solar eclipse in more than twenty years to be completely visible in the Northern Hemisphere. All along Thirty-fourth Street pedestrians and motor vehicles were slowing down, until they came to a complete stop as the shadow of the moon finished devouring the sun. Neither Adrian nor I had special lenses or little squares of X-ray film to protect our eyes, and I didn't want to see this nasty business anyway. The death of the light frightened me. The air grew murky yellow, the silence was absolute, and suddenly all shadows disappeared, and we ourselves seemed like shadows in that dense darkness. The words *nuclear apocalypse* lit up like a neon sign in my head, chilling me. As a child I'd spent the coldest years of the cold war in Los Angeles, where I experienced the absurd elemen-

tary school rituals in which an alarm would ring and we students
had to imagine that nuclear war had broken out and curl up
under our desks to protect ourselves from an atomic explosion.
Thus, supposedly, we would manage to survive—but only in
order to witness the gradual death by radiation of all humanity,
in the permanent gloom brought about by a layer of nuclear ash
that would cover the sun forever. Standing there on a paralyzed
Thirty-fourth Street, wishing with all my strength that the moon
would hurry up and finish with its ghastly feast, I thought, *This
is how the world comes to an end.* Adrian stopped inspecting the sky
for a moment, turned to look at me, and kissed me.

There was nowhere for us to go. I couldn't take him to my
mother's apartment, and he was sleeping on the sofa of a friend
who lived in Coney Island. I spoke to a friend—the same one
who had asked me about diets and constipation—and she loaned
us her rented basement room while she was at work in a nearby
restaurant. The next day Adrian announced that he had rented a
room in one of the sinister hotels for the homeless that were then
multiplying on the West Side of Manhattan. They were called
single-room-occupancy hotels, were rented out by the month,
and were the last refuge of drug addicts, penniless old people,
the desperate. As the name indicates, they allowed only one person per room, and I imagine Adrian must have bribed the night
porter to let me in. We stayed in that hotel until I left for Cuba.
The place horrified me, but I will say that the sheets always
seemed to be clean, I never found any fleas or other bugs, and our
room still had its original turn-of-the-century moldings and a
window that overlooked the street.

It was a difficult relationship. I was even more riddled with
anxiety than usual during those final days in New York, and
Adrian's complete inability to protect me—which I interpreted
as a lack of will—filled me with resentment and fury. Compared
with him, moreover, I was a spoiled, bourgeois child: at night
Adrian would put a carton of milk and one of orange juice on
the freezing windowsill, and that was what we had for breakfast,
though I would have preferred a cup of hot coffee from the corner
deli. We would walk all the way to the supermarket to buy a
cheap loaf of bread, despite my protests that for a few pennies

more we could have the delicious bagels made on the corner—
which were, as it happened, the best in New York. I doubt he
ever suspected that our room repelled me; by his standards, it
was perfect: it had a bed, a window, a table, and a chair.

And yet we understood each other. He was living his life in
earnest, and I hadn't found that very often outside the dance
world. I valued his work as a poet, and nothing could have
seemed more manly to me at that point in my life than his pecu-
liar lack of superficiality, conformism, or duplicity. It was clear
that we weren't sharing anything, that I was only occupying a
space in his life for a few days, but I felt that it did him good to
have me with him, and I liked sleeping beside him. We never
spoke of an "after," nor did I think our relationship had a future,
which was just as well; in everything that happened between us,
there was something that left me disconsolate. I needed affection, and that he could not provide. The last morning I spent
in the hotel, I noticed as I was getting dressed that the smell
of smoke was filtering in under the door. Adrian insisted it was
my imagination, but it wasn't: a few minutes later the firemen
arrived, and an ambulance as well, to rescue an old man who had
fallen asleep with a cigarette in his hand in one of the rooms. I
left the hotel before they did, in an early-morning drizzle, to
pick up my luggage and say good-bye to my mother.

And now Adrian's letter arrived to change everything. I read it in
Hilda's office, tremendously embarrassed and trying to hide my
confusion from Hilda and Tere, who were grinning like thieves.
Then I went running back to the dormitory to be alone with the
miraculous envelope and decipher the tiny scrabbled letters in a
calmer frame of mind. I wanted to suck up the ink from the
paper with my eyes and discover hidden words between the
lines. I also wanted to melt the ridiculous walls that were shut-
ting me into this room and rise into some mysterious ether
where Adrian and I would embrace. *Come back,* the letter said,
and I read it once more to make sure the words hadn't rearranged
themselves to mean something else while I wasn't looking. *Come
back,* the sheet of paper said again.

I could have gone. The letter reached me just before the last of the bureaucratic obstacles to my stay in Cuba had been resolved. Only that Monday I'd been notified that I could stop by on Wednesday to sign my contract. I had yet to be paid (though to tell the truth, it didn't much matter: Lorna had loaned me a hundred pesos, and I still hadn't spent even one).

How easy the decision would have been if Adrian were the only one! But even as I read his letter with a wildly fluttering heart, a great worm of doubt was twisting inside me. The idea of life with Adrian terrified me; I didn't feel capable of such austerity. And that wasn't all. A flirtation in Mexico, which had lasted as long as my bronchial pneumonia, had left me confused, and I now forced myself to acknowledge that Adrian wasn't the only man on my mind. Jorge was homely, but he had indisputable panache; he knew about revolutions and had taken part in them; he'd visited me almost daily while I was sick, bearing books and magazines to entertain me while I convalesced; he'd made me feel flattered and protected; and above all, he'd said *"una flor da una flor"* (a flower from a flower) one afternoon when I presented him with a camellia from the bouquet he'd just given me. I was bewitched. One guilt-ridden night dimmed much of the happiness Adrian's letter had brought, and it was easy to understand why: I missed Adrian, he had a central place in my life, I felt bound to him by a mysterious, elemental physical bond—but Jorge intrigued and fascinated me. And there was another thing: I never, ever wanted to go back to that horrible hotel room.

The students' desires counted, too. Though I thought my classes were maladroit and full of mistakes, I couldn't help seeing that the kids had placed all their hopes in my course. I couldn't let myself fail and disappoint them all the more. And sometimes my efforts had results. That very morning, for example, while we were hard at work on Martha's floor section, I was trying to make them stretch their legs into second position by opening out from the groin, rather than just shooting their feet apart as they were used to doing. I ran out of explanations. "It's like sex!" I finally yelled, to my own surprise. "You have to open yourself completely to what you're about to receive." I blushed to the marrow of my bones, but the students suddenly came alive and produced a different kind of extension, intense and full of resonance: a real movement rather than just a mechanical transition from one pose to another.

I learned the lesson: that old fox Martha wasn't so crazy after all—she knew how to deploy her dramatic and sexual tricks not only onstage but in dance class as well. And I also learned that I was capable of learning to teach. I couldn't betray the students, and I wasn't sure I wanted to go back to Adrian. To my own great surprise, I realized that though Cuba—and above all its Revolution—scared me, bewildered me, and made me feel more alone than ever, I wanted to stay.

FOUR

The Harvest

The best part about going to the harvest, Yasmina said the following afternoon, was that "you can always get fruit in the country."

"And yuca. Even *malanga,* if you're lucky," Carmen added.

Once again a group of students—Yasmina, Antonia, Carmen, and Orlando—had come to hang out in my dorm room, riffling through the drawers and practicing arabesques in front of the mirror that stood on the dresser. As he was lifting one leg behind him, Orlando knocked a chair over with his pointed toe, went purple with shame, and didn't open his mouth again. The youngest of my students never missed a visit to my room, though apart from his outburst about ballet he almost never participated in a conversation. I could only smile at his muteness and try to make him feel as welcome as his companions. To tell the truth, he was a little more so. I relished the intensity of his passion for dance, and it was always a pleasure to look at him: try as I might, I couldn't find a single flaw in his body.

"When do you go to the country?" I asked.

"Every year on vacation," Carmen answered. "We usually go to the Isle of Pines—I mean, the Isle of Youth, that's what they're calling it now."

How lovely! I imagined the joys of idyllic vacation days filled with sports and swimming on a little beach surrounded by pine trees, but the kids looked less than thrilled. The Isla de Pinos, or Isle of Pines, lies a few miles off the southern coast of Cuba; trade winds guarantee it a relatively temperate climate, making it the ideal place for growing fruit, vegetables, and in particular all types of citrus. After the Revolution large halls equipped with kitchens and dormitories were erected in all the agricultural centers: during school vacations the government sent all Cuban students from junior high on up to work for the harvest.

"It's not too bad. We eat well," Carmen added, regretting the negative impression of Cuba she'd given me.

"It's boring," said Antonia.

"There's nothing to do," Yasmina explained.

"But at night it's nice; we get together and sing," Carmen insisted.

"And you can eat all the fruit you want," I chimed in; the thought of fruit was beginning to obsess me.

"And lose your taste for it," said Manolo, the one who looked Spanish and danced the rumba as if he were black. He had just come in looking for Yasmina, who was his girlfriend. "For example, let's say they have you harvesting watermelon: that's all you do, pick watermelon all day long. When you're thirsty, you pick a watermelon, cut it in half, and eat it. When you're hungry, another watermelon! After a while you never want to have anything to do with any watermelon ever again. You're practically bathing in watermelon, *coño*!"

Yasmina shot him a reproachful glance. The students weren't supposed to use swear words.

But no, exclaimed Antonia, it wasn't true that the watermelon thing was as terrible as Manolo said! Whereupon Manolo reminded her that she herself had just said it was boring. But that's not the same thing! Antonia leaped to her feet in her agitation. Yasmina interjected in her support that even if it was boring, you had the satisfaction of knowing you were doing your duty for the Revolution, and I resigned myself to witnessing what I'd already learned to recognize as a typical Cuban argument: agitated, deafening, and all too often deaf as well.

Orlando, who'd been looking over the things on top of my dresser, cut the discussion short when he turned around with a bottle in his hand. "What's this?" he wanted to know.

It was my turn to blush. He was holding the perfume I'd felt so guilty about buying, but Orlando had no way of recognizing it as such: the packaging manufacturers of the United States had recently discovered how to integrate compressors into spray containers, and now even perfumes fizzed out from their bottles looking like beaten egg whites. The students crowded around to watch as I gave a demonstration, and each one rubbed on a little scented mound of meringue, laughing in enchantment, watermelon and argument entirely forgotten. They sighed.

"Alma, why don't you tell us about another one of Martha's dances?" I had taken to acting out highly compressed versions of the Graham repertory, acting all the roles myself, but now I worried that I was encouraging an unfulfillable thirst in my students.

"Tell me instead what this business of going to the *zafra* is going to be like," I said to change the subject. "Has anyone from the school done it yet?"

"Yes, the music students went last year," someone answered. "It's not so easy to learn how to use the machete: one of the *compañeros* in the music school, Ricardo Laborde, who was studying piano, lost a finger."

Wanting to be as revolutionary as I imagined Tere or Galo would have been, I declared that I didn't think it was any worse for a music student to lose a finger than for a worker to lose one.

"But a pianist without a finger is no longer a pianist," Manolo shot back.

The sugarcane harvest, which was the focus of *Granma*'s attention and of so much conversation at the school, was also becoming the center of my own concerns. It was clear that I too was going to be expected to volunteer in the cane fields, and the thought alone filled me with horror. I was an urban creature whose experience of the countryside was limited to a few roadside picnics on the Cuernavaca highway, and in my short time in Cuba I'd already learned to hate the heat and the blistering sun. From the students' descriptions, I knew that what awaited me was stinking latrines, sagging cots, the relentless assault of flying cockroaches like the ones I'd seen that first night, rice and garbanzo soup three meals a day, and heat and sun, heat and sun. And what would I do without a dance studio? A year of no classes with Merce or Martha had already seemed like a lot—but whole weeks without even being able to train on my own? I hadn't gone to Cuba with the intention of sacrificing everything that mattered most to me, but I realized that, if I decided to ignore Adrian's appeal and stay on in Cuba, I'd be expected to participate in the *zafra*.

By May, the *zafra* was starting to reach its conclusion. Every day the front page of *Granma* bore a graphic showing the progress of the harvest in each of the island's six provinces and the total amount of sugar manufactured to date. Anyone who took the trouble to compare the graphics could see that during the first six months of cane cutting a million tons of sugar, more or less, had been ground every three weeks. But in the last month the rhythm had suddenly slowed. Word around the school had it that this was because the cane cutting had arrived at its most difficult phase. In order to reach ten million tons, said Lorna and Hilda with concern, even the oldest, most dilapidated cane plantations had been brought back into use. And in Cuba cane harvesting hadn't yet been industrialized. The *mocha*—the cutting of sugarcane by hand—is a brutal process: you have to walk along a row, grab a bundle of stalks, hack at it with all your might, and then drop it neatly in your own wake, so that a worker who always walks behind you can strip off the excess leaves and pile the cane where others will, in sequence, load it onto a truck, transfer it to a railroad car, and deliver it at last to the sugar mill. On the old cane plantations the *mocha* had turned hellish, a slave's work that "a free man can assume only on the basis of the most profound revolutionary consciousness," as Fidel put it. Sometimes, according to the students, who brought fresh news of the *zafra* from their friends in the music school, instead of neatly planted rows there were chaotic jungles of cane. You made your way slowly in the maddening heat, searching for the base of each individual cane, cutting one here, then another one sticking out over there, then advancing one more step, perhaps forward or perhaps in a circle, since quite often there was no path to guide your way.

It was no easy matter, either, to coordinate the timing of the harvest. The right moment for cane cutting to begin had to be determined separately for each region, and then the *macheteros* had to be mobilized to get there. The deadline for completion of the *zafra* had been set for July 15—an impossible goal, but perhaps not for revolutionaries.

Her usual laughter dimmed by worry, Hilda instructed me on the global importance of this harvest and how absolutely essential it was to triumph. Full and final liberation from the yoke of dependence was at stake! Cuba would be the first small, poor country to achieve socialist prosperity on its own! Since October of the previous year, the entire country had been organized into brigades of cane cutters, she told me. "And it's been just the same for everyone, *compañera,* from the age of eighteen on up." Older people, or those who weren't sufficiently fit to wield a machete, were sent out to vast rice fields and newly planted citrus groves. "We're living out a great epic," Hilda rhapsodized, as she always did when she talked about numbers. "Just imagine that more than a million Cubans have taken part in the *zafra*—half the country's labor force. Every factory and every school, including the ENA, has already sent at least one brigade. And we'll send all the brigades it takes! We're not going to lose this race for lack of a final push." Brigades were also sent by every one of the trade unions and by the organizations of—I now learned a new term—the *masses:* the Federation of Cuban Women, the Committees for the Defense of the Revolution, the Union of Writers and Artists. The armed forces were mobilized in their entirety.

"Don't forget the international brigades," added Osvaldo, a professor from the academic track who was also a party militant.

"From France, Vietnam, Japan, Canada," Hilda declaimed with great emotion.

"Why, *chica,*" Osvaldo said in a more playful tone, "there hasn't been a single delegation of friendship with the Cuban people, however small, whether it's from Libya or Panama, that doesn't end up doing some time in a cane field!"

"And there's the Venceremos," Hilda noted. Under her gaze the teacher recovered his serious demeanor.

"Of course," he agreed, once again breaking into the odd colloquial rhetoric of all Cuban conversations on politics. "All the *Internacionalista* brigades are important, but none has the same value as the Venceremos, which is living proof for us that the imperialist government is not the same thing as the American people. The members of the Venceremos Brigade had to organize in secret, you know, and gather in Canada for the journey here, and they've had to violate all kinds of prohibitions on contact between U.S. citizens and the Revolution. Just imagine, if it weren't for those laws, the entire population of the United States would be *fidelista,* and the world revolution would take a great leap forward. The Venceremos is the best: the Black Panthers, the Chicanos are all in it—it's a tremendous vanguard."

"Will they get to meet Fidel? I'll never meet him, will I?"

"Yes, they will. It's only natural that Fidel spends quite a lot of time with them. They're extremely valuable to us."

"You see," smiled Tere, who'd just stepped into Hilda's office, "you'd have done better if you'd come here to cut cane."

"Tere, don't say that to the *compañera.* Just look at her face! Don't get upset, *chica,* none of us here has ever met Fidel, but we know he values our efforts."

Chicanos from Los Angeles, piano students from Cubanacán, office workers from Camagüey—the problem was that no one had given any thought to the low productivity of these improvised *macheteros.* That didn't matter so much where the *Internacionalista* brigades were concerned, since their contribution was strictly symbolic. But any dancer could have told Fidel that the movements of the dance of the *zafra*—elastic when stooping to the base of the stalk, where most of the sugar is stored, forceful when cutting the bundle of stalks with a single stroke of the machete, and precise when stripping each cane of its leaves— can't be learned in a single day, or even in several. The *zafra* had barely begun when already a high-level member of the Cuban Communist Party, Armando Hart, had to travel to Camagüey, the province that was second highest in sugar production, to reproach the brigade leaders for their *macheteros'* low yields. Hart thought the problem was ideological, but even the "vanguard" groups then being formed around the island—"forces that assemble an important contingent of Communists such as, for example, the Youth Column of the Centennial"—were producing very little, he complained. In all positions of administration and coordination, the poorly performing technical personnel would have to be replaced with good cadres, he said: put party militants with leadership abilities in there, and the efficiency of all the *machetero* brigades would equal that of the army.

This, in any case, was the intricate explanation Pablo offered one afternoon for the situation in the cane fields, but Galo buzzed with disdain as he listened: "If those Superman-model militants existed, they'd already be governing the country. Fact is, the Revolution has spent ten years trying to form an administrative cadre. But anyone who knows anything at all about managing any enterprise left long ago for Miami."

He'd been reading the book *Cuba, est-il socialiste?* And he now scolded me for my lack of intellectual rigor.

"You should read Dumont's book. It's very good."

"*Ay Galo,* but it's in French!"

"But you speak French."

"Yes, but I don't speak agronomics!"

"Listen to this," he insisted to the others, turning away from my ignominy. "'In the cane harvest, a competent worker will cut from 3.5 to 4 metric tons per day . . . but the very best of the average citizens, only 500 kilos. The rest of them will cut from 250 to 300 kilos, especially if they're bureaucrats or intellectuals who are in no shape for the physical effort. . . . These urban workers keep their regular salary, which is much higher than that of the agricultural workers, and nevertheless produce much less. The economy thus ends up with production costs that are far too high, and very poor outputs which then cause serious shortages.'"

I didn't grasp the implicit conclusion: that if a kilo of sugar produced by an intellectual were sold for the actual cost of its production, it would cost as much as caviar. But I did understand that the cane cutting was going far too slowly.

The workers who were producing well in the *zafra* were the members of the army—young men in optimum physical condition, responding to a vertical chain of command—and the men born in the cane fields, the historic *macheteros,* sons and grandsons of *macheteros* who had learned to cut cane almost as soon as they could walk. But there were fewer and fewer of these traditional *macheteros*: as soon as the Revolution gave them the chance, they fled from the impoverished countryside to the cities. And it was partly because of this migration toward prosperity and social services—a great achievement of which the Revolution was very proud—that an entire nation of inept *macheteros* had to be mobilized at such a high cost.

In the end, I didn't cut any cane during the harvest: to my great relief, I was exempted because of my cough. I thought about going with Nancy to work in the Green Belt of Havana, even though that program was already an acknowledged failure, but when the school wouldn't authorize that either, I didn't complain. In any case, Nancy told me that her excursion with the night brigade from the ENA was a waste of time. The van that was supposed to pick them up arrived two hours late, there weren't enough lights to illuminate the fields at night, and under cover of darkness quite a few of the *compañeros* found themselves some little corner in which to while away the hours chatting or making out. ("Such irresponsibility.") During the final weeks of the harvest I was able to continue giving my dance classes every morning, and I spent the afternoons in the empty studio trying to design my courses better and rehearsing a dance that was very important to me. The work was a gift from Sandra Neels, a member of Merce's company and the regular teacher of the intermediate class at his studio.

Sandy was such an important figure in my life that even after Merce invited me to join the advanced class, I still often took the intermediate one as well, always when Sandy was teaching. I found everything about her wondrous and exotic. Among other things, I'd never seen feet like hers. Mine were so wide and flat they seemed like spatulas, but Sandy's were like hands, with long, expressive toes that would languidly stroke the floor before gathering into a point and taking their leave of it. I think I was never as much of an adolescent as during the time I spent trying to make my feet acquire the prehensile flexibility of Sandy's.

In fact, I wanted to imitate every aspect of her, even though she was so different from me—or perhaps because of that. I had wide hips and a long waist and looked as if I were rooted in the earth, while Sandy reminded me of an ant: she had huge round eyes in a small face, a little waistless torso, and extremely long, slender legs that she moved with no apparent effort, as if they were her antennae. Onstage her elongated figure and the concentrated seriousness of her dancing made her appear to be the most spiritual of Merce's dancers, but in real life she was very funny, with a racy sense of humor that sometimes shocked me. At the same time she was perhaps the hardest-working member of Merce's company, both in rehearsals and in the classes she taught. She arrived at the studio at the beginning of each week with a notebook in which she had written out an extended series of movements and combinations, always very beautiful, that we would develop in class over the following days. Her teaching was so generous that it made me forget fear, for the first time. My aim in class was no longer simply not to look ridiculous in the mirror; I began trying to be as faithful as possible to the movement of my own body: that is, I began articulating the dance at last, and Sandy observed and corrected me with increasing care.

As if that weren't enough, this magical dancer did me the favor of treating me as if I were her friend and not her dedicated fan: she joked around with me, we talked about dance, and she even invited me home to dinner with her boyfriend. (But I was too shy to accept.)

Only a few days before I left for Cuba, she came looking for me in the dressing room after the advanced class was over. Holding out one of her extraterrestrial hands, she presented me with a gift. It was an envelope containing a series of note cards, and to my frozen astonishment the first of them said, "Dances for Alma while teaching in Cuba." I looked up from the envelope, and Sandy shrugged and raised her eyebrows. "I don't know if you'll like it." Today I understand that the moment was as risky for her as it was for me: it wasn't a fairy godmother but a choreographer full of creative doubts who was giving me the most overwhelming and unexpected gift I had ever received. I promised Sandy that I would take good care of her present, and indeed, I wrapped it in my favorite Indian scarf and carried it to Havana next to my passport and all my money. Now at last, with a slightly ridiculous and marvelously unreal sensation of having left my own life to enter a film (*The Life of the Artist*), I prepared to rehearse the work.

When she handed me the envelope, Sandy had explained the methodology of her proposal. "Every card has a complete movement sequence," she said. "Some we've already worked on in class, others we haven't. You can present them however you like: if you want, you can rehearse each sequence separately, and then just before the performance you can decide how to choose what order you'll dance them in. You could start by throwing the cards into the air, then picking them up at random, one by one, and dancing each one as you go along. Or you could give them to the spectators and have them hand you the cards they would like you to perform. You could also learn them all from memory in the order you like best." I understood clearly that she would be disappointed if I chose that last option. To get the first rehearsal started, I put all the cards facedown on the floor, moved them around a bit, and chose one.

Adagio—from first position, facing front: plié on left leg and curve the spine while the right leg brushes toward front *coupé*. Stay in plié as right leg lifts to the knee and passes to back *coupé*. Slide the right foot in front of the left knee again to fourth position *relevé* on a left diagonal with the back still curved and left knee bent. Shift weight to right leg, extend left leg back, with spine stretching toward front diagonal. Semicircle with left toward front to fourth position, curving the spine again, and come to fifth position *relevé,* keeping knees bent.

In the enormous studio I translated the words, one by one, from the card to my body. It was strange, dry, sterile work, but I was confident that if I read them enough times, the words would start to move. Or maybe they wouldn't. Had anyone ever learned a choreography by correspondence? I should have started working on it with Sandy, in her living room or in Merce's studio. Or we should at least have talked about it, going through my questions, seeing where the obstacles lay, setting up a code. But of course at that point all I was concentrating on was Adrian. Let's see: Where it says to pass the foot over the knee to the floor—

which foot was it, and which knee, and which of the two goes to the floor? Obviously, obviously, I hadn't given Sandy's gift the attention it deserved.

This would have been infinitely easier with a mirror, I thought. I knew my teacher's kinetic logic so well that whenever she demonstrated a sequence for the first time, I could predict each movement before she performed it. Now I couldn't even see myself, and my intuition was blindfolded. *Elfrida strikes again,* I muttered with rage. The woman demanded blind obedience, I thought. That was why she'd had the mirrors removed, so that the kids wouldn't even have the freedom to control their own image. She wanted the obedience of a soldier, not an artist, but I was never going to stand at attention and salute her. I went on smoldering like that for some time, until suddenly I found a latch for the sequence "shift weight to right leg, extend left leg back," which allowed me to open up the following movement, the circle with the left leg, and find the balancing point where I liked to be: deeply rooted into the floor, and opening out wide from that base to embrace the air around me.

"Well, that wasn't such a bad start," I decided sometime later, toweling off sweat in the dressing room. "Maybe I'll show that to the class tomorrow and see what they think of it."

It was turning out to be impossible to communicate a vision of Merce Cunningham's work and worldview on the basis of a few exercises, which for the most part hadn't even been invented by him but by me. Unlike Martha, Merce did not structure his technique classes around a fixed canon of movements other than a brief series of warm-up exercises. What came next depended on the creativity and inspiration of each teacher and the needs of his or her students, but always in accordance with Merce's principles—which, as one might expect in a student of Buddhism, he had never codified in words. But the exercises I put together for Cunningham class were my first attempt at choreography, and I was struggling. When the air cooled in late afternoon and the birds profited from the winds' cadence to rehearse their last arias of the day, I worked on the movement sequence we would practice in class the next morning. I was never sure, though, that the exercises I invented were a satisfying reflection of Merce's dynamic structures. Now, thanks to Sandy, I had whole sequences, beautiful sequences, of a dance piece created by someone in complete harmony with his work.

The structure of a Cunningham class—the sequence in which the different types of exercises had to be presented—was complicated, but beyond that I was becoming more and more certain that the cultural abyss between Merce's vision and the students' could not be bridged. How to explain to a teenager raised in the Cuban Revolution that the most important word in Merce's vocabulary was *still*? That lone syllable summed up Merce's attitude toward life and toward dance, and it couldn't even be translated into Spanish. *Stillness* is the quiet that things and beings achieve when they have no consciousness of themselves, when they simply *are,* without intention or aim. *Consciousness,* however, was Fidel's key word—self-consciousness, class consciousness, revolutionary consciousness—and in Cuba a human being without aim or intention was inconceivable, unless of course he was a *vago*—a slacker—who, as Fidel began proposing around that time, deserved to be thrown in jail.

During class I stood in the center of the studio and tried to make the students see *stillness*—an absolute quietude, like an animal's, growing out of a harmonious position of the body— and it was futile. It made no sense to seek stillness in the middle of a Revolution, and the kids looked bored in the Tuesday and Thursday classes. It was best to try to generate some enthusiasm by teaching them about the freedom of movement in the legs Merce gave, which Martha's exercises did not impart: the marvelous adagios, the swiftness in the feet, the impossible shifts in direction. Perhaps through these technical achievements the students would manage to grasp one of the essential qualities of Merce's work: its extreme modernity. For what else did the Revolution aspire to but the latest, most advanced, most perfect modernity?

But how to teach a student to draw semicircles in the air with one leg when he didn't know how to stand firmly on the other, sustaining leg? I imagined Sandy observing me in the middle of the studio and put the question to her.

"Start with the feet," Sandra suggested, elegantly caressing the long toes of her own feet with her extremely long fingers. "If you can't begin from the center, which is the torso, and stillness, then begin from the base, and work with their feet."

I was walking to the studio after breakfast, thinking about feet and the difficult class that was about to begin, and about the snarl of still-unresolved conflicts that Adrian's letter had plunged me into, when Elfrida signaled to me from the door of Hilda's office. In the cool penumbra of the room, I was met with an expectant silence. Behind her little desk Hilda gave a faint smile. Standing beside her, Elfrida, with her usual haughty glare, said there was a small matter that had to be cleared up with respect to certain reports that had reached her. She turned to give the floor to Hilda. Indeed, the school secretary and party delegate stated, there were reports that some students were meeting with me in the dormitory reserved for foreign guests. Could that be true?

"Of course," I answered.

Well, then, said Hilda, I should know that this was not allowed. The proper place for exchanges between professor and students was the classroom, and if in the dining room during the lunch hour I happened to feel like imparting some aspect of my knowledge and extremely valuable experience to them, she, in the name of the school and the Revolution, would thank me for that right now. But I had to understand that at the Escuela Nacional de Danza—where the students were all young people without any knowledge of life, entirely unprepared to evaluate the very great differences that existed between their world and that of an internationalist such as myself, who came from such a different reality to share wholeheartedly in their destiny—any undue, or rather not undue but inadvisable, fraternization could lead to situations that none of us would want for the young people we were all helping to prepare for a better future.

I thanked the party delegate for her advice. After class was over, I headed straight for the dormitory and hid under the sheets. It was as if some sort of succubus had taken possession of Hilda. I was afraid of her, and enraged with Elfrida, who hadn't even tried to avoid the little auto-da-fé that was now making me burn with humiliation. I was even more ashamed of myself, for having heard out and accepted my condemnation without protest. Could it really be against the rules for a group of students, among them several who had already reached legal adulthood, to converse with a teacher in her room? The idea struck me as offensive and impossible. Every explanation that occurred to me struck me as vulgar and incredible. And who had seen us? Had the kids themselves denounced me? All of them? Which one? I pictured my students, one by one, standing in front of Hilda to make their accusations, hands crossed respectfully behind their backs, and I couldn't imagine which of them was suited to that role. But my most intense embarrassment arose not from the vision of my imaginary betrayer but from my own awareness—persistent, repressed, and now further unsettled by all the treacherous comings and goings of my heart between Jorge and Adrian—of how much I liked the body of teenaged Orlando. Had someone noticed? Could that have been my sin?

The next day I went to the administrative offices of the ENA to sign my contract. Before that I had a talk with Elfrida. I was surprised by the tone I used with her; it was identical to the one Hilda had used with me in her presence, and I now employed it to perfection without prior rehearsal. I was very sorry, I told her, but after taking various factors into consideration, I had reached the conclusion that my health problems—I still hadn't stopped coughing—and the absence of any adequate way of pursuing my own professional training made it inadvisable for me to stay in Cuba until the date she and I had, some time ago and under different conditions, originally agreed upon. Instead of staying at the Escuela Nacional de Danza until May of the following year, as had been proposed, I thought it best to return to New York at the end of the current semester, in December.

Why December? Why not now? And why not simply keep my promise to stay a full year? I had no idea. I didn't know what I wanted or what I was doing, but I felt a certain relief when

I saw Elfrida's face. For once the little smile that twisted the corners of her mouth had vanished, and for once we were in agreement.

I ran into Hilda in the corridor, and before I could spin on my heel and run in the opposite direction, she greeted me with the same smile as ever. "¡*Compañera!* How are we doing this morning?" Did this mean she was sorry that she'd humiliated me the day before? Or perhaps the initiative hadn't been hers—had it been Elfrida who received the reports against me? Impossible: no one in the school had enough respect for Elfrida to inform her of anything. Had Hilda received the order from higher up? From whom? Or perhaps the incident that had upset me so much was simply a normal occurrence in Cuba, a thing of no importance, a tranquil word of advice about the norms of the Revolution. But this last explanation is only now occurring to me. At the time I squirmed in bewilderment and uncertainty.

Learning Sandy's dance gave my afternoons purpose and also heightened my conflicts. It was impossible to rehearse this choreography without asking myself why I would want to dance it in Cuba. I lacked even the most elementary preparation for that kind of reflection. When I chose a form of abstract dance as my vocation, and a relationship with the audience that was very intimate but also arbitrary, I was simply exercising one freedom among the many offered me by the immense artistic panorama of New York. I was guided entirely by my own tastes and instincts, and no one ever asked me to justify my decision. Even during rehearsals the very abstraction of the artistic form I had selected freed me from the need to ask myself why. Someone performing a narrative work has to interrogate herself constantly: Why am I making this movement? What is motivating or leading me to do it? In theatrical dance, both the choreographer and the dancer must know what emotions are impelling their character to raise an arm or leap across the stage. But someone interpreting an abstract choreography has to think about rhythm, dynamics, nuances, contrasts, and impulses—and never motivation. Now those questions could no longer be postponed. Why this dance? For what reason? For whom? Alone in the studio, I tried to close the door on these questions, but they knocked louder and louder.

I was beginning to feel that being an artist and a revolutionary in Cuba was very difficult—or at least, being an artist of the Revolution. One night I went with Galo to see an "oneiric homage" to Gabriel García Márquez's *One Hundred Years of Solitude* that he and his friends from the experimental Studio Theater were putting on that year. The actors were stupendous, their physical training alone was extraordinary, and everyone involved participated in the production as if it were a sacred cause. Nevertheless the work was leaden, pretentious, and long, and the theater was empty. At that point the inhabitants of Havana were working from eight to twelve hours a day, spending another couple of hours getting to and from work, and at least another hour standing in line at the corner store to pick up the foods that were authorized by their ration cards and happened to be available that day. What resident of Havana in that arduous year wanted to spend his night off sitting in a theater watching seven actors stuffed into black leotards writhe around on a bare stage shouting, "Macondo! Macondo!"?

I asked my friends if there were any painters whose work was worth seeing. It was a Saturday night, and Pablo, Carlos, Boris, and I had gathered in Galo's cool, spacious apartment to eat macaroni with Australian butter and garlic. "There's Wilfredo Lam, but he's always painted the same way, Revolution or no Revolution," said our host. "And he's in Paris, where you can live the Revolution divinely well." And what sort of music was there? There was nothing. "Although, well"—Galo corrected himself— "for music that's a bit more popular there are the kids in the Nueva Trova. They appeal to Pablo's sentimental side." Pablo looked daggers at him. "The teenage girls go crazy, especially for one of them, Silvio Rodríguez, who strikes me as the best, though his talent as a sex symbol is invisible to me. A skinny white boy with a high-pitched voice. But the girls like him, and he has some pretty songs."

Theater? Only what we'd seen. Dance? What I already knew,

though we would have to go see the Ballet Nacional: nothing new, but their *Giselle* and *Sylphides* were really worth the effort.

Literature? "Well, it gets a little better there, though in fact it's the same thing: the great ones are those who came up before the Revolution. Alejo Carpentier, still living in Paris and drinking fine wine. Eliseo Diego, as a poet, who isn't even a revolutionary but stays on here. If you insist, we can include old Frog Face, Nicolás Guillén. But how you disappoint me, Alma! '*Soldadito de Bolivia, soldadito boliviano*' [Little soldier of Bolivia, little Bolivian soldier]. To make you happy, I'll concede that that's poetry, but the truth is, his best period ended in 1959." Galo thought it over, then added something that was hard for him to say. "There are some good people, but they haven't figured out how to understand the Revolution and haven't wanted to see Fidel for the great man he is. Virgilio Piñera: you should probably read him, but his books aren't available anymore, and you'd have to come and read him here, because I don't loan out books. And then there's *el gordo* Lezama Lima, who's written the masterpiece of this century, but I can't say that and you can't repeat it because we'll both get into trouble."

Why?

Galo looked at Pablo, Pablo looked at Carlos, Carlos looked at Boris: "Because the author of *Paradiso* is as big a *maricón* as you'll ever find," said Galo with a wicked grin.

Homosexual?

"No, *maricón*. The homosexual part isn't such a problem anymore: now that the whole UMAP thing is over, we can more or less live in peace, but you always have to be careful about appearances—and you have to be a revolutionary, of course, and José Lezama Lima is one faggot who doesn't worry about either of those things."

UMAP?

"Unidades Militares de Apoyo a la Producción," said Boris. He consulted with the others. "Shall we tell her?"

"No, because it might confuse her. It's not easy to understand," said Pablo, looking at me.

"Go on and tell her about it, *chico*, tell her! *Coño*, what's all this going around keeping the truth from everyone?" Carlos said in exasperation. "Let's leave that to the people who edit *Granma.*"

Then Boris told about how in 1965 the Castro regime had declared a campaign against antisocial elements who were threatening to undermine the Revolution from within. There would be no jail or penal servitude of any kind, it was explained: the Revolution did not seek to punish conduct, because a person's lifestyle or behavior cannot be considered criminal in and of itself. It was simply a matter of removing undesirable elements from the healthy part of society and giving them the opportunity to contribute to the nation's production, in the hope that through healthy physical labor and revolutionary shame they would recover their self-esteem and incorporate themselves anew into society, as useful members. Hence the creation of agricultural centers placed under the command of the armed forces, where people considered maladjusted or unwholesome—not only homosexuals but also a number of priests, Jehovah's Witnesses, and artists, including the young singer of the Nueva Trova, Pablo Milanés—would work sowing, tending, and harvesting basic foodstuffs for the people.

"But don't be shocked, *chica*!" Boris interrupted himself. He was the only one of the four friends to have been interned. "Look, it wasn't *that* bad. I think that in the end the regime did away with the UMAP because the army officers kept complaining that they didn't want to go on baby-sitting a bunch of *locas*. It was the officers who were going crazy, because you know how when two *maricas* get together, the first thing they do is start decorating. But of course! We even hung curtains in the barracks, and with little flounces too, made of the same sacks we used for harvesting. And the guards and their superiors were conflicted: Were they supposed to punish us for that? At night we cooked our own food—always with that nice homey touch, don't you know, which is so comforting. If there was an onion, so much the better, we chopped it and added it to the rice. If someone got hold of a tomato, we had some sauce for the macaroni. And since there was no electricity out in the countryside, we ate by the light of kerosene lamps—so romantic! One of the barracks became famous because a handful of the most outrageous queens got put

in there together, and they didn't just make curtains out of the
sacks but a whole backdrop, and they put on a show that was the
greatest thing you can possibly imagine. So then, of course, Raúl
Castro—who's Fidel's brother and the leader of the armed forces,
and who they say is himself . . . but no, I'm really not going to
talk about *that*—Raúl must have worried that his captains and
majors and colonels were losing control, herding *maricas* around
like that, so they let us go. It only lasted a couple of years: no one
even talks about it anymore. And we all came out tanned and
with physiques to die for—though my mother, so oblivious to
aesthetics, poor thing, spent about two months stuffing me with
food because she thought I'd been stricken with tuberculosis, I
was so thin."

Galo had been watching me. "You're wondering why people
like us still go on believing in the Revolution, aren't you? And
believe me, we've had a lot of opportunities in the last eleven
years to ask ourselves the same question. I don't want to play the
big martyr, because I imagine that there have been moments
when the cane cutters felt betrayed by Fidel or when the workers
asked themselves why on earth, *coño,* they go on taking orders
from our *compañerito* Minister Jorge Risquet. The revolutionary
process can't have been easy for anyone, but even so I have to say
that those of us who've had to endure the most—and not only
scarcity and neglect but affronts, insults, and public humilia-
tions, because mark my words, from Fidel on down, everyone
who's had anything to do with the leadership of this mess has
shit on us—those of us who've suffered the most, I repeat, have
been those who work in the arts. I've often wondered what would
happen if all the artists in the country piled onto a gigantic raft
and went rowing off to the ends of the earth. You can bet there
wouldn't be a single member of the honorable Politburo of the
Cuban Communist Party or of the whole Central Committee
who would shed a tear. *Coño,* they wouldn't even notice! And yet
I stay. Because if I were to abandon this process, then for the rest
of my life I'd have to live with the consciousness of being nothing but a *comemierda,* a shit-eater. This Revolution is the only
thing that has given my life any meaning.

"Do you know what it is to wake up in the morning and know

that what you're eating for breakfast hasn't been stolen from anyone else's mouth? That if your son or your nephew graduates from medical school, you don't have to feel guilty, because the son of the guy who cleans your building can be a doctor too if he wants to? Do you know the pleasure of *not* sitting down at the bar of the Yacht Club to be served a daiquiri by a black man in a tuxedo? Have you felt the relief of walking through Vedado and seeing its beautiful mansions—in ruins, with clotheslines out the windows, old sofas rotting on the balconies, and whatever else—but without seeing a single beggar knocking at the service entrance? I know you can appreciate this, because they know a thing or two about humiliating the poor in Mexico. And it's all because of Fidel and Fidel alone. Not Raúl, and certainly not that old windbag Carlos Rafael Rodríguez—he and his whole Popular Socialist Party—who almost shat with fear the day they started talking about taking up a rifle to topple Batista. And not that bureaucrat Osmany Cienfuegos either, or that little mouse turd Vilma Espín, or anyone else. Not even Che, though almost. It's because of Fidel; he's the only one who had the balls to transform this Yankee whorehouse into a real country. Unfortunately—"

"Galo, *chico,* come up for air!" Boris shouted. "Or just stop, why don't you!" Galo, who hadn't interrupted his monologue even when Carlos had started applauding, waved his hand vaguely as if to shoo away a fly and kept right on going.

"Unfortunately, as I was saying, I wasn't back in Cuba yet when Playa Girón was invaded, but I returned afterward. I returned, and I'm not leaving. And if you doubt that all Cuba thinks the same way, wait for July twenty-sixth and you'll see."

"Galo, quit it!" Pablo scolded him. "What's gotten into you? Look at the time! Lydia and Mireya must have been waiting for us for hours already—"

"And we'll have to find some bicarbonate of soda for this poor child here, to help her keep down all the patriotic chorizo you've been stuffing her with," Boris concluded.

It was getting late. As if in answer to my initial question, my friends had offered to take me to a festival of Cuban film, where they would show me the best that the Revolution had produced, artistically speaking. We sped off to the Cinemateca.

Now that I think about it, that Saturday must have been my last evening of relative peace in Cuba, the last moment when the world retained its logic and the things that mattered most to me had some reason for existing. I had asked about Cuban art, and my friends wanted me to see *Memories of Underdevelopment,* by the great Tomás Gutiérrez Alea; we'd see another outstanding film the next day. *Memories* was astonishing not only as an exceptionally fluid act of filmmaking, Boris said, but because of the freedom Gutiérrez Alea had had to make a film that cast such a quizzical glance at the young Revolution. The night was promising and should have been pleasurable. But before the movie started, the Cinemateca showed a newsreel from the Instituto Cubano de Arte e Industria Cinematográfica—the ICAIC—and in that newsreel I, who had no television, who had never seen a news broadcast, now saw the Vietnam War for the first time. I saw the Vietnam War, filmed from the Vietnamese perspective.

After the movie Galo and Pablo gave their friends Lydia and Mireya a lift home, and Carlos and Boris went with me to the bus stop. "Are you all right? You're very quiet," said Carlos, scanning my face. The bus finally chugged into view.

"I'm perfectly fine. I'll see you here tomorrow. I know how to get here now."

Before the main attraction began the next evening, I saw the same images in the same newsreel once more. Images of dead Vietnamese, burned alive by napalm, of children fleeing their thatch-roof homes in terror. The shrill whine and unbearable thunder of falling bombs dug in under my skin and stayed there. Later that evening, when I turned out the light in my room, they came alive and I could find no switch to silence the bombardment of questions that echoed through my head. *If a thousand bombs are falling, can anyone know where they'll explode? If it's useless to run, how many seconds do you have to wait to die? How does napalm feel when it starts to burn your skin? What does your own burning flesh smell like?* After that evening at the Cinemateca, I was incurably altered by the consciousness of living in an obscene world; whenever I was sleeping, and even sometimes while I was awake, I would experience my own body as a vast cage for storing corpses. If a country insisted on being independent and Communist, too, did it deserve to be burned alive? If a woman had five children, would it hurt her less to lose two of them? How could I understand the image I'd seen in the movie theater of an enormous gringo with a horrible smile, proudly holding up what was left of a human torso?

I suppose I had some sort of breakdown, though it wasn't a change any observer—much less I myself—would have noticed. Day by day I simply lost the logic of things and their pleasure.

Monday afternoon found me back in the studio with Sandy's dance.

From first position, big jump into second position *plié.* Stay in *plié* and sweep the left leg into *attitude* behind. Stay in *attitude* and rotate slowly outward on the right leg. Turn.

I ended the rehearsal after fifteen minutes. What kind of dance was needed in Cuba? The kids were right, I thought. No one here was interested in socialist realism, but neither did it make any sense to reproduce the latest innovations of the New York avant-garde. If Cuba was so resolutely Cuban, what was I doing here with my abstract dances and aleatory "events"? What in hell had I come to Cuba for? What was I doing here? Turn turn turn turn. From one moment to the next, Sandy's dance had stopped making sense to me. Whom was it for? By what right could I ask an audience to witness this unrelated series of movements? I couldn't justify the solitary performance I was rehearsing on the basis of the pleasure it might give someone to see me: I was not beautiful; I was not a great dancer. I wasn't going to take anyone's breath away with my technical prowess. I had nothing to say to people living in a country that faced, day after day, the danger of atomic annihilation, invasion, a war like the one Vietnam was waging against imperialism. It made no sense to do what I was doing. My dance had no meaning. For what? For whom?

I sat down on the beautiful worn mahogany floor and jotted

down a few ideas in my notebook for a possible dance, or event, to take place in the school, making use of its strange architecture that was somewhere between modern and prehistoric, its labyrinth of jungle paths. I stopped writing and raised my eyes. The brick vault over my head reverberated with a silence that suddenly grew heavy and threatened to crush me. I felt the walls and ceiling collapsing around me, but when I focused carefully, I realized that all the bricks were still in their places. And what was more, they could be counted, one by one, and thus their threatened collapse could be warded off. I lay on the floor for some time, counting bricks, until the heavy silence that was pressing me against the floor lifted a little and allowed me to go back to the dormitory.

I don't think the internal fracture caused by the newsreel images of the Vietnam War resulted from any excessive ignorance of horror on my part. Perhaps it was more the opposite case. Among the readings that had fallen into my hands when I was a child were two books by John Hersey, one about the explosion of the atomic bomb in Hiroshima, the other about the extermination of the Jews in the Warsaw Ghetto during World War II. These reports were written with minute attention to detail and without rhetoric or undue emotion. I wasn't yet twelve when I read them, and I imagine they contributed something to the bad taste that, in general terms, the world left in my mouth. The description of the victims who were gassed in Auschwitz and burned alive in Hiroshima endured in my mind not as nightmares but as a kind of absolute proof of the existence of Evil. What I had just discovered in the ICAIC newsreels, with their appalling images of war and its butchery, was that Evil wasn't something that existed only in that prehistory before I was born. I had lived alongside Evil—and in willful ignorance of it! It was in the air I had breathed; it existed with my complicity and bloomed because I had allowed it to. It was as if my own blood had become a poison. The images of Vietnam, cruel death, and senseless destruction pursued me. So did the questions: How? How did they resist so much horror, so much hatred, in Vietnam? How had this happened? And above all, how had I allowed it to happen? Very small children were dying while I went on

living, effortlessly and painlessly, and I hadn't done so much as
raise my voice in protest. I could no longer sleep in peace or
breathe freely. Nor did I do the only thing that might have afforded me perspective, companionship, and consolation: I didn't
talk to anyone about what was happening to me. I was ashamed.

The day after the ceiling threatened to collapse on my head in
Cubanacán, the battle for the Ten Million Ton Harvest abruptly
came to an end. It happened without warning. I don't remember
who told me about what took place on the night of May 19,
but the first ones to learn the news heard it from Fidel himself,
during a speech with which he welcomed back eleven fishermen
who were said to have been kidnapped by mercenaries who kept
them in captivity for several days on an unidentified cay in the
Bahamas. Their liberation and imminent arrival in Havana was
announced, and in great jubilation thousands of Cubans went to
welcome them at a platform built for that purpose, as if in defiance, right in front of the building that had once belonged to the
U.S. Embassy. There, in the midst of an anti-imperialist fervor,
Fidel announced the failure of the harvest. Six months earlier
he had proclaimed that a single kilo less than ten million tons
of sugar would be an inadmissible ignominy. That night he acknowledged that it would take a mighty struggle to reach even
eight million tons.

  The demonstrations in front of the former embassy had been
going on for almost a week when Fidel made the announcement.
On May 13 a front-page article had announced the fishermen's
capture: TWO FISHING BOATS SUNK AND THEIR CREWS
KIDNAPPED BY AGENTS OF IMPERIALISM. I imagine some
kind of call must have gone out, asking people to show up at the
Malecón that night to protest the crime, but I didn't hear about
it—or maybe I just didn't want to go. Those who did go gathered in front of the embassy building, now occupied by a small
delegation of Swiss diplomats who were charged with representing the interests of the United States. That first protest was not a
particularly memorable event.

The next day, a Thursday, *Granma* devoted considerable space to the demonstration but gave priority on its front page to an endless article about the courtesy visit of a Soviet naval detachment. For the first time, that day I didn't find the little graphic that I was in the habit of monitoring in the paper, showing the amount of cane milled in each of the six Cuban provinces. In the edition of Saturday, May 16, the lead story concerned the assassination of two black students during a demonstration in Jackson, Mississippi. That same night thousands of students demonstrated again at the same spot on the Malecón, and *Granma* printed the news in red ink in its Sunday edition. *"¡Nixon, jutía, te quedan pocos días!"* (Nixon, you swine, you're running out of time!) the demonstrators chanted, and also *"¡Nixon, fascista, somos comunistas!"* For the first time Nixon's name was written with a swastika in place of the *x*. That same Sunday the demonstrators filled the Malecón almost entirely and swore they wouldn't leave until the fishermen were returned. A photo of the demonstration and a gigantic headline—200,000 PEOPLE MARCH PAST THE YANKEE LAIR—took up the entire front page of Monday's *Granma*. Inside were photos and interviews with some of the most prominent demonstrators. My heart leaped in my chest with guilt and amazement. So many people had gone! And I hadn't. A Vietnamese diplomat. A Brazilian guerrilla. A boy Pioneer. Alicia Alonso. Nicolás Guillén. A star *machetero.* I could have seen them up close if I'd bothered to go to the Malecón. The morning of May 19, *Granma* announced *"¡Victoria!"* and published a photo of the fishermen, who had reportedly been abandoned by their captors on the Bahamian cay the day before. Men weathered by sun and salt water, they were all small, skinny, and gap-toothed except for one, who was as beautiful as a Greek god, monumentally tall and muscular. Standing with his companions on an outcropping of coral, he gazed toward the horizon, clenching his fists. I looked at the photo for a long time and noticed later that Hilda had cut it out and posted it on her office wall. Inside the paper was the story of how that triumphal night had been celebrated in front of the embassy. But the real celebration would come the following night, Tuesday, when the liberated fishermen would be given the greeting they deserved. I didn't go that night, either. But Fidel did.

Standing on the improvised platform in front of a dense crowd of jubilant *fidelistas,* the Comandante en Jefe spoke in detail about the epic deeds of the fishermen and their people, and about the Swiss diplomats' dangerous flirtations with the Yankee enemy, but it seemed that he couldn't keep himself from mentioning the failure that was tormenting him. He repeated several times that there were problems with the harvest, that the possibility of not reaching ten million tons had to be considered, and then suddenly, in what appeared to be an uncontainable outburst, totally unexpected by anyone in the audience, Fidel said, "But if you want me to tell you in all clarity what the situation is, it's simply that we're not going to make it to ten million tons. Simply that. I'm not going to beat around the bush."

He announced that the following day, on television, he would explain in detail the reasons for the failure to reach ten million. And thus ended a battle conceived and organized by people who believed, literally, that the human will could move mountains.

After class on May 20, I went to Galo's house to watch a rebroadcast of the speech Fidel had made that morning. It was the first time I'd ever listened to the man who had almost single-handedly altered Cuba's destiny. I remember that as I watched him speaking, I privately raged against my mother: she really was brainless, and her lack of enthusiasm for Fidel was one charge more to add to all the others I was stockpiling against her, for there had never existed a more lucid, heroic man. His physical beauty itself was the confirmation of his extraordinary spiritual energy. His thin voice, like silver paper, the long hands that moved like fish, the Roman profile, his singular stubborn will to share his thoughts, to make his own intellectual processes public, to repeat and repeat an idea until he felt sure that there wasn't a single Cuban on the whole island who didn't understand and share it, the high flights of rhetoric and the infinite gaze—it was all spellbinding. And so was his failure. To see Fidel in defeat was to see the hero, naked and unarmed, awaiting the tiger's mortal assault. For more than three hours I lost myself in a rapture that was produced not so much by the speech as by the sonorous undulation of his words and his expression of pain.

I didn't hear, nor was I interested in understanding, the very harsh reality he was announcing, and I imagine many Cubans reacted the same way. The failure of the harvest was too great a disaster to allow most of us to take in that this was, in fact, the failure of the revolutionary project itself. But thirty years later I can see that this was what Fidel was saying, and indeed without much beating around the bush. Or at least he let it be understood that the Ten Million Ton Harvest had been an attempt to achieve a certain independence from the Soviets and that that attempt had failed.

The initial plan for the great harvest had emerged from a series of incontrovertible realities. To begin with, the one thing Cuba really produced in abundance was sugarcane: across the island there were more than enough cane plantations and virgin land to sow the hundreds of thousands of hectares of cane that would be needed to grind and refine ten million tons of sugar.

Next, since the beginning of the Revolution and the nationalization of the sugar industry, the sugar mills had never operated at full capacity. It was logical, then, to think that those mills had more than enough capacity to grind all that cane. The numbers added up: for the most successful capitalist *zafra,* in 1953, the sugar magnates had sown more hectares of cane than ever before, and the total amount of sugar refined had come out to something more than seven million tons. Obviously socialism, with its superior mode of production, would have no problem breaking the capitalists' record, the revolutionaries said when they studied the plan.

Still, the technocrats at the Juceplan and the Ministry of Sugar, known as the Minaz, did foresee some problems. It was indisputable that in the last three years sugar production had plummeted—from six million tons down to five and then to four and a half—but skeptics were helpless in the face of Fidel's enthusiasm: it was all a question of organization. The country's 138 sugar mills, or *combinados*—factories for grinding the cane, cooking the molasses, and refining sugar—all of which were considerably older than the Revolution, would have to be reconditioned and repaired, and in particular the *colosos*—half a dozen vast mills that refined the greater part of each year's total—would have to be brought up to date.

Nature was uncooperative that year, and as had already been acknowledged, the goodwill of the improvised *macheteros* did not prevail over their inexperience, but the Ten Million Ton Harvest was above all an industrial fiasco. Ultimately, sugar is an industrial product, however rudimentary its manufacturing process may be, and as the maximum leader of the Revolution now had to acknowledge, he and his most faithful colleagues were all guerrillas, not managers or industrialists.

So absorbed were we in the explanation for its failure that many of us didn't pay much attention to Fidel's account of why the harvest had been undertaken in the first place.

After the aggressions by the United States, Fidel now recalled, facing the cameras, the Soviet Union had begun to buy most of Cuba's sugar, generally at subsidized prices.

"Of course," he said, "in the situation in which our country found itself, needing to import all its petroleum, along with a whole series of raw materials, foodstuffs, and equipment, there was no possibility of acquiring these things except from the Soviet Union."

But as the needs of the Revolution grew—partly because under the new regime a growing proportion of Cubans were gaining access to education, nutrition, housing, and health care, and also because the total number of Cubans was on the rise—the country's ability to pay for social services did not increase. The economy did not generate any more income, said Fidel. An entire generation of Cubans would be unable to forget the look on Fidel's face as he listed Cuba's real export possibilities—its true opportunities to generate wealth—as if he were understanding this terrible reality for the very first time. Cuba was not only a very small, very poor country: it was a country with very little hope of ever ceasing to be poor.

"Of the products that we export," he explained now, "sugar is number one. . . . That is: sugar, nickel, and small amounts of tobacco and rum. Fundamentally, those are the exports that our country has."

A revolution cannot be sustained on the basis of sugar, rum, and tobacco, and the economic embargo decreed by the United States generated another set of difficulties. Cuba could not engage in trade with most capitalist countries because they had tacitly or openly joined the blockade, so it was hard to obtain dollars. Without dollars, Cuba could not turn to Europe to buy the products it had once imported from the United States.

"As a consequence of that and of the needs of a developing— and disorganized—country, as any country is in the initial phase of a revolutionary process—our commercial imbalance with the Soviet Union grew greater each year," Fidel explained. "At the same time our need for imports for the development of the country grew. . . . We then proposed a long-term agreement to the Soviet Union, which depended on our own ability to increase sugar production."

In other words, Cuba agreed to take out a loan from the Soviet Union for an amount larger than its entire existing debt. In exchange, it would hand over for the long term, at guaranteed prices, practically all of its sugar production. If the country could maintain a steady output of sugar, it could stay afloat and avoid disaster. *But* if it managed to generate a gigantic increase in sugar output—no matter how temporary—the surplus might be enough to finance the construction of the island's only other feasible source of development, a large-scale mine on the site of the world's largest deposits of nickel ore. And—Fidel did not say this on that long-ago May 20, but Pablo did—the mine could then be built without Soviet participation.

Those were the regime's calculations when, in 1966—just when sugar production began its slump—Fidel decided to prepare a ten-million-ton harvest four years in the future. Calculations were made—miscalculations, actually, but calculations all the same—of the amount and type of cane to be sown, of harvest schedules and the number of cane cutters required. But— when he reached this point in his speech, Fidel had been talking for a couple of hours—they forgot to take the sugar mills into account.

The result, as Fidel now revealed, was that almost from the moment the harvest got under way, in October 1969, the highest spheres of the Cuban government had been informed by their on-site delegates that the sugar mills were not grinding well. Worse, some of the *colosos* hadn't even begun to grind because the new equipment hadn't arrived yet or hadn't yet been installed. By December, only two months after the harvest began, the situation was already critical and the ten-million-ton goal was in jeopardy.

Perhaps that would have been the moment to reconsider. It would have made sense to ask whether, given the broken-down and inefficient state of the mills, it was worth going ahead with a plan to mobilize the entire country for a harvest that was already in jeopardy. But, Fidel now explained, he and his planners did something else instead.

"That is when the decision is made to seek means, seek railway lines and construct forty kilometers of railway track so that the excess of cane could be transported to other sugar mills. . . . The decision was made to stop work on all mountain roads and highways, all roadwork not related to sugarcane. And all of those resources, all of them, were concentrated on roads."

In other words, construction on key intercity highways was stopped so that tracks that would be used only once could be built. The goal was to solve the emergency: to transport fresh cane from a mill that had broken down to one that hadn't. Even the construction of dams was stopped. The universities were emptied of engineers and technicians, who were all sent to the *centrales* to figure out how to get the mills working, said Fidel.

But even then, he went on, it often happened that one of the *colosos* would apparently be ready to produce, with all the *alzadores* ready to stack the cane and all the trucks from another damaged mill ready to carry it to the new railway lines, and nevertheless what got produced wasn't sugar but "constant breakdowns and production halts. Then, in order not to pile up cut cane on the ground, forty or fifty thousand laborers had to suspend work." These were campesinos, mobilized at a high cost from the most remote regions of the country, and because of the constant work stoppages they never felt that all their effort was leading to anything.

"This had a terribly demoralizing effect," noted the Comandante en Jefe de la Revolución.

And to top it all off, "one day, finally, the *coloso* would be grinding well, and that day there would be no cane."

Fidel talked on forever, sparing no detail of the *zafra* in which nothing had gone well, even for a single day. It wasn't until April, a month earlier, that the engineers and technicians who spent all day climbing around inside the *colosos* trying to figure out what was wrong made the most terrible discovery of all, the discovery that led everyone to the now inevitable conclusion that the Ten Million Ton Harvest would never be achieved: the "agro-industrial complexes" that had not been repaired or had not benefited from any new equipment were grinding very badly—at less than seventy-five percent of capacity. But the complexes into which so much of the country's scant resources had been poured—those that had been allotted the greatest share of the investment in rehabilitation and from which the greatest share of the triumph was expected—were grinding even worse.

Socialist effort had not even been capable of correctly installing the machinery of the country's basic industry.

Thus ended Fidel's explanation of the sugar disaster to an exhausted people who were now in a state of shock. His voice almost gone, the *máximo líder* of the Revolution declaimed for the first time the slogan that would accompany him for so many of the subsequent years of his government. "*¡Convertir el revés en victoria!*" he shouted hoarsely. Transform defeat into victory! Pablo was crying. Galo switched off the TV.

There was almost complete silence on the lunch line in the cafeteria the following day.

When it was my turn, I saw the usual chickpea gruel and rice, but no fresh vegetable on the tray (the slice of green tomato had disappeared days before), nothing for dessert, and once more the heavy cube of *jamonada*—a "meat by-product," as I had learned the pastes made from the residue of slaughter were called—that was our protein ration almost every day. My stomach clenched. I decided that it was absolutely necessary to ask that the large spoonful of oil not be ladled over my rice: others probably needed it more, and it robbed me of any pleasure in eating and did further harm to my already rebellious digestion. But as I'd been told that the oil was a special privilege reserved for only a few people, I tried to make the request diplomatically.

"You see, it'll make me fat, and we dancers have to watch out for that," I told the *compañero* in charge of the kitchen.

"If you manage to get fat in Cuba, we'll take you to see Fidel so you can share the recipe with the rest of us," the man answered, and poured half a ladle of oil onto the rice.

It was the only time I ever heard him speak.

FIVE

Coming of Age

I turned twenty-one eight days after the failure of the harvest was announced. Following a series of complicated negotiations with the telephone operator—which must, I imagine, have included some notification on the New York operator's part to the Central Intelligence Agency in Washington—my mother succeeded in communicating with Hilda's office, which sent for me. It was like getting a phone call from another galaxy. The person speaking to me was my mother, but she didn't like Fidel. She was calling to tell me how happy she was that I'd been born, but I was besieged by the suspicion that my entire life had been a grotesque mistake. She wanted to know how I was, what I was eating, how my classes were going, but any sincere answer would have caused her terrible anxiety. I resorted to monosyllables and evasions, feeling all the while a great urge to punish her for being so frivolous, for understanding so little, for having interrupted my class, for having brought me into the world. My mother, whom no one could ever accuse of being overprotective, worried.

"Is it cold down there? Do you need a sweater?" she asked helplessly.

I hung up without managing to tell her that I loved her or that I missed her, and I felt more orphaned than ever.

Obsessed now with reading the paper, I devoured the copy of *Granma* in Hilda's office every day, paying special attention to all the articles about Vietnam and to everything that had to do with the war's nauseating slaughter. Only a few weeks earlier, on my flight to Mexico, I'd changed planes in Dallas. About twenty recruits boarded the airport bus with me, on their way to a military base to learn how to make war. At the time they horrified me but also made me sad; they were so ignorant of the world, so terribly innocent, and they were being sent to the other side of the planet to kill and be killed. Now I could no longer think of them like that. I saw them as giants towering over their victims, hairy, carnivorous, violent, and guffawing: wild beasts. And I had lived alongside them.

I fell prey to what would turn into decades of unforgiving insomnia; for the moment I managed to adapt to it by reading. The books I'd brought from New York were left in their trunk, replaced by the ones Tere, Galo, and Hilda had lent me. I read *Paradiso* by José Lezama Lima—the rotund homosexual who was guilty of insufficient love for the Revolution—in a Mexican edition Galo had gotten hold of with some difficulty. (In 1968 a limited edition of the book came out in Cuba, but it sold out immediately and was never reprinted.) The novel was a variegated mannerist concoction that described the journey of a strange and possibly homosexual being, who was conceivably identical to the book's author, through an extraordinary world that was unquestionably Cuba. The language was dense and difficult, full of metaphors that took on a life of their own, and I sometimes thought that Lezama—like Jorge Luis Borges's Pierre Menard, the other author of *Don Quixote*—had wanted to write Proust's Cuban novel. I pored over every detail of the book with joyful astonishment and without guilt, since I could detect no criticism whatsoever of the Revolution in its pages. But the question that now intrigues me never occurred to me then: Why, precisely, was it determined that this text should not be made available to any Cuban who might want to read it? In contrast, Alejo Carpentier, who was certainly Lezama's literary kinsman in the organic development of his writing and its all-encompassing ambition, was almost a national hero. Thanks once more to Galo and his friends, I was able to read some part of Carpentier's vast literary output. His eighteenth-century Cuba, trapped between European forms and formalities, the revolutionary fragmentation of those forms, and its own chaos, sometimes seemed more real to me than the country that lay before my eyes, and at the same time helped me to understand it.

It was hard to make the transition from those blazing, lucid pages to the pamphlet titled *Assault on the Moncada Barracks* loaned me by Hilda, who had renewed her friendship with me without ever once alluding to the day she had censured my conduct. I remember submitting to the pamphlet as if it were a punishment I was voluntarily and passionately accepting. "Look," said a torturer to Haydée Santamaría, who in 1953 had accompanied her boyfriend, her brother, and Fidel Castro in the attack on Batista's Moncada barracks. "Look: here are your brother's eyes. And we're going to bring you your boyfriend's testicles the same way." *Look at them,* I told myself. *That hard kernel of horror is what you've refused to see.* Haydée Santamaría was known and admired throughout the island, a living martyr, but she was also in charge of a large cultural center, the Casa de las Américas. "Casa," as everyone called it, formed a bridge between the Revolution's intellectuals and creators and those of the rest of the hemisphere. Over the following months I had several opportunities to meet Haydée in the beautiful art deco building that was Casa's headquarters. I couldn't do it. Every time I had to pass by that building, I crossed the street to the sidewalk opposite, so as not to risk an encounter with the woman who had been shown her brother's eyes.

Casa de las Américas published a magazine, and Tere loaned me her treasured copy of the issue that came out after Che's death. "We will be like Che!" Fidel had sworn at the end of the speech in which he confirmed the news of the hero's death, but reading through the articles by leading Latin American and European authors—Julio Cortázar, Eduardo Galeano, Italo Calvino, Luis Cardoza y Aragón—made me despair: being like Che wasn't hard, it was impossible. "The revolutionary is consumed by this uninterrupted action which has no other end than death, unless the construction [of socialism] on a global scale is achieved," Ernesto Guevara had written. So I could find salvation only by dying? A number of the magazine's articles compared Che to Christ, or at least cast him in the role of universal martyr: "Those who are incapable of achieving one of these states must say so and abandon the struggle," and so forth. Everyone remembered his words with awe and devotion, because they were spoken by a man who had lived up to them. But I was frightened by his marmoreal temperament—hard, scathing, and intolerant of any lapse.

In a poem by Mario Benedetti I found a description of my own situation vis-à-vis this prophet:

it's shameful to see
paintings
armchairs
carpets
open the refrigerator and take out a bottle
type the three global letters of your name
on the rigid machine
the ribbon was never
before
so pale
shameful to be cold
and move closer to the heater, as usual,
to be hungry and eat
such a simple thing
to open the record player and listen in silence
especially if it's a Mozart quartet

What should I do? I asked myself. *Live in shame? Give up Mozart?* Once more I read Che's Bolivian diary, which contained nothing but death and horror. On the last day of September 1967, a week before he was captured and assassinated by agents of the CIA and the Bolivian army, Ernesto Guevara noted in his diary the loss of almost half his men. A few months before, the surviving members of the original column of twenty-four men had split in two. Without means to contact half his men and with all communication to Havana cut off, lacking adequate ammunition, food, and above all water, Che fought off despair with increasingly scant resources. He heard on a radio news program that the other guerrilla column had fallen in an ambush, and he hung on to shreds of hope: "The news about the deaths of the other group appear to be true, and we must assume they've been liquidated, though it's possible that a small group is still on the move, fleeing contact with the army, since the news of the death of all seven could be false or, at least, exaggerated." It was terrible to see the hero like that, doing his best not to understand that he wouldn't be the only one to die, that inevitably all of them would be exterminated. I felt him raging at the thought that the death awaiting him would be not an epic climax but a pathetic defeat: "We went out at nightfall, the men exhausted for lack of water and Eustaquio making a spectacle of himself and weeping for lack of a mouthful of water."

Could it be true that in order to save Vietnam, two, three, or many Vietnams would have to be created? In New York, almost three years earlier, following the daily news articles about the hunt for Ernesto Guevara with appalled fascination, I thought more or less in passing that I would like to be able to be heroic, to live and die like Che, memorably and passionately, without ever descending into the trivial and inconsequential spheres of existence. But as I went deeper into his life from my room in Cubanacán, I found it intolerable to think that he'd lived out his destiny in a barren no-man's-land like the Bolivian *altiplano,* a dreary expanse of shrub cover devoid not only of water but also of any form of joy or consolation—music, for example, or dialogue. The fact that he chose precisely that death, so far removed from all the beauty of human creation, kept me from wanting to be like Che. And it tortured me to accept the idea that a human being's only moral salvation consisted in imitating him.

Yet how I loved knowing that heroes did exist, and that I was now living on a green island led by one of the greatest heroes of all time! Fidel's daring attack on the Moncada barracks, at the head of a scant handful of warriors; the audacious speech— "History will absolve me!"—with which he began his own defense before the dictator Batista's judges; his remarkable meeting with Che in Mexico; the landing—mad, mad and inspired!—of the poor rebel band that in 1956 traveled from Mexico aboard the *Granma,* an old and battered yacht, to the island's coast, and of whom survived, according to the history books, barely a biblical dozen men who under Fidel's command proceeded *hasta la victoria siempre* . . . The history of Cuba I was piecing together on the basis of these readings was, like all self-taught knowledge, fragmented and highly subjective, but it was also mystical, since my only sources were Cuban pamphlets, which had a great deal in common with the stories of the lives of the saints. In any case, I read the lives of Fidel and Che as if that was what they were; I wanted intensely to believe in their beatitude. The revolutionary faith to which the two of them were continually referring was the faith I wanted to inhabit, Fidel's faith, which hadn't been destroyed by the humiliation and death of his former comrade-in-arms or by the cataclysmic failure of the *zafra*: the patently unproven conviction that the perfect union of science and the human will would succeed in transforming the miserable destiny of the human race, and that socialism represented the ideal conjoining of those two ingredients.

But oh, how contrary I proved when faced with all the disciplines of this new faith! From the twenty-odd scribbled pages of my journal, preserved in the one surviving notebook from those days, I'll copy the following:

> At some point I find that all the references to the word "possession" in any Marxist-Leninist treatise about anything start to set my teeth on edge. "Man enters into possession of himself, of the means of production, of nature, etc." Why this zeal to possess everything? Marxism is just as much the product of bourgeois materialism as any other system, a kind of inverse mold. (I would say death mask, but it sounds disrespectful.)

> Nancy, the teacher from Chicago, was counting the days until her boyfriend arrived with one of the Venceremos Brigades, and never asked herself these sorts of questions but lived happily in the Revolution and the school. I spent my nights wide awake.

"Put just a little more sugar in that coffee, Hilda; after all, it's the one thing we're not going to have any shortage of." Tere, who smiled when she spoke of terrible things, didn't have much of a gift for making jokes, but in the days that followed the failure of the harvest, she was one of the few people who at least attempted a little humor. The school secretary was not grateful. "*Coño, chica, make it yourself!*" Hilda kept her head low, immersed in the task of preparing the agenda for the general staff meeting that was about to begin. Only Elfrida and Lorna were still missing. Those of us who were gathered in a classroom—Nancy, Tere, Hilda, me, and the two academic professors, Osvaldo and Chaina—didn't exchange a word. "Hilda, I'm sorry; I wasn't complaining about you," Tere murmured. "I was just trying to make a little joke, but in Cuba these days not even our jokes are successful, you know?" She directed the rays of her luminous smile at me, but then leaned her temple against her fist and rubbed her forehead. "I don't know, I don't understand. I don't understand how an entire country can give all of itself, tear itself apart, give the very last drop of its sweat—for a just cause, for the most just of causes!—and then fail like this. Can it be that there really is a god, and he doesn't like us? Or is it our own fault? Can it be that we're wrong and just can't see it?"

No one answered. During the long silence Osvaldo went on sketching the rows of rifles he was filling his notebook with.

"We're all feeling like that: the hardest part for me too is not understanding what else we could have done," Hilda said finally. "We talked about it yesterday in the party meeting. Of course mistakes were made: the whole issue of the machinery, the failure of the agro-industrial complexes. But the end result of our discussion was: Did we have to risk everything for the ten million tons, or not? Because we'd already tried industrialization, and that didn't work; that project was way too ambitious, and we were short of everything from capital to skilled labor. We had to fall back on what we really are good at, and what else is that but sugar? And now it turns out that sugar didn't work, either. So what I'm wondering is, if we're not a sugar-producing country, what are we? What other choice did we have? And what alternative is there now? Was Fidel just terribly wrong, or is there no way out?"

Nancy: "I do not know what one I think is worse: that Fidel is mistaken or that he isn't."

Everyone smiled at her tripped-up Spanish. Lorna and Elfrida came in and took their seats. "We were commiserating over the *zafra,* Elfrida," said Tere.

Elfrida pinched her lips shut and ended all discussion of the matter. "We're not here to speak of the past. The Revolution needs all of us to dedicate ourselves to doing our duty now and doing it well." She locked her shiny, beady gaze on each of us in turn. "Shall we begin?"

Who could make sense of Elfrida? Her sudden shifts in mood and perspective, her unforeseeable jumps from unpretentiousness to the most absurd authoritarianism, and from authoritarianism to sensibleness, alarmed and infuriated even those who liked and respected her. Tere's smile was now congealed on her lips.

Elfrida cleared her throat, straightened out a stack of papers, gripped a pencil as if it were a prophet's staff, and launched into her remarks. There was a consensus in the Escuela Nacional de Danza, she said: we were doing badly. The students in the school's inaugural class, who were about to graduate after five years of training, had not attained an acceptable level of proficiency, while the kids who came after them—who had been more rigorously selected, were more homogenous in terms of age and educational background, and lived in the school as boarders— were still worse, lacking even the fervor for dance and art that those in the fifth year indisputably possessed. (It was, I thought, a bit like the new machinery imported for the harvest that produced even less than the old equipment.) But that was not, perhaps, the fundamental thing, Elfrida continued. In all the students a disturbing dissatisfaction could be detected. This sentiment could not be ignored, much less censured. The students' obvious discontent, irritability, anxiety, and even skepticism undoubtedly had a cause. She and Lorna, following Fidel's revolutionary example, did not want to evade or sidestep their responsibilities. It was now up to all of us to find solutions and improve the situation.

We looked at one another in astonishment. Once again the winds that moved Elfrida's spirit had changed from north to south, and our sails had to be adjusted accordingly. Encouraged by the terse, clear presentation that the school director had just given, the teaching staff embarked on a discussion of key problems, in particular the lack of an overall study plan for the program's five years, the absence of coordination between the modern and Afro-Cuban sections, the poverty of the academic program, and the lack of any stage practice for the students.

Almost two hours had gone by when Tere, in the heat of the discussion and her enthusiasm, said that if the kids—with the exceptions we all knew—didn't know how to present themselves in front of an audience as dancers rather than as students, if they didn't know how to project their personalities and didn't have much stage presence, it was in large measure due to the lack of repertory. The simple dances taught to the first-year students at the end of the year were appropriate to their needs, perhaps, but we'd have to start thinking about promoting new choreographers, because the fifth-year students needed real choreography, high-level work that would stimulate those who danced it to develop as artists, and none of us was qualified to provide that material.

Elfrida, who up to this point had been attentively taking notes, slammed her notebook shut. Once more her eyes were glittering, and again she raised a tremulous and defiant chin. When I came to this meeting, I never thought I would have to face such harsh judgments, our director declared. She knew she wasn't a great choreographer, but it seemed cruel to have to listen as her best efforts were misunderstood and denigrated. She couldn't believe her own colleagues would humiliate her in public like that. She would never create another dance. She burst into tears, picked up her purse, and left. Lorna smiled in distress, as if she were the one who needed to apologize for her behavior. "The failure of the Ten Million Ton Harvest has upset all of us," she rationalized.

After the meeting I walked Tere to the bus stop. Normally she would accompany me to the cafeteria after our classes, before she went home to the lunch her husband had prepared, but that afternoon I stood with her during the long wait for the bus. "Who's last?" she asked. Someone among the half-dozen pedestrians scattered in the shady patches across half a block raised his hand, and Tere acknowledged him with a quick nod. A few yards

away from the others, perspiring, I tried to keep thirst from dis-
tracting me from the conversation, anguished at the prospect
of spending the remainder of the afternoon in the sole company
of my lacerating guilt, but comforted to know that the ever-
equable Tere was suffering, too. "With all of us walking around
under a dark cloud like this, I don't know where this Revolution
is going," she told me now. "You saw Elfrida just now, acting
like a madwoman. As for me, all my life I've slept like a saint,
one long sleep from bedtime to morning, and now I wake up
while it's still dark, as if someone were shining a flashlight into
my eyes. Last night I had to get up and walk around; I was in
such agony that there wasn't room for me anymore in the apartment. At least Mariano didn't wake up."

She sighed. "Do you think we're in any condition to help the
kids? Because they're slipping away from us. We need to be
strong, clearheaded, and above all united. But with Elfrida like
this we can't. And the fifth-year students are heading for graduation, and I see them worrying more and more every day about
what their lives will be like once they're out of here, and every
day we're in less of a state to give them any guidance."

In the distance, from out of the burning light that liquefied
the pavement, came the metallic flash of the bus. Idly I noticed a
handwritten sign pasted to one of the bus stop posts: XCHG 1/2
HOUSE, IN MARIANAO, PRIME LOCATION, COMFORTABLE,
SPACIOUS, FOR 2-BDRM APT IN VÍBORA. Throughout Havana
these kinds of advertisements for exchanges could be seen, most
of them long since bleached out by sun and rain. Exchange
Elfrida for a director in her right mind. Exchange this universe of
madmen for a normally dysfunctional country. I slammed down
the insidious counterrevolutionary who had just raised her serpent's head inside me. "It pains me to leave you, *niña*," said Tere,
signaling for the bus to stop. The dozen people who by now were
scattered across the entire block rapidly formed a line in the sun,
each one placing himself behind his "last one."

"I wish you could come home for dinner with me," said Tere.
"I wish you'd come every day, to have a little bit of home life, but
the rations we're receiving lately are so much worse than usual. I

don't want to leave you any hungrier than you are!" She smiled and left. I wished I could go with her—it always did me good to leave the school's dense, solitary atmosphere. Now I lacked even the energy to stick my head into the cafeteria and investigate whether the evening's menu offered rice with *jamonada* or rice with omelet.

I woke up before dawn without noticing the humidity, the mosquitoes, the distant murmur of the brook, or the concrete-hard bed. Tangled in confusion, I found myself facing a Chinese banquet, fork at the ready before a table full of platters heaped high with colorful exotic dishes, each one more fragrant and tempting than the others and all of them just out of reach. Dazed, I raised my hand to my mouth and, thinking to find a shrimp, bit down on air. I stretched my arm toward the platter of fried rice and touched a rough surface that was the sheet. The dish of kung pao chicken was closer: was it made with peanuts or almonds? I bent toward the dish to see better and saw the night. Not even when I realized that I was hallucinating did the delicious, tempting, just slightly greasy fragrance disappear. Avid, salivating, I felt my entire body fill up with frustration, and at the same time I found it completely absurd that I was about to weep from hunger. If putting up with a few hunger pangs was part of every Cuban's revolutionary duty, why did I feel so famished?

There were hours to go before the cafeteria would open.

Something happened that morning, thousands of miles away, in a steep fissure between two Andean peaks in Peru, that for a good while stripped us all of our obsession with appetite and of the melancholy of our failure. In the early hours of May 31, the earth reverberated as if it were giving birth to a dragon, rose up, broke into a thousand pieces, and buried alive thousands of inhabitants of the towns and villages in a canyon known as the Callejón de Huaylas. In the epicenter of the earthquake, at a point exactly in the middle of the Callejón, all the water in a lake just up the mountain from the little city of Yungay catapulted into the air and then drowned the entire city in mud. All in all, the earth swallowed seventy thousand lives in the first minutes of the quake.

The awful news jolted Fidel into immediate action. Once again the energy of his presence on the television broadcasts and every page of *Granma* swept us up with him. Concerned, stirred, horrified, he gathered the experts together and learned, along with all the rest of us, the exact dimensions of the tragedy: how many deaths and where, how many victims, what obstacles the rescuers had encountered. We all understood the intensity with which he turned his attention toward Peru: someone was suffering even more than we were! And in confronting the disaster that had taken place in a fellow Latin American nation, the Revolution discovered that it was neither defeated nor helpless but, on the contrary, that it still had enough resources to help the most unfortunate. Only a few hours after news of the disaster reached the world, Fidel sent his minister of health in person to Lima with a planeful of first-aid supplies. A couple of days later he himself went to the airport, along with his closest men— Lorna's husband, Manuel Piñeiro, among them—to welcome the messengers back and announce the departure of more airplanes. *Granma* cited his explanations of the earthquake extensively. In Cuba, he pointed out to us, we suffered a great deal from hurricanes, but all in all the island's situation was a privileged one, because hurricanes are a phenomenon we can take precautions and safeguard against and thus save many lives. "But earthquakes destroy bridges, destroy dams, destroy factories and whole towns," he warned. "They're worse than ten atomic bombs, because that type of bomb affects an area with a radius of ten kilometers, but an earthquake like this one covers a radius of two or three hundred kilometers. . . . Few countries in the world have a more rebellious landscape." Horror and shock led him to reflect: "This makes their struggle extremely hard . . . but the Peruvians have always confronted the difficulties of nature with immense valor and have constructed great feats of human ingenuity. Inca civilization developed in one of the most difficult natural sites in the world."

Exhaustive, encyclopedic, always full of fascinating figures and dates, as baroque as Lezama Lima or Carpentier in the organic and voracious development of his thought, Fidel was marvelous when he gave himself over to speech, I thought. And there was no limit to his generosity. He sent off fifteen of the country's doctors, fifteen nurses, and ten sanitation workers to help the Peruvians. I studied his beautiful manly profile on the newspaper's pages and thought that if I hadn't toiled away at the stupid routine of dance, I could have mastered a profession that would allow me to go out and help the world. Blankets were being sent, doctors were being sent, food was being sent to Peru, and I would be sent, too. I saw myself with a sun-browned face and a backpack, boots torn by the mountains' rocky paths, receiving a warm, electrifying embrace of welcome from Fidel, the hero who gave himself entirely at every moment. What incomparable jubilation! What a wasted life was mine!

Four days after the earthquake a campaign to donate blood for the wounded was launched, and the long lines normally seen when a scarce product became available in the shops began forming in front of the blood centers. In their crisis, their poverty, and the infinite limitations imposed by their own failures and the U.S. blockade, the Cuban people were giving away their blood— and felt some consolation at having something left to give.

Fidel may have thought that his constant appeals to the world, seeking support, sending reinforcements, always needing to be seen, and seen in a good light, were born from his obedience to the doctrine and practice of proletarian internationalism, but in other socialist countries—the Soviet Union, let us say—this was not the most extolled principle. It was, rather, an essentially Cuban condition: the fertile island planted in the middle of the Caribbean Sea was destined to be a melting pot. The Revolution was internationalist because the country had for a very long time been cosmopolitan. And though it did make strategic sense to avoid isolation in Cuba's confrontation with the United States, the main thing was that Fidel—so inescapably Latin— didn't like feeling alone any more than his compatriots did. The Comandante's hunger for people and his gigantic curiosity about anything going on anywhere on the planet even brought him into conflict with one of his primary impulses, which was anti-Yankeeism.

And that was why, in 1968, he had decided to invite the famous American anthropologist Oscar Lewis to Cuba. After an initial encounter lasting some twelve hours, during which the anthropologist said very little and the Comandante spoke a great deal, Fidel made Lewis an offer. He had read with admiration, he said, the portrait of a very poor Mexican family that Lewis had published a few years earlier and that became so famous that it was made into a Hollywood movie. As Lewis's wife later recounted, Fidel said that the book, *The Children of Sánchez*, was "revolutionary" and worth more than "fifty thousand political pamphlets." Now the Comandante proposed that Lewis, along with as many field researchers as he might need, carry out a similar project in Cuba. Similar but, of course, much more ambitious: the study would include not only the poor but all social strata across the entire country. Fidel even proposed—to ensure that the project would be authentic and complete—that the Cuban exile community be included in the study. For Lewis, who had already suffered the censure and opprobrium of the Mexican government and part of the Mexican intelligentsia after *The Children of Sánchez* was published, the dangers were obvious. He made it clear to Fidel that he would demand total freedom in his work. Moreover, he asked that the Revolution promise not to punish anyone he interviewed for collaborating with the study, regardless of the political convictions that a person might express. Of course, said Fidel, "We're not going to kick up a fuss the way the Mexicans did. This is a socialist country, and the only thing that matters to us is that you do your work honestly." This siren song proved irresistible, and Lewis arrived on the island early in 1969 with his wife and various members of his research team.

I learned this story from a singular dancer I had known in Mexico named Alicia, who was also an anthropologist. She had been part of Lewis's research team for *The Children of Sánchez,* and now she had joined his Cuban team. One evening at the beginning of June, Hilda handed me a message: Alicia had just returned from a short trip to Mexico and had a package for me, forwarded from New York. She invited me to drop by that evening at the house she was sharing with the other members of Lewis's team.

At the spacious home where some of the members of the team—researchers from Cuba, Mexico, and the United States—were housed, people were talking as if their work and the Revolution was inseparable, as if a lifetime was too short for the great goals they had to achieve. This was a historic project, they said happily: to chart the map of a country's social classes, understand how class consciousness determined each person's degree of revolutionary participation, to create a true portrait of Cuban society—what an opportunity! Lewis himself came in for a moment. I remember him as being short of stature and large of ego. He had a stocky body, gray hair, and an impatient demeanor; his speech and gestures were abrupt and hurried. He seemed aware that his obsessive character made people think he was rude, and he made an awkward effort to seem friendly. The Cuban government was enormously interested in his project, he told me, almost the moment Alicia introduced me. Those in charge of supervising it had found top-level young people to help with the research, had placed three magnificent houses at his disposal—two for his colleagues, and another for himself and his family—and had guaranteed them transportation and the state's full cooperation. Manuel Piñeiro himself had stopped by just the day before to say hello and personally assure them that they would lack for nothing. Having said that much, Lewis clearly felt that he had fulfilled the basic requirements of social exchange. He arranged a few details with his team, said goodbye, and left the room.

Fidel's direct backing afforded Lewis's team privileges I hadn't seen in Cuba. The house the Cuban government rented out to them was large, breezy, modern, and surrounded by a garden. The entire neighborhood of Miramar was like that; it looked like a residential suburb in Florida. The few pieces of furniture in the house seemed to have emerged the day before from a warehouse maintained by the government for just such cases: sojourns of some duration by distinguished foreign visitors, level two. I seem to recall some wicker rocking chairs in the living room around a glass-topped table; the dining room contained a heavy mahogany table and several mismatched chairs. Every surface was covered with documents and folders except the walls, which Lewis's team had papered with maps, graphics, and the schedule of interviews they were going to carry out.

Alicia opened a refrigerator bulging with cheeses, yogurt, butter, milk, cucumbers, tomatoes, and even a monumental slab of meat, and offered me a banana milk shake. Wide-eyed, I couldn't help mentioning my astonishment at her privileged situation. Of course, compared with what was available to Cubans, the food here was good, she admitted, but it wasn't anything extraordinary. But all the Cubans I knew went around perpetually irritated by the scarcity of food, I answered. She looked at me as if wondering how I'd managed so quickly to surround myself with counterrevolutionaries, and I decided it was best not to tell her a joke that was making the rounds and that always made me giggle, no matter how many times I repeated or heard it over the following months. Fidel is listening to a report by a secret agent he sent to Miami to find out just how badly capitalism has deteriorated. "Comandante, you wouldn't believe it, those people are way, way behind us," says the spy, squaring his shoulders. "Just imagine, they're still devouring things we stopped eating years ago: steak, milk shakes, buttered toast . . ."

I gloried in the taste of the anachronistic milk shake, trying and failing to drink it in measured sips. "Piñeiro's opinions seem to matter a lot to Oscar," I commented to Alicia, wiping my mouth. "Is he really all that powerful?"

"I think he's the person closest to Fidel," she answered. "They say the two of them get along very well. And on all matters of state security, at least, he's the one who has final say."

It wasn't entirely clear to me why the man in charge of state security—I imagined Piñeiro activating the antiaircraft missiles that would protect Cuba from the coming Yankee attack—was so interested in Oscar Lewis's project.

In the *guagua* on the way home I extracted the envelopes from the package Alicia had delivered and examined them one by one. Some were from my mother: a letter, a cassette, the latest dance reviews from the *Times,* and some funny clippings from *The New Yorker.* Elaine sent a note containing the devastating news that the U.S. Immigration Service had finally managed to deport both Sheela and Graciela. There was also a letter from Adrian, but most of the envelopes were from Jorge, the Mexican man who had visited me so often when I was sick. He sent books—an anthology of twentieth-century Mexican poetry, a little book by Efraín Huerta, another by Octavio Paz—magazines to entertain me at night, and several letters. One was long and scrawled on a legal pad. In another envelope came a postscript, typed on a note card like the ones Sandy used for her choreography. Finally, hiding in a manila envelope, lay a sheet of rice paper flecked with gold on which, in large architect's script, he had written fragments of a Baudelaire poem with a purple marker. The author of the letters hid from view, then showed himself, referred to me but without mentioning me, evoked the rainy season that was just beginning in Mexico City, our city, and that left the afternoon skies blue and gleaming. He spoke of the water that ran down the dilapidated walls of the old ruined palaces in the center of the city, which both he and I loved so much, of the still unwashed blood of the students killed in Tlatelolco two years earlier, of the terrible nostalgia brought on by the sight of rain in Mexico City, nostalgia for what you have experienced and for the things that you'll never experience, the life that passed you by. He wondered whether the absurdities of daily life in Cuba, the infinite frustrations and scarcity, might be keeping me from understanding in all its full, magnificent, audacious, and historic dimensions the epic tale that the Cuban people were living out.

I didn't remember Adrian's letter until I was back in the dormitory. *He can tell I'm forgetting him,* I thought when I opened the envelope. *That's why he's sending me his picture.*

As the days went by, Hilda began to smile again and Tere stopped trying to make jokes, but the failure of the Ten Million Ton Harvest still weighed on us during the only celebration that took place during the months I spent at the dance school.

Though I can't recall the reason for the party, I know it was in June because it was an evening of inconsolable sadness, like all those that followed Fidel's *zafra* speech. In any case, it must have been an important occasion because even Manuel Piñeiro showed up, in gleaming boots and an olive green uniform so pressed and starched that it crackled. That was how I finally met Lorna Burdsall's husband. He sat down at a table in the dining room, at a distance from everyone else, and his bodyguard brought him a bottle of rum and a bucket of ice. Lorna then escorted me over to introduce me—with a certain deference and even shyness, I seem to recall—to the imposing figure who was her husband.

Perhaps if the entire personnel of Cubanacán had not been in mourning, Piñeiro would not have felt assailed by the same infinite melancholy that gripped everyone else and would not have installed himself in an isolated corner with his rum and his bodyguards. Perhaps I would then have a memory of the legendary charm that so many visitors to Cuba describe in their memoirs—the intensity of his interest in the world and the beings that inhabit it, and the lively humor of his anecdotes. The Piñeiro I spoke to that night, however, was capable of an almost catatonic indifference when faced with someone who could not be useful to him. Bearded, with russet hair, perhaps even taller than Fidel—but no one could ever be taller than Fidel!—and with the same gift for occupying much more space than his body actually took up, the Comandante de la Revolución in charge of state security bowed slightly in greeting and squinted at me for a moment in the exasperating darkness of Cubanacán before eliminating me from his field of vision with a small movement of the head. "I'll see you later," he said to Lorna. But Piñeiro must have been bored, because as I made to leave, trailing behind his wife, he called me back. "Come here. Sit down."

Without asking, he filled a tall glass with ice cubes, poured in rum to the brim, and set the drink in front of me. In considerable distress, I told him that I didn't like alcohol. "Have you met the director of the ENA?" he asked, paying no attention. "Look. This is Mario Hidalgo." He gestured to a gray-haired man of about fifty who was sitting at the table with him. "He's your boss, the man in charge of this whole big *miedero* [shitpile].

Here's your chance to get to know him. Have a drink with the *compañera,* Mario."

It didn't take the Comandante long to realize that I was not the one to help him chase away his blues. I didn't drink, I didn't talk, I didn't sing the praises of the Revolution, and since no one was telling jokes, I didn't laugh, either. After two or three quick questions—he wanted to know if I'd been treated well in Cuba and if I needed anything, and I may have told him that I desperately needed some mirrors and a different kind of diet for the students—he forgot the Mexican dance teacher who was so inept that she didn't even know how to come up with some pretext for leaving the table. He and Mario Hidalgo, whom I'd never before seen at the school and who hadn't said a single word to me, went on drinking in silence.

"So how are things going at the school?" Piñeiro finally asked the general director of the Escuelas Nacionales de Arte.

"Well, *mielmano*"—that was how *mi hermano* sounded in Hidalgo's thick Cuban accent—"you see . . ." Graying and wiry, Hidalgo looked like a military man, or at least very much unlike an artist, even though he was wearing civilian clothes. Now he was trying to think of some information to give Piñeiro about his work as the head of the school. "We've had a few little supply problems, you know. We keep having power blackouts, so we've got to get the generator working again: we really need it, especially in the kitchen."

Piñeiro, who had been absorbed in his drink, now threw himself back in his chair and shot Hidalgo a glance that was both amused and irritated. "No, no: I'm asking you how the students are, what you think of the teachers."

Hidalgo began to grow alarmed. "Well, you see, Manuel, we still have a little problem with absenteeism, but of course on the other hand we've had a pretty high turnout for the volunteer work campaign, especially where the dance school is concerned." Hidalgo gave a little smile to Lorna Burdsall's husband.

"No, *coño,* that's not what I'm asking about, either. I mean, is this school serving any purpose, in the end? We aren't too sure what artists are good for in this country, we're not sure of their commitment to the Revolution, they continue to be the most

unpredictable"—the displeasure on Piñeiro's face increased—
"not to say vacillating sector, and from the beginning we've
counted on this school to breed a new kind of artist. Good, clean
people, without vices. So what do you think of these kids?"

There followed a very long silence. Mario Hidalgo was hunched
over so low that his forehead almost touched the table. Finally,
he lifted his gaze. "Manuel, you know me. You know who I am.
You can say I'm ignorant or uneducated, but you can never say
that I'm not a revolutionary or that I don't believe in Fidel. From
the time on board the *Granma* until this moment, I've always
been where Fidel and the party wanted me, in the mountains and
in the city, fighting it out on any front that arose, *mielmano,* that's
how it's been. And I've never complained, I've never asked for
anything, because I only want beautiful things, good things, for
this Revolution, which is like a mother to me. That's what I'm
telling you, *caballero*! Because without the Revolution I'm worth
nothing, my life is worth nothing! But listen to me, Manuel, I
have to ask you a favor now. I have to ask you so you can ask
Fidel, because I know he listens to you."

Piñeiro was still gazing at the director of Cubanacán with
both irritation and amusement. Now he raised his chin slightly
in interrogation.

"Get me out of here," said Mario Hidalgo.

"*¡Oye, chico!* What's all this?" Piñeiro shifted forward in his
seat and gave his former comrade-in-arms a couple of quick pats
on the back. "This is no time for discouragement. What happens
if we all get discouraged? (And there's no denying that some of
us have plenty of reason to.) No, *hermano,* no. No way. The Revolution doesn't always send us to the battlefront we might have
chosen. Look at me—do you think I like being a police dog? But
as it happens there aren't many of us who are good, unconditionally good, really unshakable, *hermano,* and we have to distribute the tasks in accordance with what the cause demands and
not with what our subjectivity wants. I don't need to tell you
that! Wherever the struggle places us, that's where we wage the
battle—"

Mario Hidalgo interrupted. "Manuel, look at me, *mielmano:*

look at me. I'm a baker by trade." Piñeiro glanced at him in surprise. "Yes, that's what I am, you should have remembered that, and neither the *Granma* expedition nor the war in the mountains took the baker out of me. I thought they had. I thought that when a man became a Hero of the Revolution, everything changed, that all of us could take on any task and help Fidel save this country, from whatever post we were assigned to. *Coño,* if we could overthrow Batista! But now I've learned that that isn't true. I can't do everything. Ask me to organize an ambush for you, and I'll organize it—perfect, lovely, without a single casualty on our side. Ask me to figure out how to supply a factory, and I'll figure it out. If Fidel wants me to bake bread, I'll bake bread. But I'm asking that the Revolution use me for what I'm good for and give me a chance to serve. Because for this, for administering this shithouse full of artists and *patos* and intellectuals—I'm no good for this. And why should I lie to you, *chico?* I'm no good for ideology, either. I have one single ideology in life, which is Fidel and *Patria o Muerte.* Anyone who strays from that had better look out because he's going to get it right on the head from me. But around here they're always telling me it's more complicated, that I have to be careful, that artists are very special people. *Coño, chico,* tell Fidel to get me out of here!"

Piñeiro took a last swallow of his rum and signaled to his bodyguard that they were leaving.

"I'm begging you," Mario Hidalgo said.

"I'm going, *hermano.*" Piñeiro took his leave. "Tomorrow we've all got to take up the machete again."

The two of them got up, having forgotten me entirely. Mario Hidalgo left. Piñeiro walked out. I noticed with some alarm that the Comandante could barely hold himself upright.

"What are *patos?*" I asked Tere the next day.

"That's what people call homosexuals. Who used that word in front of you?"

"*Maestra,* may I speak to you for a moment?"

"For just two minutes, Orlando, and only if you'll stop calling me *maestra.* This is the fifteenth time I've asked!"

Orlando gazed at me with adoring eyes. He looked at the ground. He blushed. I was suddenly having trouble breathing. A long time later I decided I would have done Orlando a great favor if I'd had fewer scruples about the fact that he was sixteen and I was twenty-one. But that was mere speculation. The boy's body and soul were visibly tied up in a hundred knots of conflict, and it wasn't feasible for someone as insecure as I was, with so little experience myself in such matters, to take charge of his amorous initiation. On the contrary, to conceal my little weakness, I was often exaggeratedly severe with him.

"Orlando, those shoulders, for the love of God," I shouted at him every day in class. "You're not in the army. This is a dance class! Pull your shoulders down, relax!"

And Orlando would lower his shoulders and twist his lips and wrinkle his brow and clench his fists while continuing to advance on the diagonal looking as if he were the Nutcracker prior to its transformation into a prince.

There has to be a prince in him, I thought. *It's simply not possible that a body like that is useless for dancing.* But neither Orlando's body nor his spirit succeeded in expressing itself. He was a Cuban mulatto, but in folklore class he moved like a Norwegian.

"It's because I don't like folklore, *maestra.* I like your classes," he would say, looking at me like Saint Barbara contemplating the cross.

"All right, here's your minute. What's up?"

"*Maestra,* do you think I'm improving?"

"Of course you are, Orlando, but not enough, I'm afraid. It's very strange: you have a dancer's body, a dancer's instincts, and an extremely elegant line, but you don't know how to move!" Orlando was gazing at me in anguish now, his mouth contracted in a poor imitation of an attentive smile. I tried, too late, to soften my evaluation. "I think you live with a great deal of tension. If you could just relax, if you could enjoy yourself more in class instead of always fighting to catch up with the other students, I'm sure everything would change."

Orlando's smile twisted even more. His face muscles were sculpted very close to the bone, and at moments like this his beautiful, rounded features looked more like a skull. "How can you tell me to enjoy myself when my life here is hell?"

"What do you mean, *hell,* Orlando? How can you say such a thing?"

"They can't forgive me for wanting to take ballet classes, they can't forgive me for having come here on my own because I really wanted to be a dancer. That's the only thing I want in life—to dance. But the students in my dormitory brag about how their parents brought them here or the school chose them. Even if they like dance, they say they're not here because they want to become dancers. They say male dancers are almost all perverts, and ever since I said I wanted to study ballet, it all got worse. And you tell me I need to relax!"

I had neither a solution nor any helpful advice for a Cuban teenager whose classmates accused him of being homosexual. I wanted to encourage him, but for a reason I wouldn't have been able to identify as cowardice, I preferred to pretend I hadn't quite understood what he was explaining to me. "That prejudice against ballet is very old-fashioned. Tell the others that I say ballet is just fine." I left him with his skull's smile plastered across his face.

Dear Jorge,

It's so hot! One of the things I've learned here is that you can obviously take the tropical heat much better than I can; I spend only ten percent of my time enjoying the beauty of the things you told me about (and other things I've seen, too, like this school, which I don't think you've visited and which is very strange and beautiful), and the other ninety percent of the time lying prostrate in a puddle of sweat. Why is it only dictators have those portable fans that shoot a perpetual breeze into their faces? I desperately need one. Fortunately, the rains are starting here, too. A fat little cloud appears on the edge of a blue sky and summons all the others, the wind comes to keep them company, the leaves go into a dance of happy agitation, and the water party breaks out. Two or three deluges come down, then the black sky clears and the

*leaves and the wind calm down, still letting little cool drops fall here
and there, all of them having decided to keep it a secret that only a
moment ago they were having an orgy. I won't breathe a word of it
either, as long as they promise to do the same thing again tomorrow.*
¡Viva la lluvia!

*There's a lot I could tell you about, but in heat like this, news of
water is much more important. Well, that's not true (you always
accuse me of exaggerating, so I'm going to try to be serious). The most
important thing is that my students are absolutely wonderful and I
love them all very much. I've also met Galo, the friend Azucena told
us so much about, and he and his friends are marvelous. I'm doing all
right with the classes, I think, but planning them is a lot of work.
Sometimes I think that I explain the importance of Merce Cunningham technique better to you than I do to the students. Sometimes my
thoughts just seem to evaporate when I'm in the middle of a class.*

*What's turning out to be hardest for me is this Revolution. Or
rather, understanding what one must do in order to be a revolutionary. I'm beginning to understand that I've been greatly deformed by
capitalism before coming here, and I see that what you were saying
about the dangers of individualism is true. It takes a great deal of
effort for me to stop thinking about myself. The other day, for
example, I was actually glad, deep down inside, when they told me
that because of my cough (which is a lot better now, by the way) I
wouldn't have to donate blood for the people injured in the earthquake
in Peru. Even though they're in the most desperate situation imagina-
ble, and we've been following it on the news here each day, and even
Fidel himself went to donate blood. I acted as if it frustrated me not to
be able to go, and it did, a little bit, but not enough. I understand
that this is a serious failing, and that I should have insisted until I
convinced the people at the school, but I don't know how to change. I
mean, I feel that if I were to transform into a revolutionary like Che,
I would cease completely to be myself, and I can't help being scared
of that.*

*Furthermore, outside of Che and Fidel, I can't keep from feeling
that the people who are in charge of the Revolution, or many of
them—along with those who write about it and support it—are
a bunch of jerks. For example, that magazine you'd told me about*

put out a special issue on Che, in which a guy named Emanuel Carballo—I think he's Mexican—wrote that one should always distrust all intellectuals. The other night the director of the ENA, who I think is a Hero of the Revolution because he survived the landing of the Granma or something like that, said that all artists are a pack of shit-eaters (when he says comemierdas, it comes out as comemieddas). But what I want to know is, what harm have we artists done to the world? Compared, say, to Hitler or Nixon or Charles Manson, who didn't kill as many people as Nixon, but then . . . I've been feeling very guilty because everyone here thinks that since I lived in the United States and then came to Cuba, it means I participated in demonstrations and the fight against the Vietnam War, and you know that isn't true. It's something that will pain me all my life, especially after the massacre of the students at Kent State. But it's also true that none of the waitresses who worked with me at the cafeteria had ever gone to any demonstrations, and they really are proletarians. It isn't that I want to sidestep my guilt, but I don't think my poor conduct is due to the fact that I'm an artist. It may be that I'm a useless creature, but all in all I believe the work we do is important (or, in Cuban, impottante). Isn't it?

All right, I'll stop here so as not to bore you. Really, I just wanted to thank you for all the gifts you sent. Thanks for the book of Poesía en movimiento: I loved the poems by José Juan Tablada, and also by Ortiz de Montellano—I'd never heard of him before:

I am the last witness to my body
I feel myself feeling
the cold of marble
and the green
and black
of my thoughts
I am the last witness to my body

That's how I feel sometimes. Pacheco's climbing vine sounds to me as if you had written it.

    Alma

  P.S. Elfrida Mahler is a horrible witch.

By the time I finished writing the letter, the start of the afternoon's deluge was only seconds away; if I didn't leave immediately
for the dance studio, I'd spend yet another afternoon without
rehearsing. Where were my tights with the patched-up crotch? I
kept my best practice clothes for the class and used the shabbier
things for rehearsing Sandy's choreography. Now I couldn't find
the most worn-out set of all, and as my departure for the studio
was further and further delayed, my mood grew worse. I yanked
the clothes I'd used that morning out of my bag and threw them
on the floor. The *Granma* I'd pilfered from Hilda's office flew out
with the leotard and flapped open to a photograph I'd tried to ignore that morning. It was taken in Cambodia, the country adja-
cent to Vietnam, invaded by U.S. troops two months earlier on
the eve of my arrival in Cuba. Years later I saw that photograph
again, in the *Granma* archives of the Benson Latin American Collection at the University of Texas at Austin. In the background is
a helicopter. Front and center stands an American man in combat uniform, his sleeves rolled up, a helmet on his head. He must
be about forty years old, and unusually, he has a mustache. He's
smiling. In one hand he's holding a lasso, apparently made from
some ordinary material, leather or rope. The other end is tied
around the neck of a Cambodian. The captive is barefoot and
wears only a skimpy loincloth. He is blindfolded, and at the
moment the photo was taken, he's just stumbled. Alone in my
room in Cubanacán with that photo, I had the feeling that I was
witnessing something intolerable.

The rain caught me halfway down the path, and for a few
moments it brought some relief. The path through the jungle
was an undersea landscape, and I felt I might become amphibian
at any moment. I reached the studio with water, leaves, and perhaps even algae pouring off me and quickly changed into my
practice clothes. But then, as I stood in the middle of the studio,
all the energy that had accompanied me there evaporated, and I
couldn't persuade my muscles to engage with my brain. I tried
out a few phrases, lost my balance, then distracted myself trying

to fix the barre, which had been detached from the wall for the past two weeks. I went back to the center of the studio and again felt the weight of the silence and the vault over my head, threatening me. I wanted a drink of water; my mouth tasted like a bitter communion wafer. I sat down on the beautiful worn mahogany floor and wrote out in my notebook a couple of ideas I'd had for a dance performance. This was a piece that would make use of the school's strange architecture and the labyrinths of its jungle paths. As the spectators walked toward the little plaza in the heart of the dance school, they would see, first of all, a hung dog; then they would come to a bonfire with four young men dancing around it naked, smeared with blood. At the end of the path, I wrote quickly, having at last recovered my concentration, the spectators would reach the little plaza, where they would find another hung body, mine, but I would really be dead.

As he'd promised, Boris took me for a stroll through the splendors of Old Havana one morning. Thin and quick, Boris was, of all Galo's friends, the one with the most stereotypically gay demeanor—which may be why he was the only one who'd ended up in a forced labor camp. He was also the most conservative, in the strictest sense of the word. In his artistic work he was less involved than the others in avant-garde movements: he had been a classical ballet dancer, and now he was an administrator for Alicia Alonso's company. He was also the one who expressed the least fervor about the Revolution. It might reasonably be hypothesized that Boris's lack of enthusiasm was a consequence of the time he had spent doing involuntary agricultural labor, but such is not the logic of revolutionary feeling. I think Galo would have gone on loving Fidel even if he'd had to spend two years in a UMAP, while Boris, with or without the UMAP, would always have preferred the classic to the experimental and order to chaos.

We had gone to the Museo de La Habana on the Plaza de la Catedral to see not the collection of furniture and old paintings that the colonial building housed but the stained-glass *medios puntos* that made Boris so happy. At every door and window topped with a semicircle of glass, he stopped to explain the evolution, over the course of the colonial era, of these transparent ornaments that, with the light of the tropics filtering through them, tinted the stone floors with their candy colors and at the same time helped to cool them off.

"You see, Alma, how Cuban we Cubans are?" Boris explained with sudden intensity. "This seventeenth-century house is not the Escorial, these stained-glass windows are not the cathedral of Salamanca, even if stone is stone and leaded glass is leaded glass. This is a merry seaside flutter of wings, playful and a little clumsy, without much affectation, without much technique, if you like, but also without any colors or forms but our own. That's why I don't agree with the people who say that we Cubans were always mentally colonized until Fidel came. When Galo says that, he's forgetting where he lives and what he reads and what he eats. I agree that Cuban culture was born in the colonial era, but that doesn't mean it isn't profoundly Cuban. And that's why it's important to preserve the *medios puntos* and the palaces and the houses in Vedado, too. I don't know if those forms are decadent or not, authentic or not, and I don't care: I think they're beautiful, and they're Cuban, and if we destroy our most fully achieved buildings, as many of those idiots around Fidel keep wanting to do, we'll destroy the evidence of what it is to be Cuban, and we'll lose our way."

Boris kept silent for a while after that declaration, while we strolled through elegant rooms full of carpets and elaborate furniture. Perhaps he was thinking he had spoken too loudly, though the museum was almost empty. Maybe he was talking to himself. When we left the museum and headed for the fort known as the Castillo del Príncipe, he started talking again, picking up what seemed to be the continuation of an internal monologue.

"But look how unexpectedly a man can be visited by regret. I was just thinking that in another time or another life, I would have devoted myself to museum work and restoration. But I'm only thinking that now because it's been my lot to live precisely during this period, the revolutionary period, and revolutions generate so much destruction that you need someone around who knows how to repair the damage afterward. There's been an urgent will to destroy the past; right now we Cubans think we have to finish off everything that's old—only what's new is good. People see the past as a dead weight that won't go away but stubbornly remains alive. When, if you think about it, it's really extremely difficult for the human mind to remember anything past, even when you find yourself face-to-face with something as solid as this stone fortress, or as impossible to eliminate as history itself. We can rebuild, imagine, interpret, dream that we are remembering. But we can't remember."

We were going past an old building, which in my opinion was rather graceless. "Look," Boris, who noticed everything, pointed out. "This is exactly what I'm talking about. See that window? Until a couple of years ago it had some wonderful stained glass in it, half art deco, half cabaret. And look what's left now. And no one cares. No one feels any need for such things."

Back in Galo's cool, breezy apartment with a distant view of the sea, I tried to recover from the blasting sunlight of our excursion. Recently Galo's mother had managed to get hold of a bit of yuca—by trading a cup of the powdered milk I'd brought from Mexico with a neighbor lady who had a nephew who lived in the country. We were drinking water and eating some delicious fritters made from the bartered yuca when the phone rang.

Pablo answered. When he hung up, his face was grave. "It was your friend Alicia. She's coming over to say good-bye because she's going back to Mexico, she doesn't know exactly when. She says Piñeiro came to Oscar Lewis's house yesterday and practically tore the whole place apart, and the project, too. He confiscated all the archives and will not return them. He said their work was counterrevolutionary; that objectively, Lewis was working for the CIA. Lewis insisted on speaking to Fidel, and Fidel wouldn't meet with him."

Galo's face darkened. "*¡Coño!* I wish she hadn't said all that over the telephone."

June came to an end. In the strange, willful trap of my memory, I can't seem to find any explanation for why Alicia ended up staying on in Cuba several weeks after Lewis left, or how I explained to myself what Piñeiro had done, with Fidel behind him. (Lewis died of a heart attack six months later, without having made any public reference to the disaster in Cuba.) But in those intervening weeks we did manage to glean that one of Piñeiro's main charges against Lewis, after he had seized and read his files, was that his research team had interviewed at length a person who was opposed to the Revolution (and who, worse still, was related to a top Cuban official). We also learned, a few weeks after Lewis's departure, that despite his explicit demand and the guarantee he'd been given on that point, the government arrested and imprisoned the anti-*fidelista* relative who wasn't known to have committed any crime but that of participating in the interviews. We found out as well that Piñeiro, in trying to excuse his own actions while simultaneously reproaching Lewis for his blundering audacity, had mentioned that Fidel was very sensitive and that the criticism of the Revolution in the books *Les guérilleros au pouvoir: L'itinéraire politique de la révolution cubaine* by K. S. Karol and *Cuba, est-il socialiste?* by René Dumont, had profoundly wounded the Comandante en Jefe, since the foreign traitors who wrote them were once thought to be friends of the Revolution, in whom Fidel had placed all his confidence. And we learned that in a dispute over Lewis's financing, Piñeiro had finally triumphed against another faction in Fidel's entourage who had supported the project. The anthropologist had received funding from the Ford Foundation, and the head of state security insisted that aid could not be accepted from a supposedly humanitarian organization that was in fact a front for the CIA or was infiltrated by it. Today I wonder whether Comandante Piñeiro's zealous pursuit of the sociologist and all other things Yankee, had anything to do with the fact that he himself was united in matrimony with a blond citizen of the hated country where he had also studied. Perhaps it was himself he didn't trust. But I don't remember the incident clearly enough to speculate any further.

I do have a very sharp image, however, of an incident of no importance that took place one morning before class began and that still delights me even today. Perhaps I remember it because, without realizing it, I lived during all those months in Cuba in a state of permanent self-vigilance and control, and this was one moment when the students and I were free and silly and therefore happy.

As usual, I had arrived at the studio a few minutes late. In the steamy dressing room I'd taken my shoes off, struggling to tug on a leotard and tights that kept snagging on my sticky skin. At that point in the morning I was always strangling on the day's worst attack of anguish, and I had to fight down a muscular impulse to cancel the class, flee to the dormitory, and hide in bed for the rest of my life. But the first touch of bare foot against the studio's naked wood always rescued me, as if my entire being gathered together and came back down to earth there, knowing what it had to do.

"Ready," I shouted, clapping my hands to hurry the slackers who were still in the dressing room or the corridor outside. "Class time!" They came running in, freshly bathed like me and not quite put together, tugging at the crotch of their threadbare leotards or rolling up one leg of their tights so a run wouldn't travel any farther. "All right, turkeys! We're starting!" I was still clapping. "Carmen's missing. Yasmina, why don't you go get her? She's still in the dressing room."

Carmen came running out, hopping on one foot while she smoothed down her tights. "Alma, how did you know it was me in the dressing room?"

"Because I saw your heels underneath the door, how else?"

"And just from my heels you knew it was me?"

"Of course I did, silly girl. Don't you know that your heels, your knees, and your arms are every bit as unique and expressive as your face? I would recognize you from your shoulder blades, and you'd recognize me, too. That's why we're dancers, because we believe that the most important things are said with every bit of our bodies!"

"Then let's all go to the dressing room and try it out, Alma! Each person will go in and the rest of us will see if we can recognize the heels underneath the door."

"You may want to do that, but not on my time—I didn't

come all this way to waste my class on such nonsense. All right, monsters! For indulging in such foolishness: one hundred sit-ups before the class begins!"

Groans and howls of protest echoed through the studio, amplified by the brick vault, and then we all stretched out on the floor and shouted out the count for each sit-up, happy as kings. During class I was astonished to note that Carmen was working very consciously with her heels and ankles, and so were Orlando and José.

SIX

Tourism and My Conscience

It was July, the holy month at the heart of the Cuban Revolution. Thanks to Fidel, history had begun anew one July 26, almost twenty years earlier, with an attack by a group of young visionaries on the dictator Batista's second most important barracks. As the anniversary of that date drew near, the entire island was mobilized again, not to cut cane but to commemorate the founding moment. TODOS A LA PLAZA CON FIDEL—Everyone to the plaza with Fidel—was the slogan we read in *Granma,* on the walls, and on the billboards where it replaced the now outdated 1970: YEAR OF THE TEN MILLION! In offices, on *guaguas,* in the line at Coppelia, and in my studio in Cubanacán a change was in the air like the coming of the rains. In the aftermath of its great failure, the militant nation was injured, covered with bruises and on the verge of tears: now the day of communion was approaching, I was told, when the Comandante's words would allow us to understand what had happened and to become conscious of our mistakes, raising our spirits so we could go on with the struggle no one wanted to abandon. How could we, when the future of the world depended on the Cuban people and those of us who were there with them? With Fidel. Onward to victory forever. *Patria o Muerte. Venceremos.* To repeat those words sincerely was to unfurl a sail in your chest and navigate by the great winds of history.

Fidel was Urakán, I thought: the Caribbean god of tumultuous air who moves the world to a different place and turns life on its head. One day he uprooted the whole island and sent it out to cut cane. The next day everyone was standing in line to send their blood by plane to a distant country. Who else had his energy or his colossal power? Yesterday we were all sad; today we were cheerful and effervescent as we prepared for July 26 and the anniversary of the beginning of Cuba's liberation. To go to the plaza and see Fidel! I heard about the citywide rumba that would break out afterward in the avenues—the entire end of July was a carnival, with people parading around in costumes, live music everywhere, and rivers of cheap beer—and the thrill of being in the plaza with the Horse, *El Caballo* himself, everyone together, listening to his thoughts. It was a fervor that came to find me as I trotted through my daily itinerary from the dormitory to the dining room, from the dining room to the dance studio, and from the studio back to the dormitory, deeply immersed in my ongoing arguments for and against myself and my life. I was trying to work out what my—or any human being's—responsibility was in the face of horror; the validity of art as an end in itself; the pity and repulsion I'd felt toward Mario Hidalgo; the way socialism offended my exalted notion of the individual. I was increasingly unsuccessful in defending myself against my own internal prosecutor, but now all those doubts gently vanished before a distant murmur that was growing louder and louder. "*¡Todos a la plaza con Fidel!*" said my student Roberto to my student José, out of the blue. *Me, too,* I thought, grateful to have landed in such a historic moment and place. *I'm everyone now, too.*

On July 26, 1953, slightly more than a hundred young men armed with great faith and lousy rifles unsuccessfully attacked the principal military barracks of Santiago, Cuba's second-largest city. The author of that adventure was Fidel Castro, born almost twenty-six years earlier on a prosperous sugar plantation, the product of an unofficial relationship between his poor, almost illiterate mother and a thriving plantation owner. This origin was no secret, but little was said about it, and even less was said about Fidel's father, Angel Castro, a determined, poverty-stricken Spaniard who first came to the island in the 1890s as a soldier with the Spanish royalist troops. A few years later he returned, seeking better fortune than that offered by life as a farmhand in his native Galicia. He rented some land in the province of Oriente, at the opposite end of the island from Havana, and began growing sugarcane. By renting and then buying he became rich: when Fidel was born, about three hundred families—many of them Haitian—lent Don Angel their labor in exchange for a *conuco,* a plot of land on his ranch on which to grow their own sustenance. Nevertheless, the Galician was neither a man of leisure nor an oligarch: there were no luxuries on the *finca,* and the Castros worked hard. Until the end of his days, Angel Castro was a gruff man without pretensions or refinements.

In the early years of the twentieth century Angel Castro married a country schoolteacher. He had two children with her. As time went by, he fell in love with a laundress named Lina Ruz. From that lasting love affair, says Fidel's biographer Tad Szulc, were born seven more children: Angela, Ramón, Agustina, Emma, Juana, Fidel, and his younger brother, Raúl. It's quite probable that Lina and Angel were formally wed after Angel's first wife died, when Fidel was six years old. It was then, at least, that his parents had Fidel christened, and it's possible that they took advantage of the same ceremony, as many common-law couples still do in Latin America, to fulfill the other mandates of the Church. Fidel seems to have seen relatively little of his father after the christening: for reasons that remain unclear, he was sent away from the family plantation to the provincial capital of Santiago, where he was enrolled in a parochial grade school. Save for a few school vacations, he would never live at home again.

The few references to Fidel's childhood and adolescence that I found in the patriotic handbooks lent by Hilda and Tere tended to highlight other details: I learned that the young Fidel was a good student, an exceptional athlete, and a die-hard rebel. He climbed the highest peak in Cuba—the Pico del Turquino—on the outskirts of Santiago, he played basketball, and he defied the priests who tried to discipline him. Once enrolled in the National University in Havana, the tellers of his story went on to say, he chose to study law and found an outlet for his naturally rebellious tendencies in the student movement, but he was quickly disappointed by the prevailingly reformist spirit. To this biography, his younger brother Raúl innocently added the fact of Fidel's violence. He was always *guapo* (which, in Cuban, means

"belligerent"), Raúl said, from the time he was a child. At the
university he carried a pistol and was even accused of killing a
rival student leader. Heir to a certain fortune, educated in the
best schools of Santiago and Havana, tall and good-looking, the
young Fidel was also out of control and somewhat eccentric: due
to that, and to his origins, Cuban society's guardians of morality
and good breeding never saw him as anything more than a par-
venu. A series of youthful experiences such as his participation in
a popular insurrection in Colombia and a failed attempt to overthrow the Dominican dictator Rafael Leónidas Trujillo allowed
him to transform his affinity for violence into a fundamental ideological conviction: that armed struggle alone can bring about
meaningful social change.

He finished his studies and founded a small law firm, taking
on lost and worthy causes. At the same time, with his usual
manic energy, he plunged wholeheartedly into the clandestine
organization of an armed movement. And perhaps it was by
channeling his aggressive instincts into the fight against Batista
that Fidel became charismatic for the first time. The eternal
point of dissension among his enemies—at what point did Fidel
Castro become a Communist?—would appear to be simply the
wrong question, since it seems, rather, that when he distanced
himself from the gangsterish student groups who controlled the
political life of the university, Fidel opted for romanticism as an
existential posture. When he resolved to organize an attack on
the country's second-largest military barracks—an attack that
had absolutely no hope of success—he found hundreds of volunteers who certainly wouldn't have joined up if the aim had been,
for example, to get together for a close reading of *The Eighteenth
Brumaire of Louis Napoleon.*

I'm narrating the details that seem important to me now. But
when I was trying to grasp the essence of Fidel's life back then, I
thought it ignoble that my friends—Carlos, Tere, even Hilda—
should dwell openly on certain of the less glorious facts of the
Comandante's life, which they did, naturally, because Cuba is a
small island and such intimate matters were known to everyone,
without needing to consult any history pamphlets. Like so many
others, I tried to contemplate Fidel from a distance that would

eliminate the warts and the bad temper. In a violent, romantic region like Latin America, the hero who assembled multitudes, the one who excited and moved me, was not the Marxist or the troublemaker but the armed dreamer. In the same way, the great national gathering at the Plaza de la Revolución on July 26 would celebrate not a ridiculous military fiasco but the sublime audacity that at one point was defeated and then subsequently rose to glory. The event was the ideal context for a public evaluation of the results of the year the country had just lived through.

Along with tempestuous evocations of the history of the Revolution, the month of July arrived in Cubanacán with chocolates brought by Hattie, the new teacher in the dance school. Hattie Singer—a New Yorker, diminutive, fortyish, redheaded, enthusiastic, and very practical—was the biggest trophy Elfrida had collected on her headhunting trip through the dance studios of New York in search of modern dance teachers. Hattie had green, inquisitive eyes, a body full of very well shaped curves, and a happy cackle. She had finally accepted Elfrida's invitation to give a month-long class for the fifth-year students, as soon as summer vacation freed her of her duties at the university in New York where she taught. She had never been a famous dancer, but she was very capable and enjoyed teaching her classes as much as her students liked taking them. She'd been doing it for twenty-odd years, and when she appeared in the studio on the first Monday in July with her cute little body, her loud laugh, and her firm footsteps, and her unshakable confidence in herself, she calmed us all down. In a heartbeat I would have exchanged my own conflict-ridden mother for this confident, openhearted woman, but I resigned myself to simply taking her classes, which replaced mine for the advanced group.

She gave me the chocolates herself when she arrived at the dormitory in Cubanacán the night of that other patriotic day, the Fourth of July. When I opened the door of the room, Hattie looked me over with a knowing eye and then smiled with her whole wide mouth. She came in, put the box full of letters and packages she had brought from New York on the table, took a glance around the room, and reached the only conclusion that interested her at that moment: "I'll bet there's nowhere around here where I can get a whiskey with lots of ice, is there?" It was the first time I'd heard a woman ask for an alcoholic beverage just for herself. "After a trip like that, you really need a double whiskey—no kidding." She let out one of her big laughs. "I can't believe that I was in Canada this morning and now I'm on Fidel Castro's island!" To keep from being detected by the U.S. immigration authorities, Hattie had traveled to Toronto, from where she took a direct flight to Havana. "Tomorrow I'll worry about what the FBI will try to do to me if they catch me; for now I'm happy. If I had a drink, a little cheese, and a few olives, things would be perfect—but I'm not complaining." She curled up in the armchair. "Now, tell me everything. How are your classes going? What are the students like?"

Dancers are often apolitical, but in addition to being a dancer Hattie was a lifelong resident of the Upper West Side of Manhattan, which was settled by a significant number of emigrants from Europe on the eve of the Second World War. The great leftist tradition that that community upheld gave a particular flavor to the conversations and even the apparel of that part of the island— lots of shawls, loose clothes, natural hair. Hattie, who wore her very curly red hair in a kind of Afro, was not a militant leftist, but like so many of her neighbors she was a great admirer of the Revolution. She wanted it to be the next day already so she could see the school, the students, Havana. "Gus"—her husband—"is green with envy, but he told me I had to come; he'd never forgive me if I passed up an adventure like this." She found it admirable, she said, that someone as young as I was would decide to embark on this unpredictable odyssey, but I thought it was much more adventurous to live the way she did: happily open to all that life offered, without fear or guilt.

Hattie asked me for a summary of the school and its problems, but the box she'd left on the table was winking at me irresistibly. I threw myself on it as if it were a ruptured piñata and extracted its treasures one by one: letters from Graciela, announcing her expulsion from the United States, as well as from my mother,

Elaine, and Adrian; back issues of *The New Yorker;* a packet of granola; a tin of olives; the chocolates and a packet of candy; various cans of sardines; and a sweater. With exemplary courtesy, I offered Hattie some olives, and she, in a reciprocal effort that would have been superhuman a few weeks later, refused them. But she calmly accepted a tiny bite of one of the chocolate bars, since chocolate was not her passion, and looked on contentedly as I devoured the rest. *Once she leaves, I can eat another one,* I thought. But Hattie stayed on, and little by little, in a sleight-of-hand that concealed nothing, I slipped another chocolate and almond bar from its triangular box, unwrapped the silver paper, and gradually made it disappear. My mother had spent a lot of money to send me those Swiss chocolates, which had just then become the rage, and though at that point any product with a little cacao and sugar in it would have had me fainting with delight, the truth about the strange connection between brain and taste buds is that the chocolate's exotic name and familiar yellow box with red letters increased my delight as much as or more than its aroma, its grainy texture, and its flavor. To eat Toblerone at that moment was to become civilized once more.

Hattie brought news of the opening of a Frank Stella retrospective at MoMA and the latest Bergman movie. And Twyla? "I think she's talking about putting together some event that's supposed to start at dawn at the Cloisters and end in the afternoon at the opposite end of Manhattan in Battery Park. But I'm too old to go chasing around after the most *dernier* experimental *cri.* That's a job for you youngsters. There should always be an avantgarde, but not everyone should have to endure it. What's the vanguard up to here?"

Pessimistically I told her what I'd been able to glean about the dance world and the theatrical arts in general.

"I'll tell you one thing," said Hattie. "I'm delighted to have been offered a trip with all expenses paid to this gorgeous tropical island, and I'm sure you are, too, but I don't understand what we're doing in Cuba. Is there a tradition of modern dance here? Has anything of value been done in the field? And if nothing has been done, then who needs us?"

"Are you sure you don't want any more chocolate?" I said by way of response.

"No, and I don't think you do, either. Two chocolate bars when you're famished is all right, but if you eat the third one, you'll regret it tomorrow."

She stood up, yawning. Lorna would be coming to get her first thing the next day to show her around. At the door Hattie turned back once more and looked me up and down. "By the way," she said, "I met your beau."

I gazed at her blankly.

"Adrian. He brought me the letter that's in your package. I invited him in, and he and Gus talked for a while. He's very unusual."

As if the wind had suddenly blown the windows out, Adrian came rushing into the room in great gusts. His smell, his voice, his very white skin, his insidious gaze. I didn't welcome him, but I couldn't keep him from entering.

Alma Alma Alma Alma,

Why can't you come running when I call? You're young and haven't yet learned how to respect a man's desire. Let's say that for the moment I accept your banal excuses, but you know they're lies. I don't want to deny the value of the revolution in which you now seem to believe so strongly, but I doubt that someone who doesn't know how to forge the most elemental link, the bond that unites two people in desire, will know how to build anything of consequence. If the recurrent vision of what it will be like to have you between the sheets again hadn't addled my brains, I would say you had disappointed me, but I won't do that because I know how easily offended you are. Don't be offended, don't waste your time; you think you still have a lot of time ahead of you, but on average we have about seventy years to live on this earth, equivalent to 25,550 days or 613,200 hours, of which you've wasted the last 1,440 that you haven't been at my side. Get back here: we need to start making babies. I repeat, your reasons for denying yourself motherhood are banal, but to my own astonishment—I didn't know I was so generous—I forgive you everything. You're a compulsive liar and you addle my brains, but I like you. Stop playing games and come back to me right now.

I didn't sleep all night. What did this man want from me? Why did he want so much more than I could give?

That Sunday as usual we all got together for lunch at Galo's house. Each person brought some of whatever was left on his ration card, and since it was the beginning of the month and everyone knew whether the things left over from the last month's quota were going to be needed this month, we did well for ourselves that day. There was some pasta, some beans. I brought two tins of sardines. For a really special treat, Carlos's mother had got hold of ten egg whites—I don't recall the amazing piece of juggling by which she achieved this—and some lemons, and with those ingredients and a bit of sugar she had managed to make the lightest, subtlest, and most fragrant meringues I've ever eaten. Carlos, normally incapable of bragging or hogging the limelight, had good reason to feel boastful, and with a dictatorial air we'd never before seen in him, he decreed that we weren't allowed to touch a single meringue before dessert. He opened the cover of the beat-up tin box he'd brought them in and let us stick our noses in to smell the lemon. We nearly fainted.

"*Coño,* and how are we going to make a dish out of pasta and sardines that will stand up to those meringues?" Galo protested. "*Chico,* you really are a counterrevolutionary. You show up here with your meringues and reignite a whole category of capitalist yearnings in me. What shit: spaghetti and sardines when what I want is a filet of sole meunière. And champagne. Off to a UMAP with you!"

"Galo, Galo, it's a good thing for this country that it's Fidel who's in power and not you, because with those Stalinist leanings of yours, *mi hermano*—"

"Listen, is this my house or not? When you're here, my word is law."

"Not in the kitchen, it isn't! You don't even know how to boil water. Now get out—we'll come up with something!"

We ended up doing the only thing we could do: for soup, everyone got two ladles of beans, then we mixed the sardines with the pasta. I had no way of guessing that years later I would pay about fifteen dollars for a kilo of black beans in a fashionable Parisian *épicerie,* or that the dish we invented out of necessity would later appear in North American gourmet magazines as a uniquely Sicilian delight: *pasta con le sarde.* The meal would have looked better to us if we'd known it was so luxurious, but in any case it wasn't bad.

"And now what do we do?" we asked one another, after we'd finished our dessert and coffee.

Nothing was on in any of the theaters. The Ballet Nacional's season hadn't started yet. There weren't any shows worth seeing in any art galleries. All of us had already seen the twenty films that were playing at least six times each, even *Trapeze, Seven Brides for Seven Brothers,* and *The Knights of the Teutonic Order* (though admittedly not *Brother, Give Me Your Little Paw,* a Soviet production). We'd already strolled through Old Havana and Vedado. We'd already walked along the Malecón. By then it felt as though we'd already told one another every possible anecdote and piece of interesting gossip. The subject of the Ten Million Ton Harvest was absolutely taboo. Even I was no longer a novelty.

"Is it true that time doesn't move this slowly in other places?" Boris, Galo, and I asked one another.

"The fault cannot lie with the place," said Carlos, lounging next to me on the sofa. "It's just that we're still living like *consumers* of culture here. Why do we have to be given everything? Why don't we produce it ourselves? Right now we should be exercising our right to creativity, maybe writing a play, or rehearsing. But we're all a bunch of *comemierdas* who produce less and less—who knows why? Obviously, our inner resources are withering away. You, Alma, you talk so much about this famous piece of choreography someone gave you, but we haven't seen a thing. Dance some of it for us!"

"I haven't gotten anywhere with it yet," I said.

"But I'm sure you've got some new medical symptom that will have us all dying with envy," said Galo. "Do you still feel a pain at the top of your stomach when you see a piece of yellow fruit?"

"Leave her in peace, *chico*!" Carlos reproached him, not for the first time. He patted my hand while the others laughed. "Why do you find it so strange that all the pain this girl has in her heart should spill out into her body as well?"

"Do you really have that much pain in your heart?" queried Galo with renewed interest.

"No," I answered. "But Carlos is right: Why haven't you ever thought about forming your own theater company?"

"Carlos is nuts," said Pablo. "It's not about inner resources or anything else. We were just as bored before the Revolution. It's our geographic destiny. You don't have to think about it very hard to understand that the word *island* and the word *isolation* are related. This is a small, poor, isolated country. There's a reason why Carpentier and Wilfredo Lam spend their time in Paris. What are we supposed to do when an audience large enough to fill a theater for even a week simply, objectively, doesn't exist here? Where are we going to get ideas and inspiration, except from what passing ships bring us when they stop over? We're a port of call, and the only ideas that reach us are the ones that fall off some freighter while it's unloading. The only truly original cultural phenomenon this society has ever produced is, as always, Fidel."

"Look, I'll grant your point about Fidel," said Boris. "But it's also true that there were no government officials in charge of culture before, and now there are. And those guardian angels are increasingly bureaucratic: they're not creative and they're ignorant. So when they have to make a decision—what movie to show, what book to publish—they fall back increasingly on Soviet standards. And I don't know about you, *chico,* but I say that if we have to exchange one dominant culture for another, European cultural imperialism will always be a lot more fun than the contributions of our Soviet brothers. If it weren't for the Czechs and the Poles, there'd be fuck-all in terms of socialist art. In that respect, we're completely screwed."

"So you think Russian movies are terrible?" asked Pablo, who always defended the prevailing orthodoxy more than his friends did.

"They're all right—Eisenstein and all that. But I'll take Truffaut, Fellini, Antonioni, Polanski, and De Sica any day. And in theater and painting and the novel, what can you say? For the last twenty, thirty years it's all been borscht. The Soviet Union is an artistic cemetery compared to what's being done in Europe, not to mention Latin America! Even Yankee culture is more interesting. If I have to choose between *For Whom the Bell Tolls* and *Thus the Steel Was Tempered,* I know which I'm taking."

"Ay Madre Santísima," sighed Carlos. "It feels like we're repeating even this discussion for the thousandth time. Galo, read *Granma* aloud to us: sometimes you do that very well. Isn't there some extremely detailed account of the visit of a Romanian delegation on the front page today?"

"No, and by the way, I was forgetting," said Galo, going to get the newspaper. "I don't know if any of you saw this photo, which is really something.

"'Nearly fifty people wounded by bullets as police clash once more with black demonstrators in Asbury Park, New Jersey,'" said the text that accompanied the photo of the riot. "Do you know where that is?" Galo asked, and I, who until that moment had been very proud of my total ignorance of all parts of the United States beyond Manhattan and the Brooklyn Academy of Music, had to say that I didn't. In any case, though the town was in the state of New Jersey, apparently not very far from New York City, its name seemed to correspond to one of those places in the country where there is no crime or poverty or conflict and everyone has very white skin and blond hair. Black people had been forced to form a line against a wall and were then humiliated, which wasn't unusual. But this time there was gunfire, as if the whole thing were happening in Mexico or the Congo or Bolivia. And thus was Che's exhortation fulfilled, for he had urged us to create "two, three, many Vietnams!"

"What a shame, *chico,* what a shame," murmured Carlos, but I suddenly felt a kind of euphoria. I had the feeling that a door was opening for me onto an understanding of the world.

"This time the war is really starting," I announced.

It was an idea I'd been developing for several days—or rather, since there was nothing original about it because I'd read it twenty times in the Casa de las Américas magazine, let's say that for several days I'd been accepting it and further developing it in my own way. Now the idea took advantage of the occasion to come bubbling out on its own: in order for the revolution to be truly global, it had to reach capitalism's vital center—"the entrails of the monster," in the words that everyone was perpetually quoting from José Martí. We all knew that, I began, and now, I declared, warming to my theme, everything seemed to indicate that this final stage of the struggle had started.

My friends were all ears. Evening fell as I explained the coming cataclysm: the fragility of consumer capitalism, the insurrectional rage of blacks, Native Americans, and Puerto Ricans in the United States. The oppressed peoples who lived at the very heart of the capitalist putrefaction would be the agents of its destruction. I savored the new taste of these fancy Marxist terms, dug up anecdotes from my own experience of working for years alongside dishwashers, messengers, and cooks. I evoked their frustration, their emotional explosiveness after endless days of poorly paid labor, the dead-end street on which their lives played out. Ignoring the little warning bell of my conscience, I also exaggerated my own poverty and privations. Unrecognizably loquacious, I thrilled at the sound of my own words. Each sentence seemed to possess an unassailable lucidity, as I explained the logic of a revolution that emerged from the extreme vulnerability of an apparently stable society suddenly faced with erupting disorder. Guerrilla-like, I drew a map of Manhattan and its bridges, citing statistics taken from who knows what sources. Just imagine! On this little strip of land, eighty percent of the wealth of the entire capitalist world was concentrated, and what was more, it was an island. When Harlem rebelled, nothing could be easier than blowing up the bridges and isolating Wall Street. Hadn't they seen the movie *The Battle of Algiers*? Well, this was going to be just the same. Submerged as I was in all the uncertainties that were threatening to strip away the meaning and direction of my existence, I enjoyed the certitude that for those few hours was mine. There would be no need to form alliances among the Chinese, Puerto Ricans, blacks, and Chicanos, I decreed. All of them knew one another already, because they all worked together in the factories and restaurant kitchens.

As soon as Boris and Carlos dropped me off at the school,

the attacks, ambushes, and battles that had so vividly filled my imagination all vanished. What remained was the infinite solidity of the four whitewashed walls of the dormitory in Cubanacán and the reality of my own existence: I was a poor, untutored dancer who knew nothing about the world and who had to make a tremendous effort simply to structure the dance classes I'd been hired to teach. As Mario Hidalgo might say, I was a *comemiedda,* without purpose or any kind of certainty. What was I good for? I busied myself mending a leotard, putting my books in order on their shelf, washing the week's clothing in the bathroom sink with a sliver of soap. What was I good for? Impossible to know, if I didn't stop talking nonsense and telling lies, if I didn't take a long, hard look at the process I was living through. I read and reread Adrian's letter. I also had to settle things with him: Either I liked him or I didn't. Either I was going back to him or I wasn't. Determined to find some answers, I spent that whole night in dialogue with myself, and though I listened very carefully, I was impossible to understand.

Adrian, all your words arrived, the whole string of them, igniting one after another like firecrackers. I have to prepare tomorrow's class, but your flash powder explodes wherever I put my foot down. Maybe I shouldn't even send you an answer; it's so easy for the two of us to misread each other, and all the more so at this distance. . . .

You say I have such faith in this Revolution—spare me the sarcasm. I don't know if I have so much faith. I don't even know if I like this place. It's uptight and chaotic in ways that I'm not. The Revolution aside, I can't seem to detach from the general fixation with rules, or keep myself from being driven crazy by how badly everything is done: the fucking bathroom light doesn't work, and it's taken a month for someone to come and fix the barre in the dance studio. The greatest goal is absolute equality, they tell me (me! whose only aspiration is to be unique!), and any deviation from the norm is punished. And yet, and yet, this place moves me, and I want to surrender to it. You don't know dancers; we're hard workers and know how to move as a single unit. We sweat a lot, take big risks, and push ourselves to go one more step when we think we can't push any further. Of course the sugar harvest moved me: it was a disaster, but I saw the entire country com-mitted to a single heroic task.

I'm sure you find this dull; you're a Buddhist and a poet, which means you have a passive attitude toward history and an individual-ist approach to the creative life. I'm sure you wouldn't like the Revolution.

Maybe I'm lying, I can't tell anymore. I don't know where this terrible rhetoric I'm spouting comes from, or why the Revolution matters so much to me when the revolutionaries I've met all strike me as a little brutal and boring and soooo square. I don't know what I'd do if I had to spend the rest of my life here. I can't seem to distinguish between rhetoric and the guilt that keeps me awake at night—at this stage I can't even tell if my own feelings are phony. I'm not sure you'd like the person I'm becoming. Ever since I got here I've needed a floor, a floor, something to rescue me from the abyss, and I can't find anything that seems real to me. The dance I'm rehearsing now isn't real, Twyla doesn't matter anymore, my students, who were so dazzlingly real at first, so reckless and festive and awkward, are beginning to bore me. But when the memory of your white, white skin burns into me, I want to believe it will offer us salvation. In the blaze and the marble, oh love, pray for us sinners.

Adrian, I'm sorry. I don't know what I'm doing, but if there's any sort of future for us, you have to believe that certain things I've told you are true. I'd rather die than bring one more human being into the world, I'd rather kill myself. You want me to promise that I'll wake up by your side every single endless day for the rest of my life, you want me to think joyfully about an eternity in which I'll ask you every morning what you want to have for dinner that night, sweet-heart. Not a chance. I know what kind of future I'm condemning myself to, but I can't see an alternative—with you or anyone else. If you want us to watch the sunset again and spend the night together, then I want that, too, and if you complain that I'm even stingier than you are, you're right.

You know, in New York sometimes I sort of made sense. (Didn't I?) Sometimes I even managed to make myself laugh. I've tried all night, but here the sentences come out any which way. Once I was a person, and now I'm a puzzle with the pieces all scattered everywhere.

Did I mention? I've decided to cut my stay at the ENA short. I'm leaving the moment the semester ends. Until then, the days are dragging. I know you don't like Fidel, but I think you might like Havana, and I'd like to show it to you. From my friend Galo's apartment you can see the sea in the distance, and that's how I like it best. First the human tumult of the city, then a green mist of majaguas *and tamarinds with a line of palm trees marching among and above them. And finally, off in the distance, a blue horizon, and you, sometimes, on the other side.*

Hattie stayed in the dormitory in Cubanacán only that first weekend. In view of her great importance to the school, Elfrida and Lorna had been authorized to house her in the city's most prestigious hotel, the Habana Libre, but the arrangements for her move couldn't be completed until Monday. I was sad to see her go, but a few days later a radical and unexpected change occurred in my life in Cuba. It was due once again, I imagine, to the intercession of Lorna, who must have felt uneasy at the thought that one of the three teachers invited to the school was enjoying the greatest luxuries the Revolution could offer, while Nancy and I were still in the ENA dormitories. Or maybe it was Elfrida's idea. In any case, Nancy and I were notified that we too were being offered rooms at the Habana Libre. I felt a pang at leaving the students behind, but in truth, ever since the afternoon visits in my room had been brought to an end, we did most of our talking in the classroom anyway.

When it first opened, in 1958, the hotel was called the Habana Hilton. It may not have been the most ostentatious hotel of that golden age of Caribbean tourism—that title belonged to the Riviera, with its outsize swimming pool and gamboling plaster dolphins and seahorses in the vast lobby—but it was luxurious and ultramodern, though in twelve years it had deteriorated noticeably. It had an amoeba-shaped lobby with a showy staircase, and two bars, one of which shared the hotel's top floor with the kind of restaurant that served cherries jubilee for dessert. Still remaining from the old days were the conference rooms, a smelly gym, a telephone exchange that handled international calls, and an "American-style" cafeteria, with a long counter and stools that could still spin. On the list of things lost forever were a casino and the television sets that once illuminated each room with their drab gray flicker. At the very top of the list of illustrious former guests was the Comandante en Jefe, who lived there along with an inner circle of fellow guerrillas during the happy, chaotic times that followed his triumphal entry into Havana.

The building, which was tall and partook of a fine modernist tradition of ugliness, occupied one corner of the city's most active intersection, 23 and L. There was an unpleasant difference between the jungle murmur that invaded all the silences of Cubanacán and the sound of asthmatic motors that filtered in from the balcony of my new room. I was also alarmed by the view, which, from the floor I found myself on—the eleventh floor, perhaps—took in the rooftops of the apartment buildings to one side of the hotel and, if you turned your eyes to the right, the high floors of the commercial buildings of the Rampa, the street that descended from the hotel intersection at the top of the hill to the breaking waves of the Malecón. Leaning over the balcony railing, I managed to glimpse a bit of sea. The wind out there was disagreeably strong, and the aluminum railing didn't seem to be made to resist my weight. I quickly retreated back to the room. Really, Adrian was right—a person needs no more than a room to live in, and this one had all that was necessary: a good closet, a comfortable bathroom, and a little reception area with a desk and even a lamp. Two twin beds formed an L in a corner of the room, as if they were sofas. The color scheme was a blend of mud and bile, and from the aesthetic point of view my austere room in the school dormitory won out every time, but there was plenty of light, there were firm mattresses, efficient laundry service, gushing hot water, and not a single mosquito. Moreover, I was at the epicenter of modern Havana: the movie house that most often showed new films was just across the street, and the park where Coppelia sold its ice cream was diagonally across the intersection. Continuing in that direction, you came to Vedado. A few blocks in the opposite direction was the university, and beyond that, Habana Vieja. Carlos's house was close by, and Galo's wasn't far. Best of all, Tere lived around the corner.

Visitors weren't allowed in the hotel rooms, she explained when I invited her to come and see me, but no rule forbade me from going to see her.

The *compañero* who took down our information at the reception desk warned that our stay was strictly provisional and would end along with the celebrations of the patriotic month on the first of August. But a pair of Chilean actors who were in charge of the ENA theater school made sure things worked out otherwise. Seeing us heading out to 23 and L with our suitcases, they mounted a protest so loud and uninterrupted that Mario Hidalgo had no choice but to yield: a week after our arrival at the hotel, the Chileans invited us to toast their triumph with a shot of rum. They'd been living in the isolation of Cubanacán for a year, and amid the lights and hubbub of the hotel they felt as if they'd just landed in Paris. *"¡No pasarán!"* they shouted, convulsed with laughter, imagining Mario Hidalgo appearing to march them back to the ENA. "Give us the Habana Libre or give us death!"

¡Patria o Muerte! ¡Venceremos! The patriotic murmur that could be heard from afar in Cubanacán was a roar at the agitated crossroads of L and 23. July 26 was coming, and posters with images of Che or abstract representations of the Moncada barracks at the top of a hill were everywhere, firing my imagination, in which Ernesto Guevara and the Moncada were joined in a single luminous moment of history, as if Che had given his life for us on the same Calvary where Fidel, in defeat, swore to come back and triumph. This impression was not only mine: the history of the Revolution was taught as a series of irrevocably linked predestined events: the triumph of the Revolution and the very existence of its heroes was, I'd learned, an inevitable consequence of the attack on the Moncada barracks.

In fact, the attack on the barracks was a disaster, a long series of accidents in any one of which Fidel could have lost his life or lost his momentum forever. What was indisputable, both for his biographers and for those of us who saw him as larger than life and preeminent, was that in certain fundamental ways the Fidel of Moncada and the Fidel of the Zafra de los Diez Millones was the same man: daring, rash, always in search of all-encompassing action and glory. He was a great political romantic in the nineteenth-century style, but with certain twentieth-century singularities, such as Marxism-Leninism, and one idiosyncrasy that was all his own: he always bolstered his faith in the coming triumph with an inflamed and minutely detailed catalog of figures, statistics, arguments, and historical justifications. That was how he bedazzled me, and it was also how he recruited the volunteers who had followed him to Moncada years before—with the steamrolling force of his personality, but also with painstaking graphics and precise schedules, budgets, and time frames for acquiring weaponry. Before such an avalanche of objective facts there were only two choices: follow the hero, or be a coward, left behind in the dust. So meticulous were Fidel's analyses and so just were his causes—and so brave was he!—that his failures could not be judged: it was Fidel against fate, and obviously when you play against fate, sometimes you lose.

On that long-ago dawn in Santiago de Oriente, fate won. The group of activists who later came to call themselves the Movimiento 26 de Julio did not yet have a name. They were a collection of men, mainly: office and construction workers, students, and professionals who believed in Fidel and in a cause they sometimes called *fidelista*. Exactly what strategy lay behind the assault remains unknown, but in its broad outlines the plan was to occupy the Moncada barracks and thus demoralize the army and incite a popular rebellion. The attacking forces gathered in Havana over the course of several months; organized in cells to keep from arousing the suspicions of Batista's police forces. Fidel's followers—who already numbered more than a thousand—trained for combat while the leader and his closest comrade, Abel Santamaría, procured weapons. Neither of the two had any military training, but Fidel studied a blueprint of the barracks and designed the tactical movements. The action would take place during the week of Santiago's famous July carnival, he decided, to take advantage of the fact that many of the troops in the barracks would be on leave and the rest in no mood for a fight. Furthermore, as they arrived from Havana, the rebels could easily disappear among the carnival makers. With the help of a poet friend, Fidel wrote a long declaration that would be broadcast over the radio to announce the triumph of the attack. A woman who was Fidel's lover at the time, the beautiful, daring wife of an upper-class doctor, selected background music to accompany the reading of this proclamation: Beethoven and Chopin.

But the chords of the *Pathétique* did not ring out, nor was the proclamation ever heard; instead, on the morning of the attack, what usually happens at such moments happened, and everything that could go wrong did. Some of the *compañeros* got lost in the streets of an unfamiliar city and didn't make it to the rendezvous. Others were driving a car that broke down. The military patrol that was supposed to pass by on the hour went by a few minutes later, and the officer on guard duty who wasn't supposed to go by at all came by at the worst possible time. The motor of the Buick that Fidel was driving stalled at the precise moment of the attack. And so on. Several of the rebels died during the disaster, and over the course of the terrible days of pursuit and torture that followed, many more were killed. Most of the leaders managed to flee, but not Abel Santamaría, whose eyes the soldiers brought for his sister Haydée to see. And not Boris Santa Coloma, Haydée's boyfriend, who was castrated before he died.

Fidel was not yet twenty-six years old on that first July 26. During my comings and goings from the dance studio in Cubanacán, I was dogged by the idea that I was already twenty-one and my entire life could be tossed out like garbage without anyone's noticing that anything was missing. The rehearsals of Sandy Neels's work were now dead time; I often ended up lying on my back on the floor, counting the bricks in the vault above until the mandatory hour had passed. Even the classes had become labyrinths in which, unable to find the transition from one sequence of movements to the next, I ended up demanding endless repetitions of a single exercise. Orlando was growing less flexible each day. For the moment Hattie's cheerful, sensible presence and the move to the hotel were a salvation; I'd been spending far too much time alone. I was distracted by the lively tumult of Rampa and the luxury of a telephone in my room, which allowed me to

stay in touch with Galo and his friends. And above all, I was distracted by the glittering prospect of the penthouse restaurant in
our new dwelling place, to which Nancy and I, accompanied by
Hattie, repaired with famished visions dancing in our heads.

The restaurant had immaculate white tablecloths, heavy silver-
ware, air-conditioning, and a uniform institutional rigor—a lack
of interest in any decorative or sensual touch, however small—
which made it look like the dining room of a luxurious boarding
school. In fact, it was very much along the lines of what I'd initially imagined the Cubanacán dining room to be. But if the
restaurant itself lacked personality, the diners sitting around its
tables offered a panorama of the most intense and exotic cos-
mopolitanism. At one table was a Palestinian delegation, easily
recognizable by their checkered headgear. They communicated
with their Cuban *responsable* through an interpreter who translated their words into French. At another table, four serious, stu-
dious black men of around forty, wearing light-colored suits in a
rather square cut and with no resemblance whatsoever to Bob
Marley, spoke among themselves in intoxicating Jamaican ac-
cents. In one corner a Cuban man was eating with a powerfully
built black man from the United States—rumored to be, I later
learned, one of the few hijackers whom the Cubans hadn't welcomed into a jail cell the moment he landed. In the opposite corner were two loudly chattering American women sitting with
their skirts hiked up and their knees wide open, their calves covered with blond fuzz. At first Hattie, Nancy, and I headed to a
table next to theirs, with a view of the park, but the sight of
them was so embarrassing that I steered our group toward a table
in the center of the room. At the table next to it three rather
small men with close-cropped, very black hair, stocky bodies,
and skin the exact color of vanilla ice cream were peaceably
enjoying their lunch.

They were Vietnamese. I felt myself go pale and then turn red
with terror, and prayed no one would notice my distress at the
realization. I chose the chair farthest from their table. But Hattie
and Nancy were upset, too. Both of their mouths formed an *oh* of
surprise and confusion. It was too late to change tables, but it
was also very hard to sit down calmly, unfold our napkins, and

order lunch as if nothing were wrong when we were sitting next to a group of men who might have fled from a rain of bombs unleashed by the country in which I'd lived, who might have had to dig through rubble to rescue the members of their family, and who might have now heard our murmurs in English and understood that we came from the country of thunder and death. Perhaps they, the Vietnamese men, would now stand up, the pleasure of their lunch ruined by their memories, and leave to find another table or another dining room. But no. The three men went on chatting in low voices and taking occasional sips of their coffee, as if the situation was perfectly acceptable.

I noticed that Hattie's eyes were red. She went to the bathroom. When she came back, the Vietnamese men were already on their way out the door. "My tax dollars . . ." said Hattie, watching them leave. Her tax dollars were helping pay for the thousands of bombs her government was dropping every day on that green country.

Her voice was choking. "This is unbearable," she said. And then, collecting herself, she added in a calmer tone, articulating each word, "I love my country, I'm very proud of our national character, our traditions of sharing, egalitarianism, and fairness, but I'm ashamed every single day now. I can't look at the newspaper without being overwhelmed with shame and horror. It's absolutely intolerable to me to be in some way involved with the murder of thousands and thousands of innocent people, and I don't know what to do about it."

"I don't," Nancy said slowly. "I don't love my country. I hate it. It makes me ashamed to have to say I'm an American." She had reddish-blond hair, extremely fair skin, and cheeks that were always ruddy. Now, as she blushed, the whole threadwork of veins in her face became visible. "Why couldn't I have been born Cuban?"

At last a waiter arrived. In seconds all problems of conscience evaporated, and we were completely absorbed in the menu and the basket of bread now on the table, full—spongy rolls with no detectable flavor. Nancy raised her eyes and saw that on the next table, near the empty coffee cups, was a portion of butter still intact in its little ceramic tub. "Look!" she exclaimed. "I haven't seen that for three months. Oh my God, do you think it would be terrible if I took the butter"—she stuck out her hand and snatched it—"and put it on my bread?" And the bread, together with the delicacy stolen from the Vietnamese men's table, vanished down her throat.

"Of the dishes on the menu, we have only the desserts," announced the waiter. "As a main dish, I can offer you sirloin steak or frogs' legs." We grew dizzy. From rice with *jamonada* to such opulence! Hattie and Nancy asked for the meat, but my natural snobbery made me order the frogs' legs, which I'd never tried before. After that day I would not be able to offer up any sacrifices of my own to Fidel: I owed him the fact that I was living in the most extreme luxury I'd ever experienced.

"Wine?" asked the waiter. "We have a very good Bulgarian wine."

"They say Fidel went diving this week. At a place that's supposed to be paradise, very close to Playa Girón," Nancy said, over the coffee. Her friends were far better informed about the Revolution than mine. "And they told me that yes, it's definite: Celia Sánchez is his *compañera*."

We lived for news of Fidel's love life, in the secret illusion—at least in my case—that there might be some chink through which those of us who aspired to his illuminated embrace could wriggle. That was why I didn't much care for Celia Sánchez—because she was the competition, even though I thought she was even less attractive than I was. Or at least that's the only explanation I can find now for the marked antipathy I felt from the first moment for a woman who had the reputation of being hard-working, down-to-earth, and unconditionally loyal to my idol and who indeed was the most important woman in Fidel's life until the moment of her death in 1980. Nancy, who always struck me as very well informed and who was also conscientiously feminist, professed great admiration for Celia. She kept a tally of the women who enjoyed any power in Cuba because, she said, there were very few of them. This lapse, which didn't bother me, was at the center of the few negative comments Nancy made about the revolutionary process. She criticized the lack of absolute equality, after a decade of socialist progress: the racism of Cuban society—which was, in fact, pandemic, and only halfheartedly combated by the Revolution—and the situation of Cuban women. "There's Haydée," Nancy would say, making her list, "Celia Sánchez, Melba Hernández"—whose title was Director of the Committees for the Defense of the Revolution—"and Vilma"—Raúl Castro's wife, Vilma Espín, better known around Galo's house as *"la caquita de ratón"* (the mouse turd). "That's not very many, and what's more, they're all from the days of the clandestine struggle and the Movimiento 26 de Julio. You'd think that the revolutionary government would do a better job of finding a place for women than the guerrillas did, but it's the other way around."

It was true that few women had any influence, but Fidel owed those few a great deal. Together with Melba Hernández, Haydée had been an invaluable rear guard during preparations for the attack on Moncada. Vilma Espín had acted as a messenger when the guerrillas were in hiding and in the Sierra Maestra. Celia— who was messenger, intermediary, secretary, organizer, adviser, and wife—joined the Movimiento 26 de Julio while Fidel was in jail, seduced by the audacity of the hero of Moncada and perhaps by the speech that Fidel, acting as his own lawyer, had made on the last day of his trial.

At the time the entire country was still in shock from the news of the attack and eager to learn the fate of the rebels who had been taken prisoner. A journalist smuggled a roll of photos of the dead and tortured victims out of the jail. Some said that the leader of the attempted insurrection had been imprisoned and killed. Others claimed he had managed to escape.

In fact, Fidel, who had been working for ninety-six hours straight when the attack on Moncada began, still had the reflexes to understand immediately that the capture of the barracks had failed. Thirty minutes later he called for a retreat and fled into the countryside with some of his militants. On the sixth day, it was said—not in the textbooks but in private, with the pleasure of finding a crack in the man of granite—he was discovered by an army patrol in a rural hut, stretched out on the ground along with two comrades, fast asleep.

Had he been an ordinary rebel, the story would very likely have ended right there. But this protagonist was nothing like the expeditionaries who'd launched an attack against Trujillo a couple of years earlier, or those who plotted against Anastasio Somoza in Nicaragua from time to time, or, of course, the anti-Castro forces, so lavishly financed by the United States, who beat a quick retreat at Playa Girón, never to return. This was Fidel, who has never been capable of acknowledging defeat because he knows perfectly well that he cannot fail: what fails are the circumstances. Three months after he was led down from the hills in chains, the leader of the *fidelistas,* representing himself, presented the closing statement in his own case. The magistrates of the Santiago court who listened to him that morning must have been powerfully impressed: however much they disagreed with the prisoner's ideas, he was an unforgettable orator who, with orotund declarations and a dazzling store of precise information, transformed the case against him into an indictment of the regime of Fulgencio Batista, its arbitrariness, corruption, and sordid injustice: "Only one man, in all those centuries, has sunk his claws into two generations of Cubans." He read the revolutionary laws that would have been proclaimed immediately after the triumph at Moncada: abolition of Batista's constitution, land for all campesinos, ownership by the workers of thirty percent of their companies. He justified the rebellion with an outpouring of citations: "John Locke, in his *Treatise on Government,* maintains that when the natural laws of mankind are violated, a people has the right and the duty to do away with or change its government." He spoke for two hours and then finally, inflamed, blazing, exploding, he declared, "Find me guilty. It does not matter. History will absolve me!"

It was an epic speech, but in the natural order of things it should have been lost in oblivion twenty-four hours later. The judges found Fidel guilty and handed down his sentence—fifteen years on the Isle of Pines, beginning with an indefinite period of solitary confinement—and turned their attention to the next case on the list. But Fidel has never been inclined to allow anyone to forget about him. In the weeks that followed, he reconstructed and further fleshed out what he had said before the judges, copied it in invisible ink made with lemon juice, smuggled it out of jail page by page, and had his legal support network type it up and distribute more than twenty thousand copies. This was the romantic, indignant text known today as *La historia me absolverá*, the cornerstone of the Cuban Revolution.

Perhaps it was because she read that speech that Celia Sánchez decided to join the Movement. Like Castro, she was from Oriente; she too was a daughter of the middle class and already an activist of long standing (though in her case, her radical fervor was inherited from her father, a well-known doctor with many social concerns). Soon after she joined, she was put in charge of taking food to the door of the jail, and at a moment when the Movimiento was in danger of falling apart, her remarkable organizational skills made the difference. It was a Cuban tradition for the leader in power to grant a broad amnesty to political prisoners just prior to an election. Fulgencio Batista, who wanted to legitimize his office with elections after having taken power for the second time in a bloodless coup in 1952, did not do this. But thanks in great measure to Celia, a significant number of Cuban women took to the streets in support of an initiative that demanded amnesty for the prisoners of the attack on Moncada. Fidel was able to leave his prison in May 1955. Six weeks later he went into exile and traveled to Mexico. He returned to the island on December 2, 1956, aboard the yacht *Granma* (named after the original owner's grandmother) and in the company of Che Guevara. Celia rejoined him in the Sierra Maestra. Two years later, on January 1, 1959, the rebel army, under the command of Fidel Castro, occupied the capital city.

It was the greatest moment of euphoria in the history of the Cuban Revolution; the entire country seemed to pour into the streets to welcome the *barbudos*. Why, then, was the twenty-sixth of July a bigger celebration than the first of January? I wondered, as I finished reading yet another history book. Perhaps, I answer myself now, because the tale of that tragic dawn is more gripping and dramatic than that of the triumphal entry into Havana. Perhaps because the Revolution wanted to affirm the supremacy of the Movimiento 26 de Julio over all its rivals in the opposition trenches. Perhaps because January 1 was a collective celebration of all Cubans and their guerrilla offspring, while the undisputed protagonist of July 26 and of *La historia me absolverá* was Fidel. No one in Cuba had any trouble understanding this. He was the Revolution, and his female acolytes—Haydée, Melba, Vilma, Celia—underscored that fact with their exemplary feminine devotion.

Lorna waited for Nancy to emerge from her class and join Hattie and me before she made her great announcement. "I have a surprise for you," she said at last. "We've managed to put your names on the list of official guests for the anniversary of the Revolution." Official guests of the Revolution! The three of us broke into a festive polka, shouting and applauding Lorna, and she, who seemed so often afflicted with worries, laughed with us. As guests, we could attend certain special events, she explained, and we would also be taken on a tour, but the best part was that during the big event, the ceremony on July 26, we would be seated on the very platform from which Fidel always spoke. "Close to Fidel!" Manuel Piñeiro's wife laughed again, pained at the thought that we had so much to be grateful to her for. "I doubt you'll be right next to Fidel—the platform is very large. But you'll be able to see and hear with no problem, and you'll be very comfortably seated.

"There's one more thing," she added. "In order to manage this, we had to register you as a delegation, because only people who are a bit more famous than you are can attend as individuals. Otherwise it's always delegations. So, you'll have to forgive me, but you'll appear on the list as the 'Mexican–North American Delegation of Foreign Technicians.'" Now she let out a hearty laugh and looked at us half amused and half apologetic. "That's fine," I lied, raging internally that our status as artists was being concealed. But really, it didn't matter—"*¡Todas a la plaza con Fidel!*"

Being a delegate was the way to live. Along with others who'd been fortunate enough to be invited to learn more about this revolutionary paradise, our small binational delegation of technicians traveled in an air-conditioned cocoon to the top of a hill. There we climbed down from the bus and found ourselves in a cool jungle, a nature preserve, where we sighed with admiration before a multitude of orchids, ferns, and hummingbirds. Then the chilled capsule swept us away to Old Havana. We drank daiquiris in El Floridita, and a few steps away in the Bodeguita del Medio we drank *mojitos* and lost all dignity and restraint in front of enormous pyramids of fried pork—the *masitas de puerco* of which my friend Pablo dreamed—monumentally accompanied by rice, black beans, and slices of roast plantain. And more *mojitos.* I couldn't resist the fantastic combination of mint, sugar, lime, and rum; even I drank an entire *mojito* and spent the evening giggling like an idiot. We were swept up in cool pilgrimage once more, to the home of Papa Hemingway. Many of the delegates, myself included, had already seen those spacious gardens and that sunlit milieu because one of the key scenes of the remarkable Cuban film *Memories of Underdevelopment* takes place there. The protagonist, hiding from a young woman who's pursuing him, walks through the house/museum, trying to find the right perspective from which to judge Hemingway's work and its author, the compulsive hunter and intellectual tourist who lived on the beach of San Francisco de Paula for twenty years without ever taking any interest in Cuba. Why was such a great novelist incapable of understanding the Revolution?

Built next to the sea on the outskirts of Havana, Hemingway's house is like a trap for catching sunlight. A delicious light illuminates the mahogany furniture and cool marble floors, bathing everything it touches in a warm sheen. In this castle of clear air Hemingway wrote *The Old Man and the Sea.* He left it for the last time in July of 1960. He moved to Idaho, and twelve months later, beset by depression, he propped a hunting rifle upright against the floor, aimed it at the roof of his mouth, and blew his brains out.

"You're thinking about how he died, aren't you?" A bearded man with the face of a nocturnal rodent had spoken at my shoul-

der and made me jump. He was no less ugly when he smiled, as
he did now while introducing himself, but he was enchanting.
He said he was a member of the Chilean delegation and a doctor.
That was why a suicide like Hemingway's had a particular impact
on him, since he spent his life fighting against death. "He had
everything, absolutely everything, do you realize? He fought in
the Second World War, like the great man he was, he wrote the
great novels of this century, he lived through the triumph of a
Revolution like this one, and then he couldn't take it anymore.
And there I am like an idiot, doing my best with penicillin and
chemotherapy, and in the end a suicide comes and says, 'You
know what? Your poor little remedies don't solve the things that
really matter.'" My interlocutor interrupted himself and gazed
out the window. "But this garden is marvelous. It makes you feel
like giving up all your ridiculous thoughts to become a palm
tree."

And what did I do? he wanted to know.

"A dancer! Of course! What else could you be! Lean against
that palm tree, and I'll take your picture."

Manuel was one of those good-hearted, gregarious souls to be
found in every excursion group, who makes sure to meet everyone, note down every address, and take everyone's picture, then
keeps his promise to send a copy. He hastened to clarify that he
hadn't come to Cuba merely as a tourist. Two months were left
before the presidential elections in Chile, which would be won,
there was absolutely no doubt, by the candidate of the Socialist
Party. He was named Salvador Allende, and the two Chilean theater people had already told me about him. "A doctor like me,"
said Manuel, "and a full-time revolutionary. A great man, with a
great heart."

Manuel himself was not in private practice but specialized in
public health; he was mainly concerned with preventive medicine, he mentioned—a branch of the profession that, in Latin
America, was frequently limited to despairing over the living
conditions of the poor. He had come to the island in anticipation
of the work that awaited him after his friend's triumph, for what
had been accomplished in Cuba in the area of public health had
no precedent in history. "I imagine that when you see someone

for the first time—me, for example—the first thing you notice is whether he's harmoniously proportioned or not. (Not true, you say? I saw you looking at me.) But I have a very deep-rooted habit of seeing only the sick and the healthy. And since I got here I've been feeling like Aladdin in the cave of treasures: absolutely dazzled. Look around you!"

It was true. Seeing it now through his eyes, the Cuban land-scape was a gleaming panorama of healthy, muscular, active bod-ies, white teeth, skin unmarked by scabies or the dark marks tattooed by malnutrition on the bodies of the children in my own country, which I was so used to that I no longer even noticed them. My memory had been marked, however, by the funeral processions with small white coffins, the candles and flowers for *angelitos,* small dead children, that were part of the folklore of almost any excursion to a Mexican village. Now for the first time I noticed that I'd never heard of any children dying in Cuba. Every single campesino child went to school, got all his shots, and went to see a doctor when he felt ill. All Cuban adults were also guaranteed medical care. And since there was no abundance of food, very few people were fat, either. The result was an un-ending parade of physical splendor and the elemental serenity produced by the certainty of good health.

"You see? It's like leaving the city and breathing clean air. You're not aware of it, but immediately you feel better."

"And you're going to do the same in Chile? Make people as healthy as they are here? Are the Socialists really going to win?"

"You'll see. Between them, Fidel and Allende will transform Latin America."

"And Che too, no? Because he already transformed every-thing. Didn't you ever feel guilty for not leaving medicine, the way he did?"

"No, I'm a doctor. He was Che. *Hombre,* someone has to give people their shots!"

He was right. Without doctors the world would come to an end. Even in Vietnam they were a fundamental part of the war effort. But nobody would ever miss a dancer.

"You look like you're thinking about death again. And the

cure is to stand in front of this stone wall so I can take your picture one more time. Because you have to smile for the camera."

The pictures Manuel took of me never arrived, undoubtedly because my address changed very frequently in the period that followed our meeting. And then his address changed, too. I thought of him three years later, when his friend Salvador Allende, who was indeed elected president of Chile, aimed the AK-47 Fidel had given him at his mouth and blew his brains out. Troops under the command of a military junta had occupied the Palacio de la Moneda and were about to reach his office. When I heard about the coup, I couldn't remember Manuel's last name, but years later I described him to an exiled Chilean who told me that yes, he had been vice-minister of health under Allende and had managed to escape General Augusto Pinochet's terror. At that moment, strolling among the rosebushes and palm trees in Hemingway's garden, it was impossible to imagine that a revolutionary socialist like Allende could triumph peacefully, but out of sympathy with his friend I hoped with all my heart that he could.

Food and drink, days at the beach, and tourist excursions—this was the Cuba that most visitors to the island knew. But the delegates who had come to celebrate July 26 were very particularly interested in another type of outing. With the notable exception of the Mexican–North American Delegation, all of them were career revolutionaries—or people like Manuel, who had a profession but practiced it in the public sphere. They were enormously curious about the Revolution; they wanted to open its hood and see how its engine looked, and they didn't want to waste any time. In those days a leftist militant who wanted to visit the island of his dreams couldn't simply ask for a visa and go there as a tourist: he had to be invited, and the government invited very few people. Among the one or two hundred delegates who clambered in and out of the chilly buses with us, there was certainly more than one who was freeloading off the rebel cause, but most of them had earned their invitations through the hard work and sacrifice, often including torture and imprisonment, that had brought them revolutionary prestige. These were the foreigners—primarily Latin Americans—whom the Revolution wanted to exalt, and now it was taking them to see those of its own achievements it was interested in exalting. Another way of putting it is that we went to visit the things the Revolution liked to dream about. Given that all the delegates liked to dream about the Revolution, during those final outings before July 26, guests and hosts alike entered into a blissful and almost lubricious realm of shared fantasy.

The cows received the most applause. They were irresistible, so calm, fat, and stupid, so oblivious to the triumph of their own existence. They were presented to us at an experimental farm on the outskirts of Havana, from whose emerald plains and white laboratories the general misery of the Cuban countryside was impossible to deduce. It was this farm, this farm right here, that was going to do away with poverty forever, its director announced. He spoke as if he were parodying Fidel, with identical pauses, reiterations, and discursive tone.

"Our task here is not an easy one," he began, standing with his feet apart and his chest thrust forward, as if he were facing down gunfire. *"Ehta rrrevolución"*—pause—"has made a commitment"—pause—"to guarantee each of its children one liter of milk every day"—the index finger of the right hand thrust upward several times to mark the number one—"at least until they are eight years old." His right hand tossed an invisible toreador cape over the shoulder and came to rest on the back. "But as it happens, there are two sorts of cows in the world: the cow that gives milk—the Swiss, Dutch, or English cow, which gives up to thirty-three liters of milk per day—and the cow that can take the heat, which is the zebu. The female zebu, which was developed in India. But the cow that can take the heat doesn't give milk. That animal is a very poor milk producer! It gives you eleven, twelve, maybe fifteen liters of milk per day, and after that it gives you no more. So, then, what are we doing here? Well, we are going to produce a new type of cow! The cow you are looking at now is a cross between the Holstein and the zebu"—pause and then full speed ahead—"which perfectly resists our climatological conditions and has an average milk production that should be as much as thirty-eight liters per day when the crossbreeding has been perfected." His index finger turned downward and jabbed a hole in the air on every syllable; his torso twisted triumphantly while he presented the conclusion. "This little animal is named Deisy."

Pure white and not very big, with a delicate muzzle and a rounded body, Deisy gazed upon us with the eyes of Hera from her tidy stable and went on chewing her cud impassively. We all fell into an absorbed silence, surrendering to our love. Some of us must have been thinking about the great scientific achievements that a revolution makes possible, others about what it would mean to be able to guarantee a liter of milk per day to every child in their country. I thought that if my Chilean friend Manuel would like to be a palm tree, I yearned beyond all else to transform myself into this dumb, imperturbable animal and know peace. Finally, from a corner, the voice of someone with a thick Brazilian accent—a tall man, well along in years—asked, "*Companheiro,* does the *senhor* think Cuba is going to keep this great discovery for itself? Doesn't it have an obligation to share *uma maravilha* like this one with all the countries of Latin America? The children of the entire continent will be grateful."

"*Compañero,*" the director answered happily, "all that Cuba has is for its sister peoples. And of course, with our children's hunger at stake, that includes Deisy and all her descendants, too!"

And we all went off to eat and celebrate a future without hunger.

During the week of our privileged status as guests, we didn't visit a single art gallery or attend one concert or play. We were not invited to meet with representatives of the Cuban publishing industry or converse with an author or even visit the editorial offices of *Granma.* I didn't ask why, because it is an inescapable condition of organized tours that the question "Why this but not that?" does not exist. On the last day of the expedition we went to visit a Cuban insane asylum, because at that point it was one of Fidel's great enthusiasms.

When we saw the director of the National Psychiatric Hospital, who came to the door of the *guagua* to welcome us, we delegates grew enthusiastic as well. I never learned whether the doctor, Comandante Eduardo Bernabé Ordaz, was in fact once a guerrilla, but he was one of the half-dozen men who were allowed to emulate Fidel and cultivate the wilderness beard that the rebels had let grow during the war. After Manuel Piñeiro the best-known among them was Dr. Ordaz, whose hairy face now bore a smile of complete happiness as he caressed and played with his beard above his snow-white medical jacket. He gave us all the impression of a man about to break into an aria or a vigorous folk dance, or to sink his fork into a gigantic suckling pig. When I stepped down off the bus, he welcomed me with an embrace that could have immobilized a lion. For a moment I thought with some alarm—and I wasn't the only one—that he was a patient in the hospital, and in fact when we went in, the patients we saw seemed to be immersed in the same galloping happiness as their physician. We followed him from room to room with smiles that grew more and more like his as he euphorically explained: the Revolution believed that productive labor was the root and justification of the new man, and that mental illnesses were the result of a disjunction between the patient and his social environment. What grew ill—if I recall the explanation correctly—was not the person himself but his relationship to society. So then if work conferred dignity on healthy Cubans, why deny the sick the chance to work and be revolutionaries as well? Here in the hospital the patients carried out productive labor on farms and in workshops. In the new Cuban society not even the psychiatric patients would be infantilized. One example: though mirrors were banned from most mental hospitals, here in the Siquiátrico Nacional the patient had the right to recognize his reflection and contemplate himself.

Gazing blindly at a row of patients in ordinary clothes who were offering us the spectacle of their huge merriment, I thought bitterly of the absence of mirrors in Cubanacán, but at that moment my eye happened to fall on a delegate I hadn't previously noticed, and both patients and mirrors dissolved into thin air because I knew immediately that I was born for him.

His name was Luis, he was a guerrilla, and I had no more than three dialogues with him, all of them brief, before I never saw him again. During the days and weeks I spent calling out to him in my thoughts as if with a long pleading moan, there was never any response, but I am grateful to him for the experience of that instantaneous blaze of passion: it had never happened to me before and has never happened since. He didn't tell me much about his life. I had no time to notice whether he was good-looking or not. I never learned whether he had any kind of profession or whether he liked the same books I did. I understood before he told me so that he was a guerrilla and that he had been in jail; he was very thin and had the expression of someone struggling to overcome a great weariness; and something in his way of walking and slightly tilting his torso to one side made it seem as if he had been frighteningly mistreated. He wasn't tall, he wasn't short; he had large eyes and a sweetness of manner that seemed inconceivable to me in someone who had been tortured. Among other sensations, his presence brought me intense relief from the omnipresent Cuban machismo that made even my friend Galo's statements into stentorian and incontrovertible pronouncements. From all of that, from arrogance and confusion, rhetoric and exhortations, my doubts and the absolute answers that were crushing me, Luis seemed, from the first moment, to be a refuge and a defense.

"¡Hola!"

"¿Qué tal?"

"Hot, isn't it?"

Thus went the first glowing dialogue of love.

In the hospital gardens Dr. Ordaz's patients invited us to watch a musical performance. I stood next to Luis, so close I could smell the faint resinous scent of his skin. The show may have been grotesque—or in the final analysis, highly interesting for the avant-garde gap between the codified gestures of the interpreters of Cuban traditional music and this imitation of them performed by a group of enthusiastic schizophrenics—but at that moment it struck me as heavenly. Between one musical number and the next Luis and I exchanged a few phrases, though I had to make an effort to get my voice out of my throat.

I don't remember a single word we said, except that they were all trivial.

I was dying to ask him everything—Why Vietnam? Why not art? Why did I have to feel so out of place?—and finally I asked him where he was staying, and he told me, in his characteristically sweet, protective tone, that for security reasons he was not allowed to disclose that information to anyone. Then I understood that my presence made him uneasy and that although he seemed as winged and luminous as an angel to me, I was ugly and clumsy, nothing more than an unworthy dancer standing next to a redeemer of the world. I couldn't decide whether it would be worse to stay there next to him, breathing in his smell but making a fool of myself, or to push my way through the other delegates and take refuge back on the bus. Just then an old woman in flip-flops with a bandanna tied around her head walked to the middle of the improvised open-air stage and began singing "La Bayamesa" in a hoarse and off-key voice. At the same time I saw behind her a file of delegates making their way down the hill from the parking lot to join our group. "This is magnificent!" said the director of the hospital, bursting with happiness and interrupting "La Bayamesa." "Our heroic Vietnamese *compañeros* have just arrived. *Compañeros, por favor,* let's have a round of applause. These comrades are honoring us, truly honoring us with their presence. Please, *compañera,*" and he gave a smile of welcome to a girl whose beauty was as fragile as a wing, wearing a traditional *ao dai* embroidered with red. Eyes watering and throats tight, we all applauded, and she hid her head in embarrassment and bent her waist in thanks as if moved by the breeze.

"Our comrade will be spending a few months in Cuba," said the director. "She's not even twenty-one years old, but she has the singular, the unimaginable distinction of having deactivated, all by herself, more than three hundred fragmentation bombs dropped onto her land by the imperialists. Insofar as it is able, Cuba wants to contribute to Vietnam's heroic struggle and has offered this great heroine reconstructive surgery on her hands." Then I saw that the figure who smiled and smiled there in front of us had, for hands, two seared lumps of scars, adorned with a few protuberances of crooked flesh.

You're a comemierda, I told myself. *You're unredeemable.*

I found some silence and solitude in a hospital bathroom and stood looking at myself in the mirror for a while, without finding anyone there to be friends with.

SEVEN

Celebrations and Atonement

The commemoration of the attack on the Moncada barracks would be celebrated this year as every year on the great esplanade known before 1959 as the Plaza de la República and now called, inevitably, the Plaza de la Revolución. It seemed to me that the rebels who'd changed the plaza's name would have done better to demolish the awful monument to José Martí, at whose feet the Comandante always spoke. The first time I saw it, I assumed Fidel had commissioned it from some Stalinist sculptor—the huge white marble statue wouldn't have looked out of place in a Moscow park—but in fact it was erected by Fulgencio Batista. I don't know if Cubans were reminded of Martí when they sang his couplets as the lyrics to the song "Guantanamera," but I doubt they could identify him in any way with Batista's outsize caricature. In his photos Martí looks like what he was: a fevered intellectual. His charm resided in his enormous eyes, which reflected his keenly observant and wildly romantic temperament. Aside from that he was short, scrawny, and half bald, with a disproportionately large head, and the black suit he always wore only heightened his deathly pallor. The Martí of the Plaza de la Revolución was bald and big-headed but titanic, seated in a kingly fashion with the grateful *patria* in worship at his feet. Every time I passed the monument on my way to Galo's house, I wondered how such a massive symbol could possibly be loved. And as I grew more familiar with the island, another question arose: How could it be that the embodiment of patriotic sentiment in this riotous, irreverent, and licentious country was Martí? But Martí was more Cuban than I could have understood at the time, with that massive statue and the tiresomely repeated lyrics of "Guantanamera" as my only points of reference.

The first great protagonist of Cuba's romance with its own history spent the greater part of his adult life in the United States, looking for solutions to his personal and patriotic dramas. Martí was kept in jail for a year, at the age of seventeen, as punishment for a small tract he wrote in favor of independence, and then the Spanish Crown sent him into exile. A quarter of a century later he returned to the island in search of the battle that would elevate him into death. He admired the vigor of the North American culture he inhabited for so long, and by writing he found ways to keep from drowning in it. He was a journalist, essayist, and poet, a perpetually compulsive writer whose complete works fill twenty-five volumes. Cuban independence was his obsession. In the final years of his life he felt that writing was less important than going back to Cuba to fight for independence. "About Cuba, what haven't I written? And not a single page strikes me as worthy of her: only what we are about to do seems worthy." Accompanied by General Máximo Gómez, commander in chief of the Liberating Army of Cuba, he disembarked secretly on the eastern tip of his island on April 11, 1895, in his role as the *delegado* (representative) and leader of the independence party that he himself had founded three years before. He kept a diary, a lucid and delightful account of the six weeks he spent with the ragtag liberation forces. He observed the women of the countryside with pleasure and appetite as they walked by with their strong arms and starched petticoats, and he described with equal love and in equal detail the trees in the Cuban forest, the healing plants, the meals whose taste brought him home, and the fortunes and misfortunes of the soldiers he lived among. The whole diary is filled with joy, and it's worth taking a moment to linger over his transparent prose:

April 26 {the day after a skirmish with Spanish forces}:
  We form ranks at sunrise. To horse, still sleepy. The men are shaky, haven't yet recovered. They barely ate last night. Around ten we rest along both sides of the path. From a small house they send a hen, as a gift. . . . In the afternoon and at night I write, to New York, to Antonio Maceo {a leader of the independence movement} who is nearby and unaware of our arrival, and the letter for Manuel Fuentes,

to the {New York} World, which I finished, pencil in hand, at dawn.
Yesterday I cast an occasional glance over the calm, happy camp: the
sound of a bugle; loads of plantains carried on shoulders; the bellow
of the seized cattle when their throats are slit. From his hammock,
Victoriano Garzón, a sensible black man with a mustache and goatee
and fiery eyes, tells me, humble and fervent, about his triumphant at-
tack . . . : his words are restless and intense, his soul is generous, and
he has a natural authority: he pampers his white aides . . . and if
they err on a point of discipline, he lets them off. Stringy, sweetly
smiling, in a blue shirt and black pants, he watches over each and
every one of his soldiers. The formidable José Maceo parades his tall
body past: his hands are still raw from the brambles in the pine forest
and on the mountainside {after a lost battle}. José was left all alone,
sinking beneath his load, dying from cold amid the damp pines, his
feet swollen and cracked: and he arrived, and now he triumphs.

On May 19, disobeying General Gómez's instructions and
keen to take part in a skirmish with Spanish troops, Martí
mounted a horse and galloped toward the site of the combat. On
his way there he was shot three times in an ambush. He died a
few minutes later, in enemy hands, at the age of forty-two.

In the Plaza de la Revolución the sun was now shining on the figure of Martí, martyred once by the Spanish Crown, then again by
his posthumous portrait. The national hero, embodied in a marble so white it looks like plaster, rises from a concrete column
that dominates the entire esplanade; from that column a series of
ramps descend gently to the level ground. The first of the special
guests were already congregating on those ramps, looking for
their places on the great platform where Fidel would soon make
his speech.

It had rained hard that morning. The noisy throng that began
filling the plaza early in the afternoon was equipped with a few
umbrellas but mainly with laminated canvas sacks that served as
raincoats—and with the indispensable maracas and *tumbadoras.*
The drums were already sounding when a bus deposited the

members of the Mexican–North American Delegation near the monument. Shouts and slogans ricocheted from one extreme of that overflowing sheet of concrete to the other. A restless sea of arms and heads was visible in the sharp-edged afternoon light, and every few minutes a placard or a cluster of flags would suddenly surf across its waves. The shouting was dying down, then bursting out again, rising and falling, when a lightning bolt of tension ran through that teeming sea from shore to shore. El Barbudo Mayor, El Hombre, El Caballo was coming! Fidel was near! On the platform, people swiveled in their assigned seats, craning their necks like ostriches to see where the Comandante en Jefe would appear. I too searched everywhere, my mouth dry and my heart like a radar antenna, but I was looking for someone else: maybe Luis would be among the guests. "Look!" shouted Nancy. I spun around, electrified. "There goes Nicolás Guillén!" I watched indifferently as the man who transformed ordinary Cuban speech into poetry went by. Where was Luis, the guerrilla who was made for me?

Hattie and Nancy reviewed the star-studded crowd while I kept looking for the only man I needed. Nancy was very well informed: "There's the poet Roberto Fernández Retamar. I think the man walking by over there is Amilcar Cabral; he's the leader of the independence movement of Guinea and Cape Verde. Oh my God—that's Che's father!"

Palestinians, members of the Venceremos Brigade, Hungarian, Congolese, Vietnamese, and Laotian delegates all smiled and waved. "Look look look"—Nancy grabbed my arm—"that's Régis Debray's wife, I know it is." Hattie, laughing her head off, also started waving. "Why not?" she said. "After all, I'm a delegate too." And Luis?

From the back of the platform on the side opposite us a different sound was heard, like the parting of the waters. From all sides men with strong arms suddenly appeared, giving urgent orders: "*Compañeras,* please take your seats." The general reseating was accompanied by jabs and scuffling, and in our effort to get out of the aisle and into our assigned places, I didn't notice exactly when a silence descended on the plaza like a ghost.

Then another roar arose, denser and more powerful than any of
the previous ones. On the central podium, his silhouette out-
lined by the high-voltage lights, stood an olive green form that
gazed haughtily over the sea of people. All the microphones in
the world couldn't have made a single isolated shout rise above
the gigantic wave of voices that were now clamoring, but Fidel's
whisper, the silvery paper of his voice, flew very softly out across
the air. "*¡Compañeros!*" he greeted us, and all Cuba fell silent.

We heard his greeting with anguish. How would Fidel sur-
mount the dangers of this day? Playa Girón, the missile crisis,
the economic embargo, the eternal plots of his enemies, were
challenges he could conjure away with the phrases he always
used: "in defiance of fate," "not one step back," "the historic
stubbornness of those of us who have truth and justice on our
side," "the honor of a revolutionary is not cheapened or sold,"
"*Patria o Muerte.*" It was the same gladiator who stood before
us in the plaza today, but the lions were the very throng who
applauded, desperately begging him to renew their faith. It had
been eleven years of hard work and hard life; eleven years during which victory was forecast but did not come; eleven years of
Fidel's summoning everyone to the plaza to offer dazzling statistics and figures in exchange for an effort even greater than the
last one; eleven years of believing that the path of socialism not
only led to heaven but was infinitely more efficient and productive than the empire of capital here on earth; eleven years that
were culminating today with a bungled sugar harvest and the
promises of more long lines and power outages and even greater
restrictions on already inadequate ration cards. How could we go
on? And how could we give up, when the only thing we all
wanted was to follow him? The slender thread of his voice was
heard again:

"*Señores invitados y compañeros trabajadores . . .*"

I felt that we were all praying the same thing: *Fidel, Fidel,
make it a good speech!*

"We're not going to make a commemorative speech today; I
mean to say that we're not going to remember the successes and
achievements of the Revolution." The meticulously enunciated
sentences, the long roll of the *r*'s, the hypnotic pauses, now bore

an additional burden of mourning, and perhaps as we listened that day we were no longer seeking solace for ourselves in his words but the consolation that our attention might give him. "Today," said Fidel, "we're going to talk about our problems and our difficulties; about our setbacks and not our successes."

Could it be true? Would he say that the harvest had been a failure, that it was poorly planned, that mistakes had been made?

He did. Drastically and without much preamble, that was precisely what he was already doing. The heroic effort of the harvest "to increase production in order to increase our buying power led instead to a loss of functionality in the economy and lower production in other sectors, and ultimately worsened our difficulties."

Yes, he was speaking well. Once more I felt the spell that his last speech had cast on me, even though his words had plunged everyone into anguish. A similar kind of peace was floating in the silence of the plaza now, I thought. Fidel was telling the truth. He would not betray us.

"Of course the enemy made much of the argument that the Ten Million Ton *Zafra* would bring on some of those problems. Our duty was to do our utmost to prevent that." But—and oh, how hard it was to say!—"in the end we were not able to prevent it."

No, we were not able. The first person plural Fidel always used was magical: it replaced a solitary *I,* which perforce must take all guilt upon itself without finding any remedies, with a *we* of solidarity that was both us and him, that allowed the effort and suffering and destiny of this fragile island to be shared equally by all. This was the ceremony of mourning we'd been waiting for: we needed more!

Then Fidel took flight, transporting us with him on the wings of his rhetoric, jabbing a prophet's blazing finger, contorted with the emotion and the difficulty of his words, defying the thing that is hardest to defy: shame. His face must be illuminated, I imagined, watching his silhouette in the distance, my whole being given up to him. His face must be as radiant as mine is, from so much effort and internal struggle.

"Our enemies say we are in trouble!" Fidel admitted to the

world, transported by his own prophetic, reiterative rhythm. "And our enemies are right about that. They say we're in trouble, and in fact they're right! They say there's much discontent, and in fact our enemies are right! As you see, we're not afraid to admit it when our enemies are right."

Who was speaking? Who was acknowledging, who was challenging? Was it us or Fidel? "In fact, our enemies don't matter to us one bit," he exclaimed, or we did. No, it was Fidel again, with all the strength of his thin, hoarse voice, and at that moment we exploded into a frenzy of uncontainable applause that left our hands red and burning.

"And if the enemy takes advantage of some of the things we say and causes us great shame," the Comandante cried out, "then we welcome that shame!" We applauded, and applauded some more. "We welcome our pain if we know how to transform shame into strength, if we can transform shame into the spirit of hard work, if we can transform shame into dignity, if we can transform shame into the spirit that leads us forward!"

This was the climax. Close to tears, delirious, our arms aching from all the applause, we shouted "FI-del-FI-del-FI-del!" stamping rhythmically on the platform to make so much noise that even the Yankees would hear us.

There it was. Fidel had confronted shame, discredit, and punishment, and we had redeemed him. Hoarse and exalted, trying to applaud even more, the members of the Mexican–North American Delegation joined in the pandemonium, filled with forgiveness and new hope.

But the fact was—as I uncomfortably sensed even then—that it wasn't only Cuba's enemies who were warning that the path of Revolution was heading toward delirium. Many people who were sympathetic to Fidel and the revolutionary process were formulating critiques as well, sincerely worried about the Comandante's abrupt swerves and oversize enthusiasms. In order not to be left on the wrong side of the chalk circle he had so famously drawn—"outside the Revolution, nothing"—most of them silenced their objections and their consciences, while many others allowed themselves to voice only very slight criticisms. In the plaza that day, at the moment when Fidel, now on the other side of the parting of the waters of his own history, newly accompanied by everyone, listed one after another the year's terrible economic statistics, it would have been truly unthinkable for someone who was not his enemy to tell him no, a list of failures is not enough, you have to change course and leave office. It was unthinkable, and we did not think it: Fidel had asked for our forgiveness, and in the strength we gained from granting it, the figures he was citing could no longer frighten us.

In the top-priority area of meat and milk products, for example, and despite all Deisy's best efforts, the stock of fresh milk had gone down by 25 percent since the year before. Cement production was down by 23 percent. Only 8 percent of the planned manufacture of agricultural machinery was being carried out. Tire production was down by 50 percent. And Fidel's stark list went on:

"Leather footwear . . . Through May, production is down by approximately one million pairs. . . . This shortfall includes almost 400,000 pairs of work shoes. Moreover, the quality of the shoes has deteriorated, especially that of the work shoes." Shoes, ham, meat, beans, toothpaste, deodorant—everything was scarce and would go on being scarce. In all the economic collapses Latin America had suffered over the last half-century, no other crisis of even remotely similar proportions would occur until the collapse of the Soviet Union sank Cuba into an even deeper abyss. But we didn't know that then. Not even an intelligent and critical economist like Pablo could have predicted it, and Pablo was in the crowd that day, too, because ultimately his vision of economics was derived from Fidel. According to the revolutionary socialists, an economy was not a living organism, mysterious, fragile, sensitive to any intervention, and susceptible to bleeding to death just like a body if a paralyzed or gangrenous limb was severed. An economy was a piece of machinery: if one part wasn't working, you could throw it out and replace it with a better one. And an economist was, more or less, the equivalent of a highly trained mechanic. The Revolution's brilliant economic future could be achieved: it was all a matter of tightening the screws and exercising force of will.

"We acknowledge that in this statistical enumeration only

some of the causes appear," said Fidel, landing on precisely that point. "Inefficiency—that is, the subjective factor—must be included among the causes that have given rise to these problems. . . . Yes, there are objective difficulties, and some of them have been pointed out here. But we are not here to point out the objective difficulties. The task at hand is to point out the concrete problems. And the real task is simply this: man must bring about what nature and the real facts about our means and resources cannot bring about." The Comandante's stream of silvery words came to a stop. Night had just fallen in that portentous silence.

"Man," said Fidel, after a long pause, "has a fundamental role to play here. And most fundamentally, those men who occupy positions of leadership."

When we heard this, we understood that the Comandante was about to ask for the only thing besides our forgiveness that we in the plaza had the power to grant. A kind of sibilant tension was added to the fervor of our listening, one second on a tightrope stretched across an abyss, for at that moment and probably never again Fidel was acknowledging that the vast crowd that chanted his name had the ability to determine his fate.

"We will begin by pointing out, in the first place, all of our responsibility for these problems. And my own, in particular. I won't even allude to responsibilities that do not belong to me and the entire leadership of the Revolution."

We all applauded, I don't know why. Fidel was about to offer his resignation.

"Lamentably, these self-criticisms cannot easily be accompanied by as many consistent solutions. It would be better to tell the nation, Find someone else. Or even, Find several others."

The tightrope stretched almost to its breaking point in the infinitely tiny fraction of a second between that "find several others" and the first shout that rang out from the plaza: "¡No!" And then a volley of shouts—"¡No!"—that Fidel didn't even appear to hear. There was no need.

"It would be better. In reality, it would be hypocritical on our own part as well. I think that we, the leaders of this Revolution, have cost the country too much with our apprenticeship."

What was he saying? What was he saying? What was he trying to say?

"And unfortunately, our problem—not the question of replacing the leaders of the Revolution, whom this country can replace when it wants to, and right now if it wants to—!"

And now all the anguish and emotion that had been held back came bursting out. A thousand placards waved, and all the drums pounded while the people shouted half in terror and half in joy "*¡No!*" and again "FI-del-FI-del-FI-del!"

There was no longer any need for the sentence's humble culmination: "This, in fact, is one of our most difficult problems, and we are paying for a long heritage, the heritage, in the first place, of our own ignorance." Fidel had made a mistake. Fidel had acknowledged it. Fidel had been manly enough to offer himself up in sacrifice. Fidel had said he was human and had humiliated himself before us. The uproar lasted many long minutes and ended only because the gladiator was standing triumphant, and the lion in the plaza was curled gratefully at his feet.

The speech had lasted almost two hours by then, and Fidel gave no sign of approaching his conclusion. After the catharsis I felt myself returning to the reality of the uproar in the plaza, and a hot, uneasy feeling in the pit of my stomach told me that Luis might be near. How wonderful it would be to talk all these things over with him, to know whether he had been moved as well, whether Fidel had inspired his struggle and if he believed it was worthwhile to go on. "I need to go to the bathroom, but I don't know if Fidel is going to finish before I get back," I said to Hattie. "I don't think there's the slightest danger of that," she answered, fanning herself. "Go see what you can find, then come back and tell me where it is."

I was scrutinizing rows of faces in vain, walking toward the illuminated podium where the Comandante carried on with his speech, when one of the muscular men blocked my way. "The bathroom," I stammered, but the man would have made me go back to my seat if Guillén, the poet, hadn't suddenly loomed up against the spotlights, round as a drum, ugly as a toad, but resplendent in a white suit and shoes. He was walking the aisles to try to cool off, wiping the sweat from his dark face with a white handkerchief. "*Compañero,* women must always be given what they want!" he proclaimed. He folded his handkerchief as if it were a fan and made way for me with a wink and a perfect courtly bow. A few steps beyond him I glimpsed Luis and felt like offering up a prayer of thanks when he smiled as he caught my eye.

We spoke in low voices so as not to distract those who still had the energy to follow Fidel's speech, and with a bravery inspired by Guillén's mischievous gallantry I moved my face close to Luis's and inhaled his scent once more. We skipped incoherently from one subject to another, smiling foolishly for no reason, pretending not to notice that our arms were very close, that the electricity generated by our skins as they almost rubbed against each other had us both tingling: the next step was so inevitable I began to feel afraid. Behind me I heard a voice speaking Spanish with an accent I knew all too well. "Very interesting speech, but I think a little long, *¿no?*" Nancy, damn her! My colleague from the ENA had also come looking for someone: with a big smile she was saying hello to another of the guerrilla delegates we'd met the day before. Now there were four of us whispering with our heads very close together, while my heart went on jolting, suspended between relief and infinite rage. "What about you two? Aren't you afraid the Cubans will take you for CIA agents?" Luis asked, without my understanding what such a suspicion had to do with anything. Yes, Nancy replied, that really was a problem. People were constantly joking about it and that made her very uncomfortable, but she was a revolutionary and understood that if she made the greatest possible effort to do her work well, all distrust would vanish.

Something in Fidel's tone told us that now his speech really was drawing to a close. It was time to go back to our seats. "When can we see each other again?" Nancy's guerrilla asked her in a perfectly natural tone. "I don't know, I'm staying at the Habana Libre. Call me," she answered, as if it were the easiest thing in the world. The musclemen were starting to make their way through the rows of seats, looking very efficient. We had to be going, but Luis hadn't yet asked me the same question. I was about to lose him.

"I'm at the Habana Libre, too," I said, trying to act as natural as Nancy had and grinning like a fool.

"Yes, well. Good luck, I hope your dancing is always lovely," Luis answered with an equally senseless and uncomfortable smile, and he walked away.

Going down the ramp toward our bus, I clutched my body in an effort not to release the sobs that were forming deep inside me. When Hattie asked me what was wrong, I could truthfully say I had a pain that was keeping me from breathing. What had happened? What mistake had I made, what secret flaw had Luis sensed in me, what obscure pocket of elitism, individualism, shit consumption had he glimpsed to make him turn his back on me like that? Maybe if I'd combed my hair more carefully that morning? Hattie was taking off the badge that identified her as a member of the Mexican–North American Delegation. "What an unforgettable day," she sighed. And the truth struck me like a thunderbolt: of course, I spoke English and traveled with Hattie and Nancy; I lived in the United States; the term MEXICAN–NORTH AMERICAN on my badge meant "Chicana." I was the one Luis, the hunted guerrilla, suspected. Was I the CIA agent? *"Wait, I'm Mexican. I can show you my passport!"* I silently screamed. "I'll be right back," I told my friends, trying to fight my way against the tide of people back to where I'd left him, but it was too late. I never saw him again.

Fidel had one last thing to say after bringing his speech to a close with the *"¡Patria o Muerte! ¡Venceremos!"* that we all hoarsely shouted. He turned back to the lectern and asked for our attention.

"Certainly, while we were discussing these ideas . . . we were certainly forgetting something we wanted to announce today."

He spoke in a different tone, without theatrical posturing, like someone telling a child that his mother is a little sick. "We had mentioned Dr. Arguedas," he said carefully, "who saw to it that Che's diary was returned to our country. There's something else, which we would like the people to hear with, let's say, a certain seriousness. And that is the following. . . . Along with the diary, Dr. Arguedas has preserved and sent to our country . . . Che's hands."

I would later verify how this awful gift had come to be: how it was that a whole and complete human being was reduced to fragments scattered across the world, such as this package of hands that now, years after Che's death, a Bolivian government functionary had sent to Cuba. Submerging myself once more in Che's life, I would learn that this matter of the hands, like his very death, was something decided at the last moment, almost on impulse. Twenty-four hours after Ernesto Guevara was captured by Bolivian army troops near the miserable hamlet of La Higuera, the Cuban CIA agent who was advising the Bolivians confirmed his identity to Washington. On the instructions of General René Barrientos, who was governing Bolivia at that point, Che was executed. A Bolivian sergeant fired the shots that cut his life short on October 9, 1967. His corpse was buried without any mark or sign that would allow the spot to be subsequently identified, but before the burial his hands were severed. The reasons that were given—proof of his death was necessary and his fingerprints would identify him—do not explain the decision. Rather, it seems to be the gesture of any hunter with his prey (comparable to the memorable but not exceptional case, years later, of the Salvadoran colonel who kept his victims' ears in a jar). A few weeks after the hero's assassination, however, a strange character, Roberto Arguedas, the Bolivian minister of the interior, had felt the impulse to send Che's Bolivian diary to Cuba. That July he'd decided to return Che's death mask and hands to the man he considered their true owner—Fidel, who was now consulting the nation as to the fate of this delivery.

"The traditions of our country are well known. We bury our dead, that is the tradition . . . Maceo, Martí. It's always been that way, and always will be. But we are wondering. . . . What is to be done with Che's hands?"

There may not have been many who immediately understood what was being asked. "Of his physical being, this is all that remains to us," Fidel then clarified. "We do not know whether we will someday find his remains. And that's why we want to ask the people what their opinion is"—in the official transcript of the speech, "[Shouts of "Preserve them!"]" appears here—"what should we do with Che's hands?"

"Preserve them!" shouted a few more people at that point, according to the transcript, and Fidel endorsed that response.

"Preserve them!" he exclaimed as well.

Finally, a sacred relic for the martyr's shrine.

When it came down to it, I did not want to be like Che. At moments of shameful sincerity I recognized that there was something hard and intransigent in his character that repelled me. However, it wasn't just the sweet eyes and fresh scent of the guerrilla who abandoned me forever in the Plaza de la Revolución that made me surrender my heart to him, but his pact with death as well. When I met Luis, I, like so many of my contemporaries, had already unquestioningly accepted Che's principal dogma: in order to have a meaningful life and contribute to the well-being of the human race, it was necessary to die, and fast. Following Che, Luis had suffered persecution and martyrdom and—I imagine, though I never asked—had also fired weapons. I think that particular combination of blind obedience and total rebellion embodied my generation's dilemma and gave it meaning and purpose. We reached adulthood just at the moment when, with the contraceptive pill and the atomic specter now givens, the twentieth century broke its ties to the past. Other people my age were abandoning themselves to the pleasure-seeking chaos of the times—sex, drugs, and rock and roll. But we were afraid of the void and longed for the order of the Revolution, giving ourselves over to the relief of its absolute truths. From this paradox we derived another that would rule our lives: to become a rebel was to train yourself in the discipline of absolute obedience—for the mediocre among us, obedience to Fidel ("*Comandante en Jefe, ¡ordene!*"), and obedience to Che for the elect, of whom the finest example were the eighteen Cubans who followed him into the wastelands of Bolivia and died there with him.

Ernesto Guevara was born in 1928, in Misiones, Argentina—his nickname, with which he later signed Cuban banknotes during his stint as director of the Central Bank, means simply "the Argentine." He was intelligent, restless, irreverent, idealistic, and so stubborn that he refused to be turned into an invalid by the brutal asthma he suffered from. After he finished medical school, he went out to explore the world, or at least that part of it that was closest, which was Latin America. In Bolivia he experienced the relatively peaceable revolution of Víctor Paz Estenssoro, and in Guatemala he witnessed an event that would mark him forever, the CIA-backed coup against the reformist government of Jacobo Arbenz. He intended to continue his journey beyond the sea, but in Mexico he happened to meet a tall Cuban with an overwhelming personality who disrupted his journey and his life. It's quite likely that the meeting changed Fidel's destiny as well, since without a born strategist as brilliant and resolute as Ernesto Guevara, Castro's feeble troops would probably never have achieved the great feat of overpowering Batista's army.

From the moment they met, Fidel and Che were united in a single obsessive idea. The Argentine joined the Cuban expedition as a doctor, but on the night of the disastrous landing of the *Granma,* when the rebels were surprised by Batista's troops (according to the plan, it should have been the other way around), Che made a crucial decision. In the rout that followed the attack—during which most of the eighty-two expeditionaries who accompanied Fidel were killed—the young doctor had to choose between his medical bag and a rifle. He made the decision that destiny had prepared for him.

Two years later, when the bearded rebels took Havana, Ernesto Guevara enjoyed the last victory of his life. Fidel declared him a hero and a Cuban and placed him in charge of the National Bank first and then the National Institute of Agrarian Reform, the spearhead of the Revolution. The years that followed amounted to a long series of blunders. Che's utopian, absolutist programs helped destroy the Cuban economy. His differences of opinion with Soviet and Cuban leaders alike—and undoubtedly even with Fidel himself—led him to leave his adoptive land in 1965.

It's hard to understand what drove him to embark on a pathetic struggle in the Congo, with such humiliating results that it took him months to recover his pride. In 1966 he returned to Cuba clandestinely and stayed only long enough to select and train a group of volunteers who loved him more than their own lives and who accompanied him on the fatal expedition to Bolivia.

By then he was committed to the theory of the *foco,* according to which a small group of armed men—like, say, the group that disembarked from the *Granma* on the Cuban coast—could serve as a focus, or motor, for a revolutionary process. He chose to forget that Fidel Castro was a canny Cuban who knew his compatriots very well and was devoid of the slightest desire for martyrdom. He didn't remember that before organizing the rebel expedition on board the *Granma,* his friend had led a significant national movement with thousands of followers. On the basis of a couple of trips as a backpack tourist, Che thought he understood Bolivia and decided to ignore the obvious. The ever-incisive René Dumont sums it up in a footnote: Che took it for granted that once the guerrillas were present in Bolivia "a generalized revolt of the indigenous population (which did not exist in Cuba) would take place, which means he forgot that for the Bolivian campesinos, walled up in their native languages, any Spanish-speaking white arouses mistrust, for they have often been deceived."

In the pages of Che's Bolivian diary, so different from the diary kept by José Martí before he was shot down, it's hard to know exactly what Ernesto Guevara sought in death. Glory? Absolution? That, in any case, is what was sought by the thousands of young men and women who, following his example, took up arms in a great wave that crossed Peru, Venezuela, Colombia, Uruguay, Argentina, Brazil, the Dominican Republic, Guatemala, El Salvador, and Nicaragua—young men and women who everywhere were exterminated horribly, one by one (and who only in Colombia are represented by a movement that still survives, and only in Nicaragua actually came briefly to power). These armed groups were very different from the guerrilla armies that waged true nationalist wars in Southeast Asia. Following Che, the Latin American guerrillas—many of them university students—went looking for individual glory and always displayed a fatal ignorance of the poor whom they wanted to save, as if these would-be redeemers were Spanish hidalgos who could find the meaning of sweat and physical labor only in martyrdom and heroic gestures.

As for me, I'd never been to Bolivia, had barely had a first look at Cuba, and knew nothing of the fierce debates that were forming within the Cuban state on the economic path to be followed; I did not understand what relationship there might be between Che's stubborn battle against "material stimuli" and the boxful of money that was accumulating in my dresser without my having anything to spend it on; I didn't want to die under torture, and far less did I want to kill anyone. I wanted nothing more than to transcend—and what could I do but lament that a sweet-eyed guerrilla warrior had refused to show me my destiny?

"Of the dishes on the menu, we have only the desserts," announced the waiter. "As a main course, I can offer you sirloin or frogs' legs." Hattie and I looked at each other in mute dejection. You truly had to be very carnivorous to eat beef day after day, and the moldy-chicken taste of the frogs' legs was unbearable by now. It was no use asking for a salad: in the plaza Fidel had warned us that there wouldn't be any this year.

"The sirloin."

"I have a very good Bulgarian wine."

"No, thanks," said Hattie. "I'd rather have a beer." Unfathomable mystery: everything else could be scarce, but there was always beer in Cuba—good beer, and an abundance of it.

"How are your classes going?" Hattie asked. "The students seem to be enjoying them."

"I don't know. I have no idea what I'm doing. I don't think I'm following any program at this point. The kids' confusion really throws me off: it would be so much easier if they had some idea of what they wanted to accomplish, what kind of dance they wanted to do. But they have no points of reference: the only thing they've ever seen in their lives is what the modern dance Conjunto does, and they don't like it. And since the Conjunto doesn't have much of an audience, it doesn't even have any glamour value for them."

"They desperately need new choreography. As soon as I get back, I'm going to see if anyone wants to come here to stage a couple of dances. Anna Sokolow would be ideal."

"Hattie, you're a genius! Of course Anna has to come. She doesn't make any major technical demands, she's got plenty of charisma, and her work always has a lot of social content. She'd be fantastic! You've got to convince her."

"I don't get along with her all that well, but I'll see what I can do. Someone has got to come, because Elfrida is a great fighter, she's very disciplined, and she's put something good together at the school against all the odds, but she's no choreographer. And I do feel that the kids are kind of desperate."

I kept silent. Hattie and I had different opinions about Elfrida.

"You know something?" Hattie went on, ignoring the gap in the conversation. "It's just about time for me to go home, and I've had a wonderful time here; it's been a lot of fun—despite this awful constipation! The next time I come I'm packing a whole suitcase full of Ex-Lax; I think it's been a month since my damned intestines did their job. . . . Everything has been great, but I still don't understand what we're doing here. Did you know that Elfrida wasn't the first director of the dance school? I think the school didn't even have a director when it was built. They named someone to the post afterward."

"Yes, and then they sent for a series of not-very-good Mexican choreographers to take charge of it. I don't know who decided that the ENA would have a dance school, or why it seemed necessary."

"Well, the whole thing is a real mystery," said Hattie, finishing off the last mouthful of the accursed sirloin. "Let's see what you can find out once I'm gone. But you know something? I can't stop thinking that it all has something to do with Fidel's speech. It's like someone saying, 'We're going to develop a great shoe manufacturing industry,' or 'We're going to harvest ten million tons of sugarcane.' It's all done by decree, and dance doesn't happen that way. That just won't work in art."

She wiped her mouth carefully and took a lipstick from her purse.

"And you?" she said, embarking on a subject that was unpleasant to me. "What are you going to do?" She scrutinized me with her small, olive green eyes. "I don't know you very well, but you strike me as someone with an outstanding talent for suffering. And you seem to be putting it to full use."

I kept silent, struggling not to burst into tears in front of the Palestinian and Vietnamese and Angolan delegates.

"Are you going to stay here, or are you thinking of coming back later?" Hattie insisted. "They need you very badly here, but I don't know how that boyfriend of yours would take it. How's that going?"

"I don't know, Hattie, I don't know anything. I'm so confused," and I was about to open up and confess everything, about the sweet guerrilla, and my resentment of Adrian's demands, and the infinite loneliness that was overwhelming me, but someone interrupted us. It was the guerrilla who had been flirting with Nancy.

"Hello!" he greeted us, friendliness personified. "Have you seen Nancy?"

"She took a week's vacation," I told him. "She went off with her boyfriend, who came with the Venceremos Brigade." I took some pleasure in throwing out that final detail. I didn't like him.

"Oh. Too bad. And you—you're staying here at the hotel?"

"Yes."

"Well, so am I. What a coincidence! Shall we have a drink tonight?"

My affair with Eduardo, the South American guerrilla whom I always disliked, lasted two or three weeks, and during that time I learned many things. The first was that the Cuban government kept a close eye on the sexual relations of guests at the Habana Libre. Before that I don't think I'd even noticed the personnel from the Ministry of the Interior who kept watch on the hallways; maybe because Hattie and I were staying on the same floor, but I don't recall anyone ever preventing Hattie from dropping by my room for a chat, or me from visiting hers. In any case, whenever Eduardo was intercepted on his way to my room, he was forced to return to his own floor. Visits, he was peremptorily reminded, were prohibited. I also learned the advantages of having a background in clandestine maneuvers. Eduardo would let me know in the afternoon if he was going to come by that night, and following his instructions, I would slip a folded piece of paper between the doorframe and the latch bolt so that any *compañero* inspector in charge of the hallway could believe the door was locked. Eduardo would sneak down the service stairs very late, and if the coast was clear, he would slip over to my room and come in without knocking.

Our encounters were a kind of penitence. I neither liked nor felt attraction of any kind for Eduardo, though I made ostentatious efforts to feign the contrary. Eduardo didn't much like me, either, but he didn't make the least effort to disguise that fact. There wasn't a single tender interchange or hint of communication between us, but the feeling of being used by a guerrilla temporarily diminished my whirlpooling sensation of being superfluous in the world. And Eduardo was always willing to answer all my questions. He would light a cigarette, lean back against the pillow, and the lesson would begin. I had doubts about the role of art in a revolution? "That will become clearer to you as you go deeper into your study of dialectical materialism." My stay in Cuba had turned my world upside down? "That's perfectly natural, *querida:* you're a human being who's capable of reacting to reality, and the experience of a revolution contradicts all the false suppositions by which you've lived your life. That speaks well for you."

I interrogated him anxiously about torture. I needed to know what it was like, what could be done to resist it, if the mind erased the memory afterward. Was it possible to forgive, was it possible to believe in the fundamental goodness of humanity after having been tortured? On that point Eduardo defended his privacy, and his reaction was understandable: not many of its victims have been willing to describe even the physical mechanisms of torture—how many electrodes and where—much less their own reactions and the subsequent changes to their internal landscape. "Listen," Eduardo told me, "you think far too much about this kind of thing. There's no great mystery. Basically, you try to hold out under torture because you don't want anyone else to go through what you're going through. And afterward you try to forget the whole thing, because it would be stupid to stay rooted in the past when we're fighting for the future."

But the issue of forgiveness, and the problem of the fundamental nature of humanity? Aren't torturers human beings, too?

"Logically, yes, they're human beings, but you have to understand class theory. A torturer is a human being, but he's also an oppressor in the service of the dominant class. If you really want to go into it all, you'll probably find out that his daddy beat him up when he was a kid and things like that, but that's not my problem. If I were a psychologist or a social worker or a priest, I'd try to redeem him, but as it happens I'm a revolutionary. That's where this whole idea of yours about forgiveness comes in: we're not pacifists. We've declared war on a corrupt, exploitative, and murderous system: son-of-a-bitch we get our hands on, son-of-a-bitch ends up in front of a firing squad."

Only once did I try to explain that I wasn't looking to understand forgiveness itself as much as how to recover my interest in life in a world where absolute evil was manifested with total impunity. Eduardo gave me such an impatient look that I canceled that subject once and for all. But although he thought I was manufacturing dramas where there were none, he too in his way tried to teach me how to live.

"There's no answering the kind of fundamental question you like to ask. I'm more concrete. I leave all that stuff about the nature of humanity for after the triumph of socialism. For now the only thing that concerns me is how to shorten the time until that triumph, so that fewer children die of hunger, fewer men beat their wives because they have no other way to vent the rage of being unemployed, fewer women die in childbirth. It may be that mankind, here and now—you and I included—has a fundamental capacity for evil. But in socialism we'll generate the new man, just as Che dreamed, and then there won't be any need for your worries."

He smiled. It was almost the equivalent of a caress. In order to reciprocate the gesture, I kept the thought that was gnawing at me to myself: How could he possibly believe that the question of the fundamental nature of man wasn't important? If a human being was not a perfectible mechanism, if you couldn't simply take the lid off the machine and replace the malfunctioning parts with others that were good, selfless, and committed to the cause, if human beings were always going to be the same—in the best of cases, selfish and a little lazy, self-deceiving, and adulterous— then wasn't the attempt to create a new man a wasted effort from the start, and who knew, perhaps even a dangerous one?

And if the evil ones were the oppressors and the oppressed were the good guys, where did that leave me? I hadn't ever thought of myself as evil, but I'd never done anything to win a place alongside the righteous. The answer could be deduced simply from Eduardo's way of treating me: I belonged to the anodyne, undifferentiated, pliable, and entirely dispensable— shit-eating, in a word, *comemierda*—category of artists, artisans, office clerks; all that petit-bourgeois riffraff who can occasionally be of some use but who arrange things so as not to be on one side or the other of the great struggles and who are destined to wander forever in the limbo of history. As for himself, Eduardo didn't deny that he was from a more or less well-off family, but when he joined in the revolutionary struggle, he had managed to transcend his origins little by little, "proletarianizing" himself, as they called it then. At times I thought that what he had achieved was, rather, the elimination of any trace of spontaneous or distinctive personality.

"Do you have friends who are artists?"

"No, frankly, I don't. No. Of course I like art as much as the next person. I like to read, especially. There's a certain kind of novel I enjoy a lot: I like detective novels. And then of course there are the great novels. I liked *One Hundred Years of Solitude* a lot. And *Thus the Steel Was Tempered,* that's a fantastic novel—you don't know it? By a Russian writer, about the Bolshevik Revolution. Really moving, and so human."

Eduardo took care not to reveal much about his past or present activities, but one day I witnessed an explosion of bad temper. He had come in asking if I could give him a drink, though he knew the answer already. "Of course not, you don't even drink," he fumed, adding this explicit reproach to the private list he was keeping. He stood in front of my desk for a while, riffling through my books and papers and trying to make small talk. "You should read something besides novels," he scolded, looking over the titles. "Get yourself something that will give you some theoretical grounding." He flipped through one of my notebooks, then dropped it to inspect another one. He went over to the closet, whose sliding doors were always open, and pushed all the clothes on their hangers to one end of the bar and then back to the other end. He turned toward the desk once more and aimed a quick, strong kick at one of the drawers.

"This revolution is being swallowed whole by the bureaucracy, *carajo*!"

When he had calmed down a bit, he turned on the radio, lit a cigarette, and sat on the corner of one of the beds, with the cool breeze from the open balcony door at his back.

"Don't turn off the air conditioner," he said.

"But it never makes it any cooler in here! It just makes noise."

"That doesn't matter. Leave it.

"*Hijos de puta*," he said, after a while. "Once again they wouldn't let me leave."

Eduardo was suffering an attack of impatience, as he himself later acknowledged. The Latin American guerrillas who arrived on the island were often subject to such outbursts; their situation was difficult, and although the Cubans understood that, they argued that there was nothing else they could do. For security reasons, Eduardo and all the other guerrillas had to hand over their passports—real or fake, it didn't matter—as soon as they arrived in Cuba: without documents, there would be no way for them to leave without Cuban authorization. They were placed from that moment on in the care—and more importantly, under the supervision—of Manuel Piñeiro's Departamento Américas.

In later years the Cubans angrily defended this policy when they were questioned about it by comrades from other countries. Obviously Cuba was committed to promoting the hemisphere's revolutionary struggles—not only for reasons of self-interest and the most basic spirit of solidarity, but also because this was its historical obligation—yet it couldn't expose itself to infiltration or to crude accusations of interventionism from its enemy. In the first place, no guerrilla ever came in, either on a visit or to receive asylum, if his organization hadn't previously established a solid relationship with Cuba based on cooperation and detailed information. This was understood. In the second place, Cuba magnanimously gave all the help that lay within its power—from diplomatic assistance in the eternal wars of factions among the revolutionary organizations to the finest and most demanding military training—but it couldn't be expected to abstain from having a say in decisions that affected it directly: how and when a guerrilla undertook the return journey to his country, and at what moment his organization entered the phase of armed struggle.

Both the assistance and the measures of control were administered by Lorna's husband, but like Eduardo, all the guerrillas believed that if they could only speak directly with Fidel, their situation on the island would become more bearable and they could speed up their return to their country of origin. In subsequent years the case of Colonel Francisco Caamaño Deñó became known. He was a Dominican rebel with a considerable number of followers among his former army comrades, who waited almost four years for his mythical interview with Fidel and finally managed to return to the Dominican Republic without ever having obtained it. He died in the first skirmishes of an invasion reportedly organized by Piñeiro. Over the years certain of the more informed revolutionaries learned to evade the Cuban system of control. Mario Monje, for example, the leader of the Bolivian Communist Party, who was extremely mistrustful of Che's plans for insurrection, kept his misgivings to himself when Piñeiro's people called him to Havana, and in a series of tactical maneuvers to preserve his autonomy in the eyes of the Cubans and keep from being retained on the island, he accepted the military training that was being offered to the Bolivian Communists. Or at least, that was how he explained his decisions years later. Other insurgents whom Piñeiro sent for were said to have alleged reasons of health or security in order to avoid making the journey, but most sought out the visits themselves, and with great hope.

Eduardo, who had accepted with pleasure the invitation to attend the commemoration of July 26, had been on the island for only a few weeks and was already growing impatient. He didn't want to recover from the aftermath of torture. He didn't want to take an intensive workshop in Marxism. He didn't want to go on a tour of Cuban agricultural centers or even take the combat training course taught by the most experienced guerrillas of the Cuban Revolution. He wanted to go back to his country and to the organizational work that he suspected was slipping out of his hands. And now he had been told for the third or fourth time that they were very sorry, *compañero,* but he would have to wait just a little while longer before he could discuss his affairs with Comandante Piñeiro. He lit one cigarette with the butt of another, masticating three or four phrases I couldn't hear.

"What? Eduardo, let me turn off the air conditioner, please. I can't hear a word you're saying."

"Don't be an idiot. Don't you know that if you turn it off, everyone else will hear what I'm saying, too?"

Thus I learned a new lesson: according to those most in the know, the rooms of the Habana Libre were equipped not only with toilets, bidets, lamps, and armchairs but with bugging devices as well, courtesy of the state security apparatus.

But my instructor divulged the most painful information without realizing it, one afternoon when we ran into each other in the hotel lobby.

"I just saw your friend," he announced.

"What friend?"

"The one you were cozying up to the day we met."

What? Then he hadn't left?

"No, he's still here. I just saw him. He was giving a talk on Marxist revolutionary theory."

Oh!

"The success that bastard has with women!"

The analgesic effect of my relationship of mutual use with Eduardo wore off at that precise moment, but we saw each other a couple of times more. For my part, I would have gone on: in the dance world, I had always tried to apprentice myself to the geniuses, and according to the ideas I had formed about the hierarchy of Marxist knowledge, those who incarnated theory and practice in a single body were the guerrillas. I didn't yet know how very easy it would be to find another teacher, so I was interested in keeping this one, for my doubts were multiplying.

Above all, there was a knot inside me that I could not undo, and it astonishes me now that I could ever have entertained the notion that Eduardo could help me find one of its ends. It was the following:

"Eduardo," I said to him. "Many of the ideas about historical materialism are clear to me now, I think, and about revolutionary practice, too. But what worries me is that I don't like the Revolution. I don't like it because I'm an artist, and the Revolution doesn't treat us well. I don't like it because I'm anarchic, and the Revolution wants to control everything. I don't like"—here I merely pointed to the bugging device that supposedly maintained its vigil on the ceiling—"I don't like it because I don't think there's any harm in the Beatles, or that having long hair has anything to do with whether you're a revolutionary or not. All right, we won't take that last point into consideration, because even revolutions can make mistakes, and I'm sure that the Beatles issue is a simple mistake. But in the end . . . what I'm trying to say is that I don't like living here, and at the same time it's clear to me that the Revolution is absolutely necessary to the better future of humanity. But then what do I do with my own opinion? How can I fight what I feel?"

I accepted his answer gratefully, because he gave me the only possible solution to a knot that cannot be untied, which is to take a machete and cut the obstacle in half.

"Listen," said Eduardo, "I think everything you say about the Revolution's stance toward art is true—and by the way I agree with you that censoring the Beatles and popular music is a crock of shit, though it doesn't much matter. The fact is that the Revolution also does well to mistrust you, because artists—most of them, most of them—are always slaves to their own subjectivity. Like you. You attribute so much importance to your own perceptions, which are no more than a reflection of your class origins. You believe that what you're seeing or thinking is true, but your truth is dictated by your petit-bourgeois concept of the world.

You notice things that would never be important to any proletarian. He wouldn't have time to go around fixating on the details that strike you as great problems. Don't ever tell a worker that you're worried about how the artists are being mistreated, because he won't stop laughing for hours: a little *mistreatment* next to a massive wave of layoffs!

"Look," he went on, navigating happily along his own Socratic river, "let's throw some numbers at this. What's the population of Latin America? Two hundred and fifty million people. And of them, how many are like you—that is, how many earn their living without great effort? Does fifty thousand sound about right? And how many poor people are there? Have you tallied it up? Well, then, who should the Revolution give priority to? Make no mistake about it, *querida,* make no mistake. This fight is being waged for the poor. Objective truth is on their side, and that's what you have to look for and keep in mind."

Eduardo was the one who finally put an end to our encounters. He told me he was leaving, and it was at least true that he left the hotel, because I didn't see him again. We said good-bye without false sentimentality, though he did make one small attempt to be gentlemanly. "It was very pleasant spending this time with you," he said, kissing me lightly. "The truth is, Nancy was the one who caught my eye. But it was very interesting getting to know you."

EIGHT

Criticism and Self-Criticism

The talk delivered by my lost love, Luis—"Latin America: The Spoken Word and the Loaded Weaponry on the Path to Liberty" (I'm guessing the title, but I know I've got it right)—would have been a significant cultural event at any other time. I would have known all about it, and Eduardo's comment wouldn't have caught me off guard. But as it happened, Luis's speech was lost amid a commemorative flood of cultural activities that could only be compared to the abundance of pencils, pens, stickpins, nails, and notebooks, all manufactured in North Korea, that were spilling off the shelves of Havana's shops and hardware stores, and the cornucopia of tomato, yuca, and *malanga* that filled all the ration bins. This imitation of abundance was the nation's tribute to Moncada. At the Casa de las Américas, all the members of the jury that awarded the Casa literary prize that year gave talks, including the Salvadoran poet Roque Dalton, the wisest and funniest of the group. At the Cinemateca, the great Cuban films of the 1960s were screened again—*Lucía, La muerte de un burócrata, Memorias del subdesarrollo*—and there was even a premiere of a film by Antonioni. The Ballet Nacional was presenting its season at the Teatro García Lorca, and popular Afro-Cuban dance music groups like Los Van Van, the Orquesta Aragón, and the Orquesta Jorrín were performing here and there.

And in the streets, of course, there was a carnival. All of Cuba was on parade, in front of the hotel, down Rampa and the whole length of the Malecón, swaying, sweating, and euphoric from beer, indifferent to the season's cloudbursts, the women shifting their hips, left-right, to the beat of their flip-flops, the men strutting with buttocks tight and arms spread wide, faces to the sky. Not one slogan, just conga and beer, conga and rum. Cuba was celebrating the anniversary of the attack on Moncada and—perhaps with even greater enthusiasm—the end, at last, of the eighteen-month sugar harvest, the longest in history. The official name of 1970 was Year of the Ten Million, while 1969, christened the Año del Esfuerzo Decisivo (Year of the Decisive Effort), was universally known as the year of the Esfuerzo de Si Vivo (the Effort to See If I'll Live). As usual, I kept my distance from the festivities, even squirming out of the gatherings Galo and his friends were now convening. It wasn't just that the thought of meeting new people, confronting their scrutiny and judgment, and trying to figure out how to make them like me as I hid behind a screen of smiles and silence was growing increasingly terrifying. My time was taken up with other things: I was investigating the best way of committing suicide.

I imagine that the pathology of suicide is more or less uniform. On any given day, suddenly caught off guard by his loneliness, someone looks into the same mirror as usual but finds a reflection that lies at the bottom of a well. However hard he tries, he can no longer distinguish his eyes, nose, mouth, the room behind him—only a dark glitter of water that recedes until water and well have become an opaque eye he cannot look away from. I don't remember exactly when this happened to me, but it must have been during the first days of August, perhaps before things ended with Eduardo but more likely afterward, and after Hattie gave me a quick hug and left for the airport, leaving me her tweezers, an enormous ripe mango, and the remains of a bottle of rum. "So you can drink a toast with Adrian when he comes to visit," she said. In any case, the eye appeared to me on a night when I was very much alone. I remember that I paced around the cage of my room for hours. Sometimes I stopped in front of the bathroom mirror to squeeze a pimple, and other times I was startled by the unsought reflection of my frightful profile—nose, forehead, chin, buttock, all of it out of proportion. On one of my turns around the room, the mirror caught and held me, and there I was, full of coldness and hatred, unable to pull away from my own image. I saw my reflection but didn't see the person who inhabited it, as if I'd changed into a statue that was hollow inside and about to crack down the middle. The mirror became a danger after that, but anybody's gaze was, too, and solitude as well. The days wounded me more than the nights, but the nights were a long, unbearable abyss. I saw things. Sometimes when I closed my eyes, the demons of cold and hatred would invade the hollow space I now had for a body, and I would watch in horror as their bony hands gripped the little that was left of my heart—a crushed prune floating in a red cave—and squeezed it and wrung it out, while I felt nothing. At other times it was a kind of duck, its beak lined with sharp teeth, that gnawed at my desiccated heart, holding it between little kangaroo paws. I had stopped feeling the common emotions—happiness, sadness, fear, love— but in the morning when I opened my eyes and faced the sterile eye that watched me from the other side of the well, I felt something like eagerness for the relief of death.

The problem was that it was so hard to die. I quickly realized that merely wanting to do so didn't do the trick. I was astonished at my inability to fulfill a desire so intense and absolute. There can't have been as many mornings as I remember—I remember thousands—when the pink and gold light of dawn crept through the curtains, returning me to the repulsion of life, and I clenched all my muscles, trying to summon death. As the days went by and this did not work, I grew more practical. Since death was not obeying, I had to go looking for it. My brain was boiling with plans—pistols, knives, electrocution—but I always ran up against one inescapable difficulty: the distress that the sight of my corpse would cause other people. Thinking about how to successfully overcome this obstacle as I resolved the logistics of my own disappearance became the only activity that could keep me focused for hours.

One recurrent plan was based on tranquilizers. It would be easy to get them: at the hospital I'd seen Valium prescribed like aspirin for any complaint of nervousness or sleep deprivation. I could go to several hospitals and get hold of two or three vials. I would take them one midnight, after having cut the telephone wire and blocked the door with the mattress and chair, thus forestalling any last-minute temptation to call for help. But then— here I ran up against the same problem again—the maid would be the one to find my body. I didn't even know her; I usually left very early for the school, and when I came back in the afternoon, the room was clean and empty. A corpse is a horrible sight—I'd seen the corpses of my two grandmothers and an uncle—and I had no reason to burden a poor workingwoman who had never done me any harm, and for whom I'd never done any favors, with the spectacle of my dead body.

So tranquilizers were out. While I waited for another effective solution to occur to me, I worked on the problem of the note. There were people who would miss me: I would have to explain to Graciela, for example, and to Elaine why disappearing from the world was the right thing to do. It was hard. The opaque eye didn't stop watching even as I tried to compose a farewell letter. I spent several mornings ripping to shreds the note I'd come up with the night before, horrified, in the light of day, by the sheer bad taste of what I'd written. Finally, I remembered a sonnet by César Vallejo—his poems stayed with me after I read them as a teenager—and copied it out in my best handwriting:

> De todo esto yo soy el único que parte.
> De este banco me voy, de mis calzones,
> De mi gran situación, de mis acciones,
> De mi número hendido parte a parte,
> De todo esto yo soy el único que parte.

> Of all that's here, I'm the only part that's leaving,
> I leave behind this bench, my underclothes,
> My tremendous situation, all my actions,
> The sum of all I am, split down the middle,
> Of all that's here, I'm the only part that's leaving.

For some reason I felt that this struck the right tone and explained everything. In the room's little entry hall a cork bulletin board hung over the desk. I used up a whole box of North Korean stickpins trying to find one with a head that didn't snap off when I pushed it into the bulletin board. Ultimately I had to attach the sheet of paper with two needles taken from my sewing kit. It looked good, and for a few hours I enjoyed the repose that a sense of achievement can grant.

Should I throw myself into the sea like Virginia Woolf or Alfonsina Storni (an Argentine poet beloved of Graciela)? Every passing second of the day that was just beginning reinforced the need to kill myself. The cafeteria's gelid neon light; the viscous skin of milk that floated on a nauseating, lukewarm *café con leche,* which I sipped nevertheless; the stench of benzene and the dull roar of motors at the bus stop in front of Coppelia; the embedded smell of sweat given off by the armpit of my clean dress when I raised a hand toward the greasy bar; the slow greeting, like an awakening slug, of the penis some Cuban man was pressing against my buttocks under cover of the crammed *guagua*—was there even one morning when that particular offense did not occur?—the polyester of his pants against my bare calves; the suffocating heat of Cubanacán's jungle and the thorny branches that got tangled in my hair while I was holding my glasses with both hands to keep them from slipping down my nose; the exasperation of having to race down the path at top speed while a heat rash broke out on my thighs in the spot where they rubbed against each other . . . every sensation, every contact, was a reminder of the unbearable, relentless irritation of being alive.

"The others aren't here yet?" I asked, standing in front of the students, though I was the one who was late. Without giving them time to retrieve those who were still out in the courtyard, I started the class, miserable and alive.

Should I throw myself into the sea? If I'd done that already, I wouldn't have to be thinking about how to confess to Sandra Neels that I never managed to perform her work in Havana, that I hadn't even managed to practice it all the way through, because the rehearsals had become sessions like this one, in which I spent endless minutes curled up in a corner of the studio, listening to the wind or the rain, counting bricks. I no longer knew how to move. In some past time that seemed remote I had enjoyed a certain skill in executing the long adagios that Merce created, inclining my torso at an improbable angle while one leg wove its own designs in the air. Now I couldn't perform a single phrase without stumbling. "For Alma, with admiration and affection,"

Sandy had written on the envelope that contained the note cards. Should I try drowning?

But everything floated on the waves of the Caribbean. If I wore a jacket with lots of pockets and filled them with stones, I might manage to drown. But I would look suspicious walking into the sea wearing a jacket with pockets, and the movement of the waves would probably pull out all the stones. A better idea would be to get my hands on a pistol, walk into the sea wearing a bikini (but where would I hide the pistol?), swim away from the beach, and shoot myself. But if I had a pistol, I wouldn't have to go into the sea: I could simply shoot myself in my room. The problem was, I had no experience in acquiring pistols and not the slightest idea of how to do so. And on the way back to the hotel from school, I remembered that I'd already discarded the idea of dying in my hotel room.

At the reception desk I was startled to see an envelope in the box next to my key. I opened the telegram immediately in case it brought some (fatal) news.

THINK TRIP POSSIBLE. WILL CALL FRIDAY 5 P.M. HOTEL. WAIT. ADRIAN.

I hated him. How could he think of intruding on my territory, coming to Cuba and adding even more demands to a life I could barely manage as it was? Why such zeal in pursuing me? Why wouldn't he leave me alone? Already besieged by his desire, his urgent breath, I went up to my room in a whirlwind of fury, slamming doors, gasping for air. Leave me alone! What would I do what would I do what would I do with this man who had somehow conceived who knew what sick, stubborn obsession with me?

Most days I hardly strayed from my school–hotel trajectory, though I would have given a great deal to flee to any other place. I felt as if I were hauling the empty shell of myself from one place to another in a wheelbarrow, trying to keep it from shattering into a thousand pieces. Though the hollow shell wasn't heavy, the effort of pushing it along was exhausting. I was carting myself along like that one afternoon that I remember simply for the fact that I ventured out into the street: I needed to have my foreign technician's identity card processed at a nearby office. Halfway there I thought the sun would leave me plastered flat as a decal against the sidewalk, and I'd have to stay there forever, incapable of rising, invisible, whimpering, fighting for breath. I thought I would never be able to take the fifty remaining steps that separated me from the Ministry of the Interior. A Cuban man (there were so many of them!) followed close behind me, his breath on my neck, murmuring increasingly grotesque obscenities. In some kind of slow motion I turned, making a huge effort to get my voice out, and begged him to leave me alone: *"Déjeme tranquila, por lo que más quiera."*

He was startled. *"Coño, chica,* I beg your pardon. I thought you were Bulgarian."

The bureaucratic mission was simple. They took my picture for the identity card. I didn't recognize myself. Back at the hotel I discovered that I had lost the ability to read and spent the end of the day sitting in bed with the sharp edge of the headboard stuck between two of my vertebrae, staring at the wall. Two more days until Adrian's phone call.

Throwing myself in front of a car was definitely out: given the velocity at which Havana's clankering vehicles traveled, anyone would have time to brake, perhaps after crushing one of my legs or leaving me with permanent brain damage. One afternoon, though, the thought of throwing myself in front of a train came to me. "Nothing would be left at all!" The relief of this idea calmed me down for several days. It was a plan I could carry out in privacy, without any witnesses to reconstruct the event in *Granma'*s section on traffic safety, *Semáforo rojo.* ("'The girl was standing there as always, at the bus stop on L and 23, but she looked pretty nervous,' Corporal Rubén Pérez informed *Semáforo rojo."*) The problem lay in discovering the course of the tracks used by the train that left a couple of times a week for Santiago, then in finding the best way of getting myself to a section of track somewhere out in the open countryside. I tucked this idea away as if it were a special treat I could take out and enjoy anytime I wanted. Tere noticed the change in my spirits; I must have received a letter from Adrian, to judge from the smile on my face, she said, grinning. But the perfect solution didn't last long: when I told Lorna that it would be great to take a train trip to Santiago before I left Cuba and that I would love to see on a map exactly where the train passed through, she answered that she would try to get the relevant permit for me in the remaining weeks of my stay, but that road maps were banned for security reasons. That meant it would be almost impossible for me to get near the tracks on my own, and it would probably be very difficult to persuade a stranger to transport a foreign girl without the correct permit into the Cuban countryside. What kind of trap was this—a country where a person couldn't even kill herself in peace?

One Friday when I arrived at the school I found Hilda and the academic teachers in a state of sorrow and anxiety that bordered on tears. Between one class and the next the school secretary took me aside to tell me what had happened. There had been a series of voluntary labor sessions—several days of cleaning and repair work at the school—and, taking advantage of the fact that the youngest students were on home leave, the volunteers had begun with their dormitory.

"I don't know how long it had been since any adult looked in there," she said. "I don't know what is going on with the supervisors. I feel so terrible, *chica,* as if I'd lived through a nightmare."

Hilda had a mania for tearing at her cuticles, and the flesh around her thumbnail was completely raw. "Just imagine! We went in, and right away the stench almost forced us back out," she said, scraping at another nail. "Oh my god, the stink! And then in the youngest kids' dormitory, all the walls were caked with obscene words and drawings of—well, you know. And we stared and stared—and then it hit us! All that filth was painted on the walls with excrement. You cannot imagine it! With pure shit! I haven't been able to sleep, I haven't been able to eat. This is what the school, the Revolution, represents for these children? Have we turned this place into a madhouse? Do the children we chose from the countryside to give them the very best, the *guaji-*

ritos who we thought must feel pride and love for their school, hate us so much that they cover everything with shit? Things are very bad here. I don't know what we're doing, but everything is all wrong. I feel that all the work we've been doing here has been a terrible mistake, a fatal mistake."

She burst into tears. "Ay, Alma, if you'd seen it—the sheets had these stains! I can't stand to think about it. The mattresses were ripped open. The toilets were so filthy that we had to spend hours pouring buckets of water with bleach through the door before we could even go in. I threw up. We were swimming in shit. A madhouse, *chica,* a madhouse." Hilda was sobbing. "How could this happen? What good is this school? I don't understand."

Of course the fifth-year students, who were all from Havana and lived at home, had already heard the news. In class they were serious and distracted. "Manolo, we're working with the left foot," I warned the son of Spaniards. "The left foot, Manolo," I insisted to no avail. "Okay, then, the other left foot." No one smiled at the dumb joke that had always made them laugh before.

I suspended the class. "Did you know about the dormitories?"

"The truth is that we have a great deal of responsibility in this matter, for we stopped sharing our lives with the younger students a long time ago," said Manolo. The very serious and somewhat rhetorical language that young people used in Cuba, in contrast with the near-savagery of their manners, always made me smile. José was probing one of his feet, looking for an incipient wart. Antonia, seated in profile just outside the circle we had formed, stared obstinately at the wall, and Orlando shared her smoldering silence, as if we were the reason for the rage that seemed to be consuming them. Because of his age Orlando was the only one in the group who boarded at the school, though not in the same dormitory as the youngest students.

"They were supposed to be taking turns," Roberto said as if to justify himself. "They're supposed to have clean-up brigades in each dormitory, and someone should be supervising them, I don't know who. But those kids are completely wild. They don't want to be here. They don't like us. The worst ones are from the countryside. Their parents wanted to put them here because the

food is free, and for a *guajiro* one mouth less to feed is a significant gain. But the truth is that all the motivation comes from
the parents. They should be the ones studying here! At least they
understand the advantages, but the only thing the kids know is
that they used to have a mother and father and brothers and sis-
ters and the whole countryside to run around in, and the next
day they're here and no one yells at them or bothers them, but no
one pays any attention to them, either. And they're such wild
beasts that no one can control them."

"Roberto, don't call them that!" yelled Pilar, the chubby girl.
"You can't call a child a wild beast."

"*Chica,* calm down," the others whispered.

But Pilar wasn't listening. "They're not animals! We're the
animals, we're the ones who've been incapable of taking care of
them or defending them or educating them. You can't leave a
child that way, loose in the world and defenseless, because this is
what you get. A child doesn't deserve that. He gets his liter of
milk, his uniform, his classes. And love: what about that?"

We were silent. Finally José spoke. "It's a huge problem, but
we have no way of dealing with it. If you think about it, it has to
do with the very structure of the school. To solve it, we'd have to
start all over again, but the administration are the only ones who
can do that. And you know by now that nothing is ever discussed
here. You bring up something you want to discuss, and immediately everyone looks at you as if you're a traitor. The problem
isn't even Elfrida—"

"Here she comes!" Antonia suddenly hissed, and we all
stood up.

"Adagio, *criaturas,*" I said. "Let's see if you can pay attention
this time."

The incident with the dormitories increased my sufferings,
though it also took the edge off them for a few hours. At least I
had the consolation of sharing in a general disgrace, and I had
something to think about. If I'd ever been sent to boarding
school, I would undoubtedly have been grateful for the refresh-
ing absence of my parents. I couldn't imagine any circumstances
under which I would have felt like painting the walls with my

own excrement, yet the sensation of shame mingled with rage—
as if I were the one who had left my mark on the wall—somehow
pleased me. How awful everything was! What pitiless loneliness
each one of us lived in! Would it have been better to leave those
kids in the country, without a future? Distracted, pondering, I
reached the entrance to the hotel and ran straight into the vigi-
lant eye, the torturer who had been waiting for our appointment.
It was Friday: Adrian was about to call. Today, with that eye on
him, he would comprehend the poverty of my heart.

Tucked away in a small side corridor of the Habana Libre were a
hair salon, some offices, the decomposing remains of a typical
hotel shop—though without the toothpaste, maps, key chains,
and razor blades such shops generally sell—and a half-dozen long-
distance phone booths. Anyone who made an appointment and
sat through a long wait could make a call from this exchange.
Those of us who were guests at the hotel had less of a wait, and
we could also receive international calls there.

In that windowless tunnel the heat and humidity were palpa-
bly dense. The light from the naked neon tube screwed into the
ceiling brought into bright relief the operators' smeared makeup
and the sweat stains on their blue and white uniforms. Sitting
on one of the wooden benches in the waiting area and trying
to guess how many calls were left before mine would come in,
I inhaled steam and exhaled bitter fumes and couldn't calm the
incessant churning in my stomach. It was several degrees hotter
in the phone booth; if you wanted to go on breathing, you had to
hold the door open with an elbow or a foot. Everyone talked like
that, with the door open, body outside, and head inside the
booth, seeking air and privacy at the same time without obtaining either. Adrian's greeting sailed to meet me across rivers, val-
leys, seas. We didn't know each other very well, yet I realized
with a start that his nasal voice was as intimate to me as my own
saliva. He sounded extremely happy.

"Good news. Remember my friend Jonathan, the one in
Coney Island who let me sleep on his sofa? He has a friend in the

Venceremos Brigade. I'm going to talk to him next week and see if I can join the next one."

How immature! Thirty-three years old and sleeping on a sofa! And didn't he know that the Venceremos Brigades admitted only the most battle-hardened militants, revolutionaries so pure they had washed away the immense guilt of being Yankees? This ignorant man was claiming the right to be my boyfriend?

"Hello? Can you hear me?"

"Hello. Yes."

He laughed, disconcerted. "Well, do you want me to come? It doesn't sound like you're too excited about it. . . ."

"Yes, of course I'd like to see you. I don't know where you're going to stay."

"Are you saying I won't be staying with you? I'm not going to Havana to see the architecture, you know."

"Guests aren't allowed here at the hotel. But the truth is, you won't see much of me if you come with the Venceremos Brigade. They spend all their time working in the cane fields."

"But I'll escape from the brigade as soon as we get there, and spend my time working on you instead."

I interrupted his laugh with a scandalized murmur: "Adrian, how can you say that! That would be cheating!"

What would the agents from the Ministry of the Interior who were listening to us think? That I was the girlfriend of a counter-revolutionary?

"But if you want me to come, there's no other way. Do you want to see me?"

The silence stretched out horribly.

"I'd like to see you, but I think it's wrong to cheat."

"I didn't know you had such respect for traffic signals."

The pause went on and on, and I could find no way to break it. It was Adrian who finally changed the subject. "So, have you been reading any good poets down there?"

"Roque Dalton, a Salvadoran revolutionary poet."

"Really? I'd like to read him. Send me a copy of some of his stuff. I've been reading Valéry. Do you know his work? He's almost as good as I am. Usually I don't like nineteenth-century French poets; they're decadent. But this guy's form is so strong.

You look at those poems, prod them, turn them upside down, shake them—they're still good. Ironclad. You'd like him."

More silence.

"So, you'll let me know if you can get in with the brigade?"

"Yeah."

On August 11 the relentless, unparalleled monotony of the front page of *Granma* was broken with an electrifying headline from a far region of the world I had never set foot in but that was familiar to me. For the past two months, the paper's inner pages had, off and on, included some bit of news about the latest scandalous, irreverent, original, unpredictable activity of a guerrilla organization that first became active in 1963 in Uruguay, homeland of my friend Graciela. If Graciela were a guerrilla, I thought, she would be like the Tupamaros: hyperintellectual, improbable, rigorous, crazy. And indeed, though anything that had to do with political militancy and rigidity of thought irritated Graciela and made her change the subject immediately, in every Tupamaro action I saw a family resemblance. According to what I'd been able to gather from the improbable news articles in *Granma,* the favorite activity of the Movimiento de Liberación Nacional (who called themselves Tupamaros in honor of Tupac Amaru, Inca hero of the resistance against Spain) was to occupy an upper-class home, bar all the doors, and then calmly lecture its inhabitants on the evils of capitalism. Occasionally they would hijack trucks that were taking supplies to supermarkets and drive them to poor neighborhoods, where they showered the people with food. They were famous for their ingenuity, their engineering skills, and the bloodless nature of their acts of *propaganda armada*. Right in the middle of Montevideo they had spirited away hundreds of arms from the arsenal of the navy training school, without firing a shot. An Uruguayan journalist, who had just won a Casa de las Américas prize with a book about the Tupamaros, said that the guerrillas counted among their members not only an abundance of the philosophy and literature students who normally swelled the ranks of such militant movements, but also doctors and engineers. (Although there were as well, the book hastened to add, a considerable number of proletarians, particularly sugarcane cutters from the provinces along the Brazilian border.)

I was entirely delighted with the Tupamaros, certain that they were all extremely handsome and refined and wore white turtlenecks and listened to Brahms, like Jorge. They also made smooth jokes the way Jorge did; one day, for example, when he saw the new kind of toothpaste I had brought from the United States— a transparent gel that issued from the tube in magic stripes of white and green—he asked whether his voice would come out in FM after he'd brushed his teeth with it. Always cool, my heroes would redistribute the booty from their raids among the poor, but they would also know how to appreciate fine wine (except for the sugarcane workers, of course). As they began taking up more and more space in *Granma,* my perspective on the revolutionary struggle changed, and in those simple times before the ruling class of the entire Southern Cone rose up as one and crushed the bothersome subversive sprouts quite effortlessly to the cry of *"¡Basta!",* I wasn't their only enthusiastic fan. They seemed like an alternative to Che's humorless, no-holds-barred war. To snatch food and weapons from under the very noses of the bourgeoisie, hide out under their very noses, live among them undetected while turning the world upside down—what fun! With such role models even I could harbor some hope of being worthy of life and the revolutionary struggle. I might not be so devoid of imagination and valor after all, I thought, dreaming that I had a modern dance studio in Montevideo where a handsome guerrilla suddenly appeared, wounded, and I hid him in the attic. All Latin America would rush to follow the example of this just, peaceful, and friendly guerrilla organization, and in its vast wake I could happily offer my life and find an alternative to the yearning for suicide that was killing me.

Then the headline that put an end to that fantasy appeared.

TUPAMAROS EXECUTE
CIA AND FBI AGENT DAN MITRIONE
Montevideo, August 10 (PL)—Dan Anthony Mitrione, of the CIA, also an agent of the FBI in the Uruguayan police

force, who was active in Santo Domingo in 1965, and supervised political torture in Brazil and presumably here as well,
was killed today by the Movimiento de Liberación Nacional
(Tupamaros).

The corpse of the U.S. agent was found at 4 A.M., with two
bullet wounds in the head, inside an abandoned Buick in the
Puerto Rico neighborhood of this city.

He was found at four A.M. Had they killed him at three? Had
he been conscious of what was happening? A movie of his death
played against the white walls of my mind at the most insomniac
hours of the night. Three masked men enter the concrete cubicle
where the kidnapped agent has spent ten days tied to the foot of
a bed and tell him, "Let's go, Mitrione, we've been told to release
you." They put him in the trunk of a car, handcuffed, blindfolded, gagged, and he cooperates: If they're going to release
him, it's best to cooperate. If they're going to execute him,
there's nothing to be gained by resisting. He thinks of his wife,
his children, but perhaps not of the bound, blindfolded, and
gagged prisoners whom his own men have carried so many times
into the torture chamber as if they were sides of beef: *maestro*,
where shall we begin? He tries not to think that if they haven't
killed him yet, it is indeed possible that he'll be breakfasting on
café con leche and croissants at the embassy tomorrow, blinking in
the sunlight, wearing clean clothes, laughing awkwardly, surprised by the strange noise coming out of his own throat. He
tries not to think about all that, because he has to concentrate
on the present—to breathe without coughing, despite the dense
exhaust fumes; to avoid cramps by keeping his muscles re-
laxed. Someone stops the car, turns off the motor, comes around
back, and opens the trunk. To his enormous and final shame, the
kidnapped man wets himself, but he immediately realizes that
there's no point in shame, because he hears the click of the trigger. *Are they using a silencer?* he has time to think.

Seeing the scene as if it were projected with neon light, I
thought, *When the bullet penetrated the skull with the speed and heat
of light, did he have time to feel it? Even for a microsecond? How does it
feel to be shot in the head?*

I read the article a second time. So the Tupamaros weren't like Graciela. They didn't listen to Brahms, or if they did, they listened in a way that was contaminated. This meant that in order to be a guerrilla of any kind, in any organization, you had to be prepared not only to die, without the privilege of choosing your own death which I was claiming, but also to kill a bound and gagged prisoner. "Allow me to say, at the risk of appearing ridiculous, that the true revolutionary is motivated by a profound feeling of tenderness . . . ," et cetera. So that was how it was. I read the article, and other words leaped from between the lines, however hard I tried to swat them away as if they were flies. *"Considerando en frío, imparcialmente, / que el hombre es triste, tose y, sin embargo, / se complace en su pecho colorado . . ."* (Considering coldly, impartially, that man is a sad being, and coughs, and nevertheless takes pleasure in his ruddy breast . . .) Why did I have to think of the repulsive, meaty gringo Dan Mitrione and César Vallejo at the same moment? *". . . que lo único que hace es componerse de días; / que es lóbrego mamífero y se peina . . ."* (. . . that all he does is make himself up out of days; that he's a lugubrious mammal and combs his hair . . .) Ashamed before the blind eye that was again watching me, I tried to justify myself. But the fact was that I had failed once more: I commiserated with a criminal, and confused revolution and poetry.

I returned obsessively to my eternal questions: Who was I? Who could I be? Of course I was no one, but it was impossible to live without a dream, an ideal, and now I found that not only couldn't I be like Che, I clearly couldn't be like the Tupamaros, either—not, at least, if I had to face the blubbery, exhausted body of a cruel gringo and join my destiny to his with a bullet.

On Saturday morning Carlos came looking for me; he was the most affectionate member of Galo's inner circle and the one who had intuited that I wasn't happy.

"¿Y qué, mi amor?" he reproached me when I came down to the lobby. "You've forgotten all your friends? We're all worried because we haven't heard a word from you."

Did I ever know how he earned a living? Carlos looked like

a teacher, but though homosexuals were not yet explicitly forbidden to work in education, in practice the ban already existed. I don't think he worked in an office, because every time we planned an excursion, he was the one who had time to stand in line. What suited Carlos best was domestic life: he had gentle ways and a natural tendency to soothe and take care of those around him, and at that point Fidel had not yet passed the law against idleness, which made employment mandatory, so it's possible that he did some form of work in his own home. He was lovely. He had very sweet eyes fringed with long lashes, and a shapely mouth. He wasn't fat, but his cheeks were round, and his torso looked to me at that moment like an inviting pillow. He smelled good. He sat me down on a sofa in the corner of the lobby where he'd been waiting for me and held me for a long time before looking into my face. "You're not doing so well, are you?" I curled up beside him and took my time making up my mind to tell him what little I was capable of saying about what was happening to me. I didn't tell him about Luis the guerrilla or the offense I'd committed against my own body with Eduardo. But I did talk to him about my betrayal of Adrian and our awful conversation the day before, how guilty I felt about having invited him to Havana at the same time I was writing flirtatious letters to Jorge, about the perverse coldness of my heart and the fiasco of Sandy's choreography, the lack of direction at the school, the scandal of the younger kids, and especially the terrible sensation of being unnecessary in the world, devastated by the horror of Vietnam, hopeless as a dancer, useless in the war the Revolution demanded, unfit for any kind of affection, as I was demonstrating not only with Adrian but with Carlos himself, too, and my other friends—I wasn't even capable of keeping in touch with them. And I had nothing to offer them anyway.

"Well, it does a lot for me when you make me laugh, and when you're quiet and you listen."

I explained that these were two very limited and superficial talents and that he didn't know me well enough to understand how brittle and egotistical I really was. I couldn't stop myself from telling him that the reason I'd behaved so badly with Adrian was that I could no longer feel anything: my heart had

dried up like a prune. And, my confession now in full swing, I
added that this was why I wanted to kill myself.

"Really? *Coño,* you're brave, aren't you? What method are you
thinking of using?"

"Well, that's the problem: I don't know. I've given it a lot of
thought, but it's not easy, you know. I thought about an over-
dose, but if I change my mind halfway through, it could be a
problem. Then there's the idea of drowning, but that seems very
hard: you float. It would only work with stones and a jacket. I
also thought about shooting myself, but I don't know how to get
my hands on a pistol." This narration of the ins and outs of my
planning was starting to make me laugh. "The best idea would
be to throw myself in front of a train, but I need a map to see
where the train to Santiago goes by."

"What you really need is a little imagination, because nothing
could be easier than this suicide you're so interested in. All you
have to do is attach the pistol to the doorknob of your room with
the trigger cocked. Then you race down to the beach in a bikini,
pick up a few stones, and put on the jacket, and when you go
back to your room to look for the map of Santiago that you forgot, the pistol will go off when you open the door, and if it
doesn't kill you, at least it will make such a complete mess of the
room that the maid will have to come and clean up, and that way
you'll get to meet her in person and fill in that fundamental gap
in your social network. Now, as to how you're going to get your
hands on a pistol—I haven't the slightest idea."

All we could do was laugh for a while in the lobby of the
Habana Libre. The need to cry was lodged in my chest as if I'd
swallowed a fragmentation grenade, and I refused Carlos's invitation to have dinner at his house or to stand in line at Coppelia. I
would have had to go on carting my hollow shell around, and all
I wanted was to deposit it in bed for a while, though bed was the
place of my terrors.

"All right, but you behave yourself with Adrian, hear me?
He's your boyfriend, and there are always these kinds of separations and reunions between couples. And there's absolutely no
problem about him coming. You can both stay with Galo, who

has lots of room, and between all of us we'll plan your meals and excursions. It would do you good to have some fun."

I went back up to the bile-colored room. I seem to remember that during the hours that followed I kept an exact count of every passing second. I had no reason whatsoever to go out. The only things waiting for me in the street were the sun and the inevitable harassment of some Cuban man. In Tere's or Galo's or Carlos's house I would have to pretend I was alive and had feelings like those of other human beings. *"There are always these kinds of separations and reunions between couples. . . ."* I saw each second forming, slow and big-bellied, and I watched each one drop heavily down.

The truth was that I'd had no doubt at all about the best solution from the first day I woke up with a dry and wrinkled heart: the simplest and quickest thing to do was throw myself off the balcony—the balcony where, out of fear of the void, I never set foot. Eleven floors would be enough to destroy my body almost completely, I thought. There would be no turning back midway, and it wouldn't be that hard for the sanitation workers to take care of things afterward. Tere, who lived around the corner, could be summoned to identify me. It might be unpleasant for her, but she was clearly the person for the job. She didn't love me too much—not as much as my mother did, for example—but I could still consider her my friend.

At that point I would usually think about my mother. Though my atrophied heart felt that she didn't much matter to me, I knew that I was the only fixed point in her hazardous existence. (My mother had navigated across several cities, many jobs, and a few marriages, always somewhat adrift and without ever losing her own suicidal fits of depression or her radiant smile.) I imagined her holding the receiver in silence, listening to the news delivered in Elfrida's tight-lipped syllables. I saw her pounding her head against the wall, howling. I saw her packing her suitcase and going to the Cuban Interests Section to plead for permission to travel to Havana in order to bring her daughter's body home. None of this was acceptable to me. But for a few slow minutes of that dawn, I forgot to think about her. A gelid blue light was starting to come through the curtains, and it was imperative that I do something before the pinks and golds of another Cuban sunrise brought back the unbearable revulsion of life and the torment of another silent, empty Sunday. It was simply a question of joining the nauseating death that had already invaded me with a real death. I urgently needed the consolation of the cool air whistling in my ears during a sweet, vertiginous fall.

I got out of bed, opened the door, walked onto the balcony, and mounted the railing as if it were a horse. The physical difficulty of hanging on to the railing with both hands while I swung the other leg over ("The other left foot, Manolo!") onto the empty side stopped me for a moment, and when I raised my eyes, I saw the rosy light of the sky and the blue splendor of the sea. They brought me neither consolation nor joy, but I remembered that I was still alive and that in order to stop being alive I would have to kill a living human being who was myself. While I was debating this question, still astride the railing, I thought of my mother and the horrible blotch of blood, hair, and guts that I was about to leave eleven floors below. It's a miracle no one saw me. I went back into the room, got into bed, and stayed there, shaking like a castanet.

In Havana, buildings more than four stories high are the exception. In the residential neighborhoods, palm trees still stand out over the rooftops against an expansive horizon. Even Tere, who lived a block away from the hotel in the most urban and relatively modern area of the city, had a wide view of the sea from the two windows of her apartment. I loved the panorama, the sea breeze that was always blowing, the enormous number of ornaments and souvenirs that made her little apartment look like one vast shrine, and the taste of the food she sometimes had enough of to share. If I didn't visit her more often, it was only because she shared this space, where there was no room for privacy, with her husband, a writer whose elaborate gestures and phrases struck me as insincere. After the episode of the befouled dormitories, however, I went over one afternoon to discuss the crisis at the school.

"The atmosphere in Cubanacán is really strange," I mused over a little cup of Tere's coffee, which was as thick as honey. "The jungle, the isolation, even the buildings are kind of disturbing. And doesn't it seem just a little bit sinister to you to have that prison next door that no one ever wants to talk about? Every time I see the watchtower, I get the shivers."

Tere smiled. "I have a sense of foreboding about the school. The kids are at the end of their rope, and even I don't feel I have any right to ask them for more patience. You know that Hilda has called an assembly of the whole school with Mario Hidalgo, for the end of the month. I imagine she decided to take the initiative, before the scandal about the dormitories starts making the rounds and we're called in to account for ourselves. The idea is to outline all the problems and ask for some material improvements, but I'm afraid the discussion isn't going to lead to any kind of agreement."

"Is everyone supposed to come to this meeting?"

"Yes, including you."

The news took me by surprise, as did Tere's warning about the kids' state of mind. Since my move to the Habana Libre, the chats in the cafeteria and the afternoon encounters in the corridors of the school had ended. For several weeks I had forgotten to look at my students, even during class. It was true that the incident of the dormitories had affected all of them, but why, now that I thought about it, was Orlando absent so often, and why did Carmen move through the class in a state of distracted indifference? Really, it was time I looked away from the eye in the mirror and looked around me a bit more.

The meeting of the Escuela Nacional de Danza with the director of the ENA, Mario Hidalgo, took place during the final days of August. It was held in the dance school's unused cafeteria, in a corner of the complex that was separate from the classrooms. Food had never been served here, even when the school first opened; the economic advantage of serving the students from all the different schools in the dining room of the administrative building had always been apparent. The dance-school dining room was only rarely used for meetings. Like the other buildings of the ENA, it was a stark place with an uninhabited air, constructed of brick and concrete, opening to the surrounding jungle by the same concrete latticework used in the dance studios.

Benches and chairs had been brought in for the meeting. Elfrida, Lorna, Tere, and several of the academic professors presided over the event from the front row. Behind them sat most of the students, about forty in all.

When I arrived, Mario Hidalgo was already sitting, facing the others, at a small table next to what once might have been a counter. I quickly took a seat as far away from him as possible, on the low risers made of reinforced concrete that stood against the latticework, where several of the older students and some of the administrative personnel had also taken refuge. Looking around for my own kids, I was surprised by their appearance: when their bodies were covered with clothing, I lost a precious intimacy with them. They too seemed to resist the change from leotards to skirts and pants, and in order to express their status as artists and bohemians, most of them wore their severe Cuban uniforms wrinkled and haphazardly pulled on, which made them look like escapees from some Catholic school in decline. They looked infinitely younger and more innocent, and far more physically fragile, in this garb. I turned my head to look at the former *Granma* expeditionary and current director—so much against his will—of the ENA. By day, he too looked younger, and though in our previous encounter, when I witnessed his conversation with Lorna's husband, he had seemed tense and upset, today he did not. Square-shouldered, wiry, and with a little potbelly, like someone once in excellent physical condition who has quickly gotten out of shape, the director also seemed a bit more of a bureaucrat than on the night I first met him. He was flanked by two assistants and spoke to them in a low voice as he replaced the papers he had been selecting and reviewing from a heap of documents back in a file folder.

"Let's get started," he ordered. He took a pen and a couple of pencils from his pocket and placed them carefully alongside the folder. "This is a session of criticism and self-criticism, and I now declare it open." He then rose a little in his chair, moved his right hand to his lower back, and from some point between belt and shirt extracted a heavy object, which barely fit into his hand, and placed it in front of him on the table. A pistol. Immediately he had my total, rapt attention, though he hadn't raised his voice. No one breathed a whisper, no one raised a hand. Mario Hidalgo looked around.

"Who wants to begin?"

For years, whenever I told this story, I emphasized the brazenly intimidating nature of the director's action: at the beginning of a session of criticism and self-criticism he took out a weapon and placed it on the table in front of him. Today I'm certain that I misinterpreted Mario Hidalgo. It was the first time I'd seen a pistol up close and out of its holster (there was no abundance of weaponry in Havana), and therefore, inevitably, the moment had to be unforgettable. I was sure the director had deliberately intended to provoke the panic that overwhelmed me, because I couldn't imagine any other reason for someone to want to set a pistol down on a table. I had no inkling of the possibility that the former baker lived in a state of permanent nostalgia for the days of his military glory and that, like many ex-combatants, he carried a weapon the way a child carries a teddy bear. He took it out of its holster because it was uncomfortable when he was sitting down, and he placed it on the table not for the students to see, but so that he himself could contemplate it. All of which doesn't change the fundamental equation of that meeting: the director was seated in front of the students in a country where any kind of protest and most kinds of criticism were seen as subversive, and he was the one with the gun.

Elfrida began to speak. Despite all its achievements, the school was in crisis, she said, and after taking some minutes to narrate the long and beautiful partnership between dance and revolution, she came down to earth on some concrete points. There wasn't enough money in the budget, there weren't enough teachers, and in the spirit of self-criticism, it had to be acknowledged that there was also a lack of dedication and commitment on the part of the younger students.

"Forgive me, Elfrida, I believe that if we're going to try and make this a useful meeting, we have to speak sincerely. The truth is, I don't think the problem here is a simple lack of money or of teachers."

Scandalized, we all turned to look at Roberto, the black student with Yoruban features, who was now standing on the risers as calmly as if he were next to a chalkboard explaining a math problem.

"I acknowledge your point about the lack of motivation in the student body, but I ask you to reflect a little on the causes for that, and to reflect sincerely. The school is in a bad way. Or rather, it's never been good, but lately it's worse. The point is that we can go on in the same way, or we can try to make this meeting serve some purpose."

"I want to bring up a question, too." This time it was José talking. "The Escuela Nacional de Danza is supposed to be an institution that trains dancers in order to generate a current of modern dance in Cuba. But we fifth-year students, who are about to graduate, we aren't going to leave here with anything like a professional level of skill. So if we're going to discuss the students' lack of motivation, I want to discuss the school's lack of orientation and failure to achieve its objectives as well."

Faced with the two boys' daring and Mario Hidalgo's pistol, I felt, for the first time in the four months I had spent in Cuba, real physical fear. I turned to look at the other professors and students who were turning to look at José and Roberto with their mouths open, clutching the edges of the benches. I know my memory is betraying me when I see an image of Elfrida with her hair standing straight up, but I'm also sure that her students' outbursts left our director strangling with rage and fear—the fear of losing her position, among other things. Mario Hidalgo, leaning back in his chair, looked from the speakers to Elfrida and from Elfrida back to Roberto and José, who were the only ones who seemed calm amid the general state of shock. I'm quite certain that the two boys hadn't discussed anything beforehand, had not arrived at the meeting with any kind of plan, and even at that point did not understand the seriousness of what they had just initiated.

"*Coño,* these artists really are something else!" exclaimed the ENA director, with a little smile of incredulity. "Tell me, what kind of grades are you getting?" he asked, signaling with his chin toward Roberto.

"A's."

"And I—" José interjected.

"I wasn't asking you," Mario Hidalgo cut him off. "So, let's see now," he went on, still addressing Roberto. "The Revolution rescued you from being a dockworker like the rest of your family, gave you a home, food, education, and a career—maybe not the most honorable career, but it's the one you chose—and even after all that you still feel you have the right to complain?"

"Roberto isn't complaining!" Antonia was as upright as a torch, her face pale, her arms pressed tightly against her torso, dangerously indignant. "*Compañero,* no one here has complained! What José and Roberto have said is only the truth, and all of us agree with them. If you don't believe me, you can call for a vote. This problem can't be resolved by attacking just one of us. What you see here, *compañero,* is disagreement with the way this school has been managed."

"And with the level of training we've received!" shouted another student, Leonor.

"Be quiet!" Elfrida shouted in turn.

"Order!" shouted Mario Hidalgo, dealing the table in front of him a blow that echoed through the dining hall.

Please don't let him pick up the pistol, I prayed.

When the tumult had died down, José, Roberto, and Antonia were still standing. The director of the school looked slowly around him and sat down. "So, the dance students think they know how to play with fire," he said, shaking his head. "It seems to me that they're not quite ready for it yet, but all right, we'll find out about that as we go along. In the first place, we're not here to discuss whether the study program is good or bad or whether you're all headed for failure because you haven't learned to dance. The directors of the school are the only ones who have the authority to discuss the study program, and if I don't intrude on the work of *compañeras* Elfrida and Lorna, not for one minute am I going to allow the students to claim that right for themselves. What we can go over here is whether there is some way of expanding the budget a little, within the very limited means of the Revolution—which strikes you as having taken such poor care of you—so that we can invite some teachers with a more revolutionary spirit and a higher level of skill than those we've found up to now. We can discuss whether our current workforce can begin producing at a level that is closer to its full capacity. We can try to improve the objective conditions of your training a little: repair the floors, get some better-quality dance clothes, and so on—I don't know much about such things. And also—why not?—we can discuss whether the ENA can afford to risk its prestige by allowing students who, as they themselves acknowledge, have not achieved the necessary level of skill, to graduate."

"Excuse me, *compañero*, but what you've just said sounds like a threat," Antonia, still standing, said in a constricted voice.

"*Compañero, compañero*"—Efrida was standing up too now, anxious—"it seems to me that people are getting a little carried away."

"I'm not carried away, Elfrida," the ENA director interrupted.

"No, you may not be, but I think that in general the tone of this assembly isn't what any of us would want for it. I think we can all agree that we do want what is best for the school, and perhaps we can all acknowledge some things that haven't worked, and other things we still haven't tried to achieve. It seems to me that all these things can be discussed calmly, can't they?" Roberto, José, and Antonia sat down. Mario Hidalgo propped his elbows on the table.

"We could even," Elfrida proposed, "allow the students to make concrete proposals, each one, and in order, because there is one thing that has always been true in this school, *compañero*." Poor Elfrida was talking with such conviction and emphasis now that her broad cheeks were trembling. "There's one thing that is the pride of the school and a source of personal pride for me, and that is that no one has ever been denied the right to freely express his personal opinion, whatever that might be."

And it was true, at least, that while the students might be afraid of Elfrida's tantrums, they didn't fear reprisals or threats. Now she seemed to have managed to calm everyone down. Mario Hidalgo immediately approved Elfrida's suggestion and began taking notes on what the kids, relieved to be back in smooth waters, were suggesting as they raised their hands one by one and waited very seriously for the director to call on them. Pilar wanted better dance clothes, Carmen wanted a better diet, and when Manolo said it would be good to have mirrors in the dance studios, Elfrida pressed her lips together tightly but said nothing.

"I want to propose something different," said Orlando. In the earlier tumult I hadn't seen him, and I hadn't noticed him much in our recent classes either, he'd been so subdued. But now he was standing, the muscles in his face contracted as usual, speaking in great bursts and taking deep breaths between one declaration and the next. "We have a lot of problems: the academic program is extremely poor, so poor that if we injure a knee tomorrow and can't go on dancing, we'll have to look for work in the cane fields or on a construction site, because we don't have the education to do anything more. In math and history I don't know even the most basic facts." He spoke with the same urgent, ponderous intensity that kept him from having friends or being at ease with himself, and now that I think about his words, I see that his criticism, logical, well expressed, and shared by the entire student body, had to fall on Mario Hidalgo's ears—and, of course, on Elfrida's—as a terrible offense. Those of us who were seated on the risers at the back of the room—José, Roberto, Hilda, some academic professors, and I—heard him and trembled.

"Moreover," he went on implacably, as if he hadn't said enough already, "moreover, no choreographers of any kind, either good or bad, have ever come here, and the result is that we have no repertory: we have nothing to dance." Horrified, I watched as my student repeated words I now remembered uttering so carelessly weeks before. I'd given no thought to the consequences of making that sort of comment in front of a group of kids who had no way of changing their situation. "Without dancing, without ever appearing on a stage," Orlando continued, paraphrasing me once more, "we can learn everything except how to be dancers. But the problem that most concerns me after four years in this School of Modern Dance is that they can't even teach me that technique here." He took a deep breath, and all of us waited in silence for him to continue knotting the rope around his neck.

"What I want to bring up is that as long as this school is not in a position to give us adequate training"—once again he was repeating my words—"at least we should be given a way of studying ballet. That's not what I want to study, I want to study and perform modern dance, but with ballet classes we could at least count on having that skill when we graduate." He fell silent as if he'd suddenly run out of ammunition, and without bringing his speech to a close or taking his eyes off the director, he sat down.

Who was going to feel compassion for Orlando? Not Elfrida, whom he had just mortally offended. Certainly not Mario Hidalgo. Not the other students either, who were angry because Orlando, with permission from no one, had just brought them back to the very brink of conflagration.

For just a moment, though, I thought my student might be safe and that his criticism had gone so far beyond what Mario Hidalgo was capable of understanding about dance that he wouldn't even notice it. The director appeared calm.

"All right, let's see," he began. "*Coño* . . . what kind of people are these people that I'm supposed to be leading here?" He laughed. "So: we haven't been able to give you adequate training. So: the sacrifices of an entire nation to give you this privilege, simply because Fidel doesn't have the heart to deny you artists anything, all the expense, the whole construction of this school just for you, is worth a cat's turd—"

"No one said that, *compañero,*" interrupted Antonia once more.

"*Compañera,* with all due respect, I believe I'm the one who's speaking right now," Mario Hidalgo fired at her. "Now, of course, if you would like to go on talking . . ."

Antonia sat down.

"So," the director went on, with a sweeping gesture of his arm to indicate the whole school, "all this seems inadequate to you. Well. All right: I know artists are proud, and in this position it is my role to respect that i-di-o-syn-cra-sy." He enunciated each syllable with careful disdain. "But I have other reasons to be proud. It makes me proud, for example, that I fought in the ranks of this Revolution from its beginning and risked my life for it—and for you, ultimately, so that you can now enjoy the luxury of airing your litany of complaints. It fills me with pride to be a son of the people, ignorant perhaps, crude perhaps, but a revolutionary. Because I might not know much about music or dance or the marvelous 'techniques' of ballet, but unlike certain other people, I can boast that in my family"—he thrust his index finger hard against his chest—"in my family, which is ignorant, poor, and humble, we don't have a single *gusano.* Do you hear me? Not a single one. I'm no *comemierda.* And now I've had to come here and listen to the complaints of an artist who says that we're not giving him enough. And I'm telling you that if you don't like what the Revolution can give you, you can just leave for Miami right now and join all your *gusano* relatives who are lining their pockets with dollars over there. Let's see if they're prepared to give up a few of those bills so the boy can have the pleasure of studying all that fancy prancing he's so attracted to."

"*Compañero,* I think you're going too far." Roberto was the one standing up again now, while Mario Hidalgo turned a freezing gaze on him. "I'm not necessarily going to defend what some of us have said here. But if you're going to refute him, you can do so on other grounds. Because no one here is free of the accusation you've just made. I do have relatives in Miami." ("So do I!" "Me too," the others shouted.) "We all have relatives in Miami, and no one can be judged for that."

"But that's precisely what I'm telling you," Mario Hidalgo answered. "That's just it. No one can reproach me for my lack of revolutionary attitude or for my family, because I have no *gusanos* among my relatives, nor have I ever in my life come out in defense of a *pato*—"

Orlando let out a sob that could be heard across the cafeteria, and pushing blindly past his fellow students, he ran out of the room.

In the uproar that ensued I didn't catch Roberto's answer. I ran out too after Orlando and found him on the brick path, convulsed with tears. I hugged him, trying to contain his sobs with my arms, wiping away the tears and mucus that were running down his skull-like face. Someone tugged at me. It was Hilda.

"*Compañera,*" she said in a very low voice. "*Compañerita,* you shouldn't be seen here. Come back to the meeting. Orlando, tell her to go back inside." And Orlando went off running and stumbling down the path, while Hilda pulled at my arm and led me back into the cafeteria.

I had a dream. The world war had ended. The world was an endless desert of smoking slag and pulverized glass. For some reason I had survived and needed Adrian. How could I find him in that void? Wandering among the dead, I reached a shore where desert ended and sea began. There I waited in anguish. Miraculously, Adrian found me and put his arms around me. But what good did it do us to be together in a lifeless world?

As we were walking along a beach populated only by empty cans and disemboweled furniture, I woke up, overwhelmed with a choking desire for his company, his hands, his green gaze. I ran down to the phone booths, where the operators were only just arriving. I begged them to put a call through for me immediately to New York. I waited the eternal, costly minutes it took for someone to go up to Adrian's room, wake him up, and bring him down to the telephone at the reception desk in our hotel. His sleepy voice bathed me in warmth.

"Come to Havana," I pleaded.

"I can't," he answered. "They didn't let me join the Venceremos Brigade."

Somehow I understood that he hadn't been alone in bed when the receptionist went upstairs to wake him.

He asked me if I wanted him to find an apartment where we could live together, and I told him I did.

I'm ashamed that I don't remember how the assembly ended or whether I discussed what happened with the students afterward. I suspect that I went looking for Orlando, without knowing how to guide or console him, and that I didn't even bring up the subject with the others. I deduce the latter fact, because if we had talked about the assembly, what happened next wouldn't have come as such a surprise.

What I do remember is that after the meeting my spirits sud-

denly improved, as if rage had had an invigorating effect on me.
I recovered my feelings, I talked to Adrian, and I returned to my
classes with a new sense of commitment that bound me to the
students. I abandoned Sandy's dance once and for all, and thought
about creating a choreography of my own. I'd never attempted
it, but maybe now was the time. It would have to be something
very simple. I would never choreograph a revolutionary dance,
but I could make a dance with music, with a certain structure,
symmetry, and theatricality. Perhaps a small composition full of
big jumps for the boys, and then another with an adagio and a lot
of arm work for the girls. Music? I wouldn't be silly enough
to attempt something with an Afro-Cuban rhythm—I didn't
intend to betray myself once again, and exoticism didn't interest
me. But something set to strong, irresistible, danceable, enjoy-
able, happy music—a waltz! Waltzes have always transported
me with a yearning to ride their waves, obey their spins and
surges with my body, dance. I had a cassette of Johann Strauss
waltzes with me. I thought *Tales from the Vienna Woods* was the
richest in nuance and dynamic changes. *Now the kids are finally
going to realize that I'm completely incompetent,* I thought when faced
with the prospect of teaching them the steps I was sketching out,
but I invited them to rehearse with me anyway. In the Cunningham technique class I began working on the sequences I had
invented—my first stammering attempts to design movement
on other bodies.

In the Graham class we'd been stuck for a number of days on
an exercise in the floor sequence: the pleatings. It was hard even
to translate the name and very hard for the kids to understand it.
The pleatings begin with the dancer lying faceup on the floor,
legs together, arms glued to the torso. In the first impulse, the
torso contracts and the head falls back, as if in ecstasy, and while
the spine resists the impulse, the shoulders and knees rise as if a
wire were pulling them toward the ceiling. Finally, after resisting until the last moment, the torso comes up as well, until
everyone is seated with torso turned and legs folded to one side.
The students were indisputably working with much greater ab-
dominal strength and could now easily repeat this movement,
which had initially seemed impossible to them. But they didn't

understand it. I tried all possible explanations. It's the same position in which Bellini painted Saint Teresa receiving the Ecstasy, I
told them. It's as if a ray of sunlight were penetrating your navel,
which is a seed, and pinning your torso down, while your arms
and legs sprout like saplings from the earth. It's as if a lover were
scooping you up in his arms from the ground, it's as if a light
were born in your torso, I explained. We did it again, and the
movement remained lifeless. I turned to Vallejo.

"It's like this poem," I told them, citing it from memory and
getting a lot of it wrong.

> Al fin de la batalla,
> y muerto el combatiente, vino hacia él un
> 　　　　　　　　　　　　　　　　hombre
> y le dijo: "¡No mueras, te amo tanto!"
> Pero el cadáver ¡ay! siguió muriendo.
>
> Se le acercaron dos y repitiéronle . . .
>
> Acudieron a él veinte, cien, mil, quinientos
> 　　　　　　　　　　　　　　　　mil . . .
>
> Le rodearon millones de individuos . . .
>
> Entonces todos los hombres de la tierra
> le rodearon; les vio el cadáver triste,
> 　　　　　　　　　　　　　　　　emocionado;
> incorporóse lentamente,
> abrazó al primer hombre; echóse a andar . . .

> When the battle was over,
> And the warrior was dead, a man came to him
> And said: "I love you so! Don't die!"
> But ah, the corpse continued dying.
> Two men approached, and repeated the words . . .
> Twenty, a hundred, a thousand, fifty thousand came . . .
> Millions of individuals surrounded him . . .
> Then all the men on earth

Were around him: the corpse saw them there. Sad, touched,
Slowly he arose,
Embraced the first one, started walking . . .

The fact is that we were all adolescents, or almost, unafraid of being thought pretentious, and still capable of great emotion and great faith. They listened to Vallejo's poem, I asked them to go through the exercise again, and it was as if a ray of light were pinning their torsos to the earth while their arms and legs rose like young shoots, as if a lover were scooping them up in his arms from the ground, as if a light were being born in their torsos.

NINE

Art and Revolution

I wrote a letter.

Hello Jorge,

Sorry I haven't answered your postcards and letters before now, but I hadn't heard of anyone who could take an envelope to you. I still don't know of anyone, but it's nighttime and I'm thinking about you. Is it still raining in Mexico City? I like to imagine you reading this letter in some café during a cloudburst, smoking your awful Delicados (I'm glad I'm not there to smell them), and watching night descend through the dark raindrops. You'll forgive my terrible spelling. (No, you won't, but you'll just have to put up with it.)

I can't understand why you don't feel like coming to Cuba. You missed carnival. (I know you don't like to dance, but I do, and you could have watched me.) The little I saw of it was unforgettable: intense, exotic, and a little scary. (Most frightening of all are the Cuban men, sons-of-bitches, who simply cannot leave a woman alone in the street, and especially not at night during carnival. (How can it be that Mexicans seem like gentlemen by comparison? (See? if you'd been here, I would have had an escort and could have enjoyed carnival more. (This isn't a complaint; it's just that I don't understand why you haven't put in an appearance over here, since you like Cuba so much and would have no problem getting a visa.))))

Anyway, what I liked about carnival, despite the macho Cuban sons-of-bitches, was seeing something going on in the street that had to do with dance, that had deep roots and that was, at the same time, completely spontaneous. Don't imagine that's easy here. I read Frantz Fanon, as you recommended, and René Depestre too, and I understand what you meant about an art that's not nationalist but national, not Revolutionary but revolutionary. Maybe it exists in painting (I

haven't been fascinated by what I've seen, but you know that's some-
thing I don't know much about) and Cuban cinema does seem to be
going in that direction, but literature is, as they say here, maomeno
(with Mao there's menos*), and I don't hesitate for one second to tell*
you that up to this point Cuban dance has been a failure.

Or at least modern dance. I've been to Ballet Nacional per-
formances—Alicia Alonso's company—several times, and her new
stagings of the classics are beautiful. I saw a delightful Fille mal
gardée. *(She wasn't dancing it, fortunately: she's blinder every day.*
(My friends say she's guided by flashlights that signal to her from off-
stage, and in spite of that she lost track of where she was one day and
danced the whole final act of Giselle *with her back to the audience.*
(Heroic, no? and ridiculous (though the next thing I was going to
tell you is that I saw her in Giselle *(facing the audience) and*
she's absolutely overwhelming. I don't think there's ever been a better
Giselle.*)))) And a* Sylphides *that made you stand up and stamp*
your feet and clap and scream because it was so perfect. (An odd
thing: it didn't matter that the sylphides, like all good Cuban
women, had curvaceous, bouncy behinds.) But do note that we're not
exactly talking about a national, or revolutionary, art. And it's best
*not to say a word about the "*moderrrno*" repertory because it's just*
the way it sounds. (What means moderrrno? *Everyone in leotards*
and tights, without tutus or fancy vests, and lots of sex and lots of
guilt.)

But modern dance! If you were here you'd have gone with me, and
then I wouldn't have to be battling this North Korean pencil and the
enormous difficulty of conveying the magnitude of the failure to you
right now, but here goes . . . We went to the Plaza de la Catedral
(beautiful, beautiful, beautiful) to an outdoor performance by the
Conjunto, which is the only modern dance group here, and to prove
I'm not as wicked as you think, I'll tell you that I stayed until the
end of the evening purely out of respect for the dancers, though the
rest of the audience made no such display of solidarity and there
weren't many of us left by the time it was over. The piece was called
Medea and the Slave Traders, *and I don't think I need to tell you*
much more about it than that, but I can't resist: Jason whipped the
slaves imperialistically, and the slaves writhed on the ground anti-
imperialistically, and Medea was a metaphor for corrupt—though

exploited—Cuban colonial society. And no one knew how to point their feet properly.

Enough. When I think of the dancers struggling against the poor nutrition and the total lack of respect and the many hours spent waiting for the guagua after rehearsal, I feel unjust. Forgive me. I was going to say something different. I was going to say that I don't know what to do with my life, because I don't believe it's possible to make revolutionary dance (or at least, I'm not the least bit interested in making revolutionary dance; what interests me is dance, period), and the thought of having to be like Che fills me with deathly horror, and never could I ever tolerate trying to be like Tania la Guerrillera even for one second (I've seen photos of her, taken here and in East Germany and before she died in the jungle with Che: Did you know she was German? And that she liked to wear a beret? And that she played the accordion while wearing the beret?), and then sometimes I think that the best thing I could do would be to erase myself from this map once and for all.

Jorge, tell me what I should do. Mario Hidalgo called a meeting the other day in which he accused one of my students—the most fragile one—of being a homosexual in front of the whole school, and said all the others were gusanos *or the relatives of* gusanos, *which amounts to the same thing, and that this school is a madhouse. I need to understand, so I'll ask you again: Can it be that art, as I have understood it and have tried to live it, has no hope within the Revolution, and that there is no hope for me within the Revolution, and that art is worthless? Answer me, please.*

The night of September 5 a spectacular piece of news was announced: for the first time in Latin American history, a socialist had become a democratically elected head of state. Salvador Allende was the new president-elect of Chile. Thinking of all that his friend Manuel, the enthusiastic Chilean doctor, had told me about him, I pondered the importance of this outcome. Manuel was right: the peoples of the world had demonstrated that when they were given the opportunity for a truly free election, they would opt for socialism. It was nothing less than a peaceful revolution. "Undoubtedly, the future will be socialist!"

Galo, ever prudent, noted that at last a door was opening for the Cuban Revolution in the retaining wall erected by the United States, which had seen to it that all Latin American countries except Mexico cut off relations with Cuba. Fidel would finally have a place to travel within the hemisphere, a country to buy from, sell to, and mutually support and encourage. From that perspective alone, this was no small achievement, and the Comandante did not conceal his joy. The guests of the Habana Libre, which was filled with *Internacionalistas* who clung to every word of the news that night, were congratulating and embracing one another in the lobby, the bar, and even the elevator. Unhindered by any *compañero* from the Ministry of the Interior, I went up to the room of some other friends of Allende's—the two Chileans who were in charge of the ENA's theater school. They both had a bottle of Bulgarian wine in each hand and another already warming their souls, and at the end of that long day of expectation and celebration, they sang, toppled onto their beds, stood up roaring with laughter, rebounded off the wall, and then fell into armchairs, drunk with happiness. They gloried in their friend's triumph, but as Chileans they also took a different view of the experiment of the Unidad Popular, the coalition of leftist parties that had managed, it was said, to achieve socialism by electoral means. For them, this victory opened up alternatives to the continent's radical left. If Allende came to power and was allowed to govern and his example was followed by others, perhaps the strategy of armed struggle would lose its validity or at least its urgency. It would be the start of a more modern era for Latin American civil society, in which politics would finally replace violence. The television and *Granma* were filled with images of Allende, the socialist doctor now become president.

He was the perfect opposite of Fidel, starting with the fact that everyone called him by his last name, which implied a less impassioned relationship between electors and elected than the tempestuous mysticism that united the *fidelistas* with their hero. Fidel had a prophet's beard and wore a military uniform, declaring

himself to be in a state of perpetual war. Allende sported a bourgeois mustache, glasses, and the ethnic garb of all Chilean men: a
tie, a corduroy jacket with patches at the elbows, and a wool vest
that seemed to have been born from between his mother's knit-
ting needles. (He looked very elegant in his pajamas too, and he
sprayed on cologne before going to bed, a good-looking Chilean
woman who was at the theater people's party smugly noted;
unlike Fidel's, Allende's private life was not so private.) Fidel was
impetuous and demanded absolute loyalty. The Chilean was a
kindly fellow, everyone's uncle: you could raise a glass with him
at the corner café and talk about any problem. He could even
have a drink with his political opponents, though I would have
to leave Cuba to discover that these existed—all we ever saw in
the photos in *Granma* was Allende surrounded by devoted multitudes, acclaimed and adored by all Chileans. I don't remember
reading a single article that explained that the Unidad Popular
was a fragile coalition of six parties, in which a dissident faction
of the Partido Radical had secured the votes required to bring
Allende to victory with 36 percent of the vote—barely sixteen
thousand more votes than were obtained by the Christian Demo-
crat candidate. What were the 62 percent of voters who had not
opted for the socialist candidate thinking? And what about those
who hadn't voted for anyone? *Granma* was not interested in that
question: Allende had triumphed, and in revolutionary Cuba, a
triumph was not a triumph if it was not absolute.

I'm not sure if the spirit of victory that was in the air at that
point had some influence on my destiny, but when I leaned over
the reception desk at the Hotel Nacional to ask for the ump-
teenth time in fifteen days whether they had any rooms available,
the man on the other side unexpectedly told me that they did
and that I could even move in that very afternoon if I wanted.
The little dance of happiness I improvised made the receptionist and his co-workers laugh. After the black episode on the balcony, getting out of the Habana Libre had become an obsession.
Where could I go that would help me survive?

My only answer was the Nacional. I was madly enamored of
this hotel, which, with its glamorous Hollywood colonial architecture and its spacious gardens overlooking the Malecón and

the sea beyond, exuded an aura of the past. Everyone had said it would be impossible to get a room there: an office of the Ministry of the Interior decided which guests could stay in which hotel, and the Nacional's guest list consisted almost exclusively of honeymooners and visiting Soviets. This information did not cure me of my obsession, but I couldn't bring myself to ask Lorna Burdsall for yet another favor; for no apparent reason, relations between us had chilled after the general meeting at the school. I didn't know anyone else with the influence to help me obtain the room I was yearning for, and I couldn't think of any better way of getting it than spending my spare time importuning the Nacional's front desk staff. On my way back from Cubanacán every afternoon, instead of getting off the *guagua* at the stop next to Coppelia, I went on to the end of Rampa and repeated the same plea each time at the hotel's reception desk: my dream was to spend even just one night in this marvelous hotel, but I had no one to send my transfer application to. It wasn't that I had the slightest intention of operating *por la libre*—outside of the appropriate channels—but wouldn't it be possible for the *compañeros* in the hotel administration to intercede with the *compañeros* at the Interior Ministry on my behalf? When they gave me the good news, I was almost as dizzy with my triumph as my Chilean friends were with Allende's.

How many weeks would I be staying? asked the *compañero* at the reception desk. I had no way of knowing. My contract at Cubanacán would end in December, and I had decided many weeks earlier not to renew it, especially now that I had agreed to live with Adrian and he was looking for an apartment for us. Nevertheless, working with my students was fully occupying my attention again, I was in the middle of my first attempt at creating a dance, and now that I had managed to escape from the Habana Libre, I glimpsed for the first time in long months the possibility of happiness. I decided to think of nothing but the present moment: I had to make the move now. "I won't be long; I'm going for my luggage. And don't give that room to anyone else while I'm gone!" I begged the man at the reception desk. I ran up Rampa and waited impatiently for the elevator that would take me, for the last time, to the hateful bile-colored room.

At the Hotel Nacional many things that would have been un-thinkable in my former domicile became possible. I could stroll through a vast garden whose farthest limits, at the Malecón's breakwater, were banks of stones and sand. I could greet the waves, watch the sea, feel the wind in my hair, and then throw myself down on a lounge chair next to the swimming pool and ask for a lemonade. There were lemons. On weekends I could invite someone—Cuban or foreigner, it didn't matter—to share the swimming pool and the lemonade. I could invite that same peson to share my room itself, and the successors to Eduardo the guerrilla who passed through there did not find their way barred by any flunky from Minint, the Interior Ministry, or mention the possibility that a microphone might be coquett-ishly concealed next to the lamp that hung from the high ceiling. My mood became festive: I invited Tere to the swim-ming pool, strolled through the gardens with Carlos and Boris, and insisted—unsuccessfully—that my students visit my new domain, so that I could brag about the cool tile floors and the wicker chairs. Even Eduardo's successors no longer struck me as quite so odious. I'm startled by how strong my nostalgia still is for that room and the lobby's elaborate mahogany furniture, because I wouldn't go so far as to say that I was happy in that place—unless the breath of freedom that lifts a bird into the air when its cage door opens is the most intense form of happiness.

And to think that all this highly frivolous intoxication, this reconciliation with the tropics and the routine of everyday life in Cuba, this fizzy new sensation, at last, of living through a truly exotic adventure, after so much isolation and loneliness, was owed to the stolid Soviets! For it was true that the Hotel Nacional was reserved almost exclusively for the *tovarich* and Cuban honeymooners. And if there were no microphones over the bed and there was clean chlorinated water in the pool and lemonade that arrived promptly at your lounge chair on the tray of an obsequious waiter—not to mention the groaning buffet table that the hotel's baronial restaurant set out—it was because *compañero* Leonid Brezhnev, president of all the Russians, would certainly not have enjoyed learning that Cuba had failed to offer his compatriots the very best of its Revolution.

Thousands, perhaps tens of thousands, of advisers had been placed on the island by the Soviet Union and the member countries of the socialist bloc. They supervised the army and the operations of the Minint. They revised the five-year plans for economic development and made recommendations as to whether each line item should be supported with more rubles. The forms of the new proletarian architecture, built out of modular units rather than by the traditional Cuban techniques, now considered individualist, were dictated by the Russians. Czechs and Poles advised the creators of cartoons for children. Bulgarians and Hungarians supervised the production of canned products and preserves. When the Cubans asked for tractors, someone in Moscow decided that what they needed were snowplows instead, and sent snowplows. When the Revolution wanted to promote uprisings in other countries in Africa and Latin America, Brezhnev ordered Cuba to hold back. When Fidel wanted to keep the atomic missiles that Nikita Khrushchev had asked to place on Cuban territory, Khrushchev, now having reached an agreement with Kennedy, took them back again. In all aspects of Cuban economic and military activity, the Soviets had the last word.

"They're grabby and rude! And they don't use deodorant," I told Galo, setting down a few shriveled oranges, six cans of Romanian plums, and two packs of Populares unfiltered cigarettes on his kitchen table. I was just back from my first excursion to the special store for foreigners whose doors had been opened to me by the technician's ID card that the Minint had finally issued. I told Galo that it was a great triumph just to reach the bin where the only available fresh fruit was heaped, for the path was barred by a quivering wall of flesh: two rows of fat women vociferating in Russian and trying to elbow past one another, voluminous bosom against ample buttock. In minutes they had exhausted the entire stock of oranges, except for the pathetic specimens I was now offering Galo. "And it's certainly not as if they were starving to death."

"Leave them alone, you," Galo advised. "Most of those people had to survive the terrible famine of the Russian Revolution. And the Second World War. A person who has hunted rats in

order to give her family something to eat has every right in the
world to do battle for some oranges. Or more to the point: someone like you is never going to beat those women to the oranges.
In any case, you've brought us inconceivable luxuries. You didn't
happen to run across a nice piece of sirloin while you were in
there, did you?"

"There were bones for soup and an indecipherable cut of meat,
but only for people who are authorized for home cooking. My
card is for a hotel guest."

In the evenings, seated in the dining room of the Nacional, I
couldn't stop watching the Russians. Never mind what Galo said
about famines and the siege of Leningrad, I felt no pity for any of
them: they were pasty-white, fat, loud, and badly dressed. They
broke into the line at the buffet table in their desire to be first
to reach the platter of croquettes and eggs *à la russe* and the
omnipresent salad made of vegetables with mayonnaise; they
removed competitors from around the bread basket with a jab of
the elbow; they grabbed heaps of the little squares of margarine
and then left them squashed between the remains of their meal
and the ashes from the cigarettes they stubbed out on their dinner plates. They never said excuse me or thank you. Where were
the stylized, neurotic Russians with dark burning gazes whom
Dostoyesvsky had taught me to imagine? In what country did
Chekhov's exquisite repressed creatures live, if not Russia? Of
course that was Russia and this was the Soviet Union, where self-
repression was no longer practiced, I thought, watching them
shout at each other from opposite ends of the lobby in what
appeared to be a mortal argument but may in fact have been no
more than a quick agreement: "See you at the pool in fifteen
minutes! *Kharasho.* Bring me a towel." Fuming, griping, pushing, they never even glanced at the lounge chairs where the rest
of us were stretched out. I would have liked to ask them what
they thought about Cubans, Cuba, their own work, and this
tropical Revolution. I would have liked to hear them tell me that
I was misjudging them—that it wasn't true that they thought
Cubans were lazy, ignorant, unreliable, and black. That they
were grateful for the opportunity to serve.

"Galo, don't you hate them? Come on, aren't they even harder to take than the gringos?"

"It's different. It's easier to hate a Yankee. The *tovarich* are like oxen; you can't feel much antipathy toward them."

Pablo jumped up. "That's not true, *chico*." It was the first time I'd seen him talk back to Galo. "You'll say anything just to be the first to the punch line. The Soviets are here to help. They live their own separate lives and don't bother anyone, and it's stupid to make fun of them."

"Control yourself, *caramba*!" Galo spat back. "I know you're grateful to the Russians for the scholarship"—Pablo had studied economics in the Soviet Union—"but they haven't asked you to groom the hair on their balls for them in return, have they?"

"*¡Mierda!*" Pablo exploded. "Why does everyone have to control himself except you? As if you were the perfect revolutionary! As if the reactionaries were in Moscow! You're the individualist!" Spraying saliva in every direction, Pablo was tripping over his own words. "You're willful and egotistical, and you call it idealism. You want to tell me that the cold war doesn't exist? That the Yankees aren't trying to crush socialism all over the world? But you want money to be abolished tomorrow and complete creative freedom for every little faggot asshole running around with dreams of being the next Mr. Andrew Warhol. You want Cuba to go right ahead and stir up trouble in Venezuela or Guatemala, and the hell with what the Soviet Union thinks. And if the Yankees drop the bomb, then what? That's not *your* problem, is it? As long as your little poetic notions of socialism aren't disturbed, everyone else can just get fried in radiation."

"Well, well, well." Galo turned to me with a crooked smile. "Our sweet child bares his fangs at last. But maybe he doesn't really care about my oh-so-slightly critical view of our heroic Soviet comrades. Maybe he wants to let the Inquisition loose on me for reasons that have more to do with my own unforgivable sins. Or no, dear boy?"

"Oh, go fuck yourself," Pablo said in disgust.

Playing air violin, Galo crooned "Ochi Chornya" in improvised Russian.

Pablo crossed his arms and turned his back on us, his shoulders rigid.

"Pablo, all I'm questioning is the price we have to pay," Galo said after a minute. "But I'm not denying that tens of thousands of Cubans have Moscow to thank for their professional training— doctors, engineers, explosives experts, film editors—even economists," he added with a hopeful smile for his boyfriend. "That was a joke, Pablo."

Galo sighed. "Maybe I should worry more about things closer to home. But I don't really care whether the Russians are rude or don't use deodorant. They live in their special areas, they shop at special stores, and when their contract expires, they leave. Frankly, I hardly ever see them.

"The real problem is different, and we don't like to touch it. The guerrillas, even the most well-educated among them, weren't what you might call art lovers, and if no one's listening, I'll include Fidel in that. We're talking about people who, like most Cubans, have a deep distrust of artists and intellectuals. But the difference between my next-door neighbor and Raúl Castro or Osmany Cienfuegos is that those two are in power, and they can justify their fear of culture by saying that prerevolutionary Cuban art was bourgeois. Maybe so, but these people couldn't tell bourgeois or socialist or Mandinga art from a horse's ass. And they're so scared that they turn to the Soviets for help— whose idea of art, in case Pablo forgot to mention it, is even more ignorant and kitschy than our leaders'."

Pablo was still facing determinedly away from us.

"You know what the weird thing is?" Galo said, turning to me. "After all these years you won't find a trace of the Soviet presence even in Cuban movies—let alone in painting, music, or cooking. On the other hand, the United States wants us dead and keeps us in a state of siege, but if you so much as scratch the surface, you'll see their influence everywhere. It drives me crazy, but anyone who tells you that our hatred of the Yankees doesn't go hand in hand with a sick curiosity about their consumer products and their culture is a *comemierda*."

"Speaking of which, the other day a man asked me to sell him some dollars," I said.

"Where?"

"In that passageway of the Habana Libre where the phones are. I came around the corner, and it was almost like he'd been waiting for me. He was really nervous. A skinny little guy, all jumpy and sweaty. He scared me. He flashed some dollar bills at me and asked if I'd sell him more."

"And what did you say?"

"*Ay Galo,* what *would* I say? I said no. Apart from everything else, where would I get dollars? And what could he do with them anyway? I keep thinking about the time I went into a phone booth in the subway in New York and a man went into the booth right next to it and looked at me just the same way, all nervous and sweaty. Except instead of showing me dollars he unzipped his pants and showed me his sex organ."

Pablo left his corner and came over to laugh with Galo.

"He showed you his sex organ, did he?" Galo jeered, recovering his good mood. "Ah, little girl, so modest and proper. The word, dear child, is *pinga.* So how big was it?"

"Galo's wrong," Boris said later, partly just for the pleasure of disagreeing with his friend. We were sitting poolside at the Nacional, watching the day end in the undramatic way it often does in the tropics: a quick fading of the light in a flat sky.

"The Soviets *have* had an influence on art. Not so much on what gets done but on what doesn't. And our brave Soviet leaders don't give a rat's fart about what they're helping to extinguish forever, because it's something they don't know anything about and that doesn't belong to them, which is our history."

"Jesus Christ! The kind of solemn monologues you hear on this island lately! If you don't mind, I think I'll just go throw myself off the Malecón," Carlos said, sitting halfway up in his lounge chair.

Unlike Galo and Pablo, who always held themselves very straight, whether they were walking down the street or sitting around after lunch, or Boris, who moved like a windup doll, Carlos, when he felt himself to be among friends, moved with that enchanting languor that the Revolution did not hesitate to

qualify as decadent. The Nacional's swimming pool was only a
relatively private place, but it was empty, and Carlos had been
unable to resist the temptation to recline on the lounge chair
like an odalisque while he listened to my account of Pablo's
lunchtime quarrel with Galo. Resuming his recumbent position,
he waved an arm languidly in our direction. "Have you noticed
something? Everything, absolutely everything, is an ideological
issue nowadays. You can't say you like macaroni better than
spaghetti without immediately getting trapped in a debate over
dialectics and cultural colonialism."

"Too true," Boris agreed, tapping at his glass of lemonade
with his straw. "In fact, what's really going on is that Galo has
been fucking some kid at Teatro Estudio and Pablo's become a
veritable Medea of jealousy. But since personal life is no longer
important, because it's all subjective, those two have to fight
over the role of the Soviets in the development of contemporary
revolutionary culture. *¡Coño!* Why don't we go to the beach
tomorrow for a change of air?"

"I can't," I said. "I promised I'd go to Santa María del Mar
with Roque Dalton and his family."

"Did you hear that, *chico?*" Boris whooped. "'With Roque
Dalton and his family.'" He mimicked me in a flutey voice.
"Since when do we rub elbows with the crème de la crème of rev-
olutionary internationalism? Look at me, I'm jealous."

I don't remember how I met Roque. It must have been through
Nancy, who had very good connections with the whole Casa de
las Américas group. My first memory of him is in his apartment
in Vedado: I see him emerging from a corner full of books with a
copy of *Casa* magazine in his hands. He wants to show me a text,
explain something, cut to the heart of an issue with the same
obsessive urgency he brought to all aspects of the revolution. The
light from the window illuminates one side of his long face. His
hand, the size of a child's, passes me the magazine. What makes
him striking are his slight build and his large eyes, like a docile
animal's. He's as restless as a teenager. I want to explain that I
just don't have the intellect for texts as advanced as the kind of

thing published in *Casa,* but he insists: no, it's supremely important that I understand, I'll see it's very simple.

The Salvadoran exile Roque Dalton was well known in Havana for the inexhaustible hospitality that made him invite anyone who crossed his path home for a meal; for his straightforward poems; for his work as a productive intellectual who filled *Casa* magazine with brainy articles; for the long months he'd spent in the military training camps that Piñeiro's people maintained for their sister guerrilla organizations; and because he was the wittiest, funniest man whom many people had ever met. During his long and varied years in exile, which seem to have been spent mainly in various taverns and bars frequented by the Mexican, French, Cuban, and Czech intelligentsia, his implausible but mostly accurate stories were as novel as his way of telling them. He would launch into the one about the time he managed to escape from a San Salvador jail thanks to a well-timed earthquake. Or the one about the ridiculous dictator who insisted on healing the population with invisible doctors, or about the suicidal joy with which his compatriots had thrown themselves into a war against neighboring Honduras.

"It's true, *vos.*" It must have been that first afternoon in his house that I heard him say this. "In 1933 *mi general* Maximiliano Hernández Martínez filled all of San Salvador with little pieces of colored paper and, with that one single stroke of genius alone, ended the smallpox epidemic. You think I'm making it up? Check it out: as a Salvadoran, I'm proud to say that he wasn't your ordinary, garden-variety tyrant. Go ahead, *vos,* go read the documents in which his great achievements in the fight against smallpox are recorded! He ordered little blue paper banners posted on every streetlight, to trap the negative forces, like that sticky paper they use for flies. And afterward that old piece of shit stated as pure fact that he had eliminated the smallpox virus." At this point Roque made a hopeless little counterclockwise gesture with his right hand as if he were unscrewing a lightbulb, and laughed.

"*Ah sí, vos.* He was a great believer in spiritualism. He always did whatever his team of invisible doctors advised. Even one of his own sons died that way! He wouldn't let any doctor from this

world near the *cipote*." Roque's smile disappeared. "And the kid
died on him. But there he was, that dumb fuck, certain he'd
saved thousands of lives. In 1932 he had about thirty thousand
souls shot and hung, but he wasn't a man to lose any sleep over a
little thing like a massacre. He saved his nation from a Communist insurrection, and then he saved it from smallpox." He tossed
the imaginary burned-out lightbulb over his shoulder and into
the trash bin of history.

El poeta Dalton had done no more than polish the inventory
of traditional Central American anecdotes to a high sheen, but
the stock of stories in that tradition is limitless and Roque's
narrative ingenuity was great. In the years that followed his
death, more than a few people tried to take the edge off their
grief by imitating him, telling real-life stories over a bottle of
rum the way he used to, stringing together absurdities as if
they were beads on a necklace, and laughing along with his
listeners, shrugging his shoulders at the impossible, ridiculous
sadness of having been born so premodern, so godforsaken, so
Salvadoran.

The same Roque who made everyone laugh also poisoned
himself with alcohol and devoted all his innermost being to
preparing for world revolution, resolute in his determination to
bring the cause at least one small victory in El Salvador. With his
eyes on that triumph, he put his life on the line and prepared for
death. Always seeking further information, I had interrupted
him halfway through a story that afternoon, asking why the
Communist uprising against the tyrant Martínez had failed, and
I'd already had time to regret the question because Roque instantly stopped telling surrealist stories about the dictator and
erupted into a lavalike torrent of theoretical considerations that
were incomprehensible to me. He went to get the article in *Casa*
in order to explain better, but my questions were really very
simple:

"*Y vos,* do you think Che did the right thing, leaving Cuba?"

He looked at me in surprise. "*¿Ydiay?* Where'd you learn to
say *vos?*"

"From my mother, who was born in Guatemala."

He smiled a radiantly white smile. "So you've got some

Guatemalan blood in you! Well then, you're practically half related to me, *vos*. Why don't you come to the beach on Saturday with Aída and the kids? We've got enough gas to get to Santa María, and on the way back Saint Marx will provide."

We both had Central American blood, but we resembled each other in another way that neither one of us was eager to clarify: my mother, though Guatemalan, was raised in the United States and had very North American ways. Roque, who was Salvadoran, was named Dalton because he was the illegitimate son of a prosperous and prominent gringo immigrant. We were both ashamed of that part of our heritage.

Hidden among the pines and the undergrowth at the beach in Santa María, Aída and I changed into our bathing suits. We walked across the dazzling warm sand toward Roque and his sons, who were already leaping through the blue water that was as still as glass. Our silhouettes stood out in sharp contrast against the glaring landscape. Shorter than his adolescent sons, Roque was a fragile marionette. My shadow was printed on the beach, sharper and darker than a photographic negative, and I corroborated once again that my silhouette was identical to a plucked chicken's. Sitting on the pure white sand, Roque and I watched Aída walk into the sea the way ladies used to, taking cautious steps, as if the water were going to nip her, and bending down from time to time to cup some water in her hands and wet her body with it. It was clear that she was another of the many wives of artists and guerrillas who end up as their husband's mother. She nursed his hangovers, forgave him his innumerable romantic adventures, and endured fear and solitude every time Roque left his exile to return once more by secret pathways to the homeland that was his cross to bear. A friendly, generous woman with a chubby torso, she was even shorter than Roque. "In Mexico they'd call her a *chaparrita cuerpo de uva*," I told the poet as we watched her coming out of the water, a sweet little gal with a body like a grape.

"Get over here, *mamita*, I've got a new compliment I want to try out on you," Roque shouted at her, delighted.

———

Roque Dalton was assassinated in El Salvador, under circumstances I'll explain later, even though it didn't happen during the time of this narrative. What interests me right now is an issue of *Casa* magazine published the year before I arrived in Cuba. It contains the transcript of a colloquium Roque took part in, on the role of the intellectual in revolutionary society. It interests me because, as an artist, I was both object and subject of that dialogue, and because there was a time when I thought that the answers to the questions it raised had almost done me in. Today, however, I believe that it was the questions themselves—Is it possible to be an intellectual outside the Revolution? Is it possible to be a nonrevolutionary intellectual?—that were annihilating.

What astonishes me on rereading this text isn't that such questions were ever taken seriously but that they were definitive in the life of a merry and irreverent man like Roque. Is it possible to be an intellectual outside the Revolution? To say yes was immediately to become a counterrevolutionary and be out of the game. To say no, for me, meant an attempt at self-annihilation. But for Roque, impassioned and star-crossed intellectual that he was, that same answer was a call to "revolutionary coherence," as they said then.

In the debate in *Casa,* it's clear from the moment the first orator starts up the session of mea culpas that what the other panelists are actually worried about is a question that they don't articulate but that they all answer repeatedly: Why do so many intellectuals who once supported us now feel uncomfortable about Cuba or even criticize us?

"To begin with, I believe we must acknowledge that many of us have been responsible for creating an illusion . . ." says the novelist Edmundo Desnoes. "The illusion that in Cuba there is absolute freedom of expression, without taking into account the demands of a society in a state of revolution. I don't believe that freedom exists in the abstract . . . it is conditioned by the revolution, it isn't an individual, capricious freedom."

The poet René Depestre picks up the thread from him. "In bourgeois society, when the committed intellectual exercises the right [to criticism], he does so with the class interests of the proletariat as his point of departure," he says, then goes on complicating matters until he achieves such flawlessly indecipherable formulae as: "But when he himself is in power, the revolutionary intellectual is co-responsible for that power. His criticism becomes partly a self-criticism which is articulated to the collective form of critical consciousness which is the revolution, in its historic march."

The other participants in the round-table discussion understand him perfectly. "I agree," the Uruguayan journalist Carlos María Gutiérrez applauds. "Criticism must be exercised through the apparatuses of the Revolution," he states. "An intellectual's critical consciousness cannot be manifested suddenly . . . for example, when a writer wakes up one morning and resolves, obeying the dictates of his critical consciousness, *I suppose in a perfectly honest way* [the emphasis is mine] to write a book of poems in which he impugns those aspects of the Revolution which he dislikes."

It cannot? No, it cannot! The Uruguayan journalist sets forth the procedure to be followed in such cases: "This man, if he wants to do such a thing, must go through the discipline imposed by the socialist construction, through its mass organizations, in order to sidestep the ideological swamps into which he may fall."

Gutiérrez, who did not have to live through the consequences of Fidel's revolutionary practice (and who, when horror and flight had their turn in his country, chose to go into exile in Venezuela and Spain), postulates an existential attitude that could be referred to as implacability, but his Cuban counterparts occasionally succumb to the temptation to affirm that their various callings—writing, painting, criticism—have some value in and of themselves. Depestre attempts a timid defense of this thesis— or perhaps, given the context, it's a daring defense: "Not many men of action have carried out an action as lasting as the books of Leo Tolstoy or the poems of Baudelaire. That is why I think that the intellectual who does not have the qualities that make a man of action doesn't have to develop an 'I didn't fight in the Sierra Maestra' sense of inferiority. He needs only follow the truth of his own life with the utmost honesty."

The Uruguayan journalist, always attentive to any ideological deviation and far better versed in Lenin than his colleagues, rebuts him. "René, when it comes to the accomplishments of artists throughout history," he warns benevolently, "allow me to remind you of something Lenin said in 1905, anticipating the confusion that removes the work of creation from its social conditions: 'The organized socialist proletariat'"—Gutiérrez was citing from memory, I imagine—"'must closely follow this labor, the labor of the intellectuals, and must control it and introduce into all of it, without exception, the vivid torrent of living proletarian activity, thus doing away with the old semi-mercantilist principle that the writer writes when he wants to and the reader reads when it strikes his fancy.'"

No more spontaneous reading! If a worker in a factory works on a fixed schedule and produces what he's told to produce, why shouldn't the privileged intellectual be proletarianized? The panelists humbly accept the warning and continue, still flagellating themselves and seeking along ever more tortuous paths the answer to that unconfessable question: Why do I have such a strong desire to say what I think? And to another one: Why can the proletarians say what they think, while I have the revolutionary obligation to shut up? And yet another: Why is the fieldworker's purpose accomplished when he cuts cane, and the mechanic's purpose accomplished when he repairs the motor, while I, after having written, or painted, or criticized, have to go out and cut cane in order to fulfill my commitment to the Revolution? And the answer that the intellectuals in this colloquium find, following the path illuminated by their Uruguayan guide, is that intellectuals, with their uncontrollable tendency to critical thought, are not trustworthy.

Rereading the debate with which I punished myself so long ago, I think that a desperate offer can also be read between the lines of this piteous text: *I'll diligently apply the whip to myself,* the speakers are saying to the power that they support, *if you'll acknowledge some value to my existence or, at least, allow me to go on existing.* But the margins for negotiation were narrow, for the truth is that at the very moment when Roque Dalton and his colleagues were debating the question of whether spilling their blood or sacrificing their calling was the best way of contributing to the Revolution, that same Revolution had already managed to dispense with them almost entirely. If it weren't that the intellectuals served as a tourist attraction for so many members of the international leftist movement, as at some point the Uruguayan Gutiérrez brutally points out, the Cuban regime wouldn't mind in the least—as Galo had said—if it saw even the most loyal of these supplicants board a boat and disappear over the horizon.

Perhaps I'm judging the befuddled writers who were gathered around the table with Roque that afternoon too harshly. Like everyone else, like the overwhelming majority of the Cuban people, they wanted to believe and they also wanted to survive, and again like most of their fellow Cubans, they hadn't enlisted in the ranks of the Revolution until the very last minute. But only they had merited a tongue-lashing from Che, who said that the intellectuals' original sin was their failure to take up arms in the fight against Batista. The truth is that Roque Dalton was the only man of action, in Depestre's terms, who was sitting at that table. And at the same time he was one of the very few Latin American revolutionaries who really was an intellectual. Out of those two planks he nailed together his cross.

"The moral affliction of the Latin American intellectual who has come to understand the real needs of the Revolution can be resolved only by revolutionary practice," he declared at that table. "He has an obligation to answer his avant-garde thinking with the facts, even at the risk of negating himself. . . .

"Do I attach more importance to the work of finishing my all-important novel, or must I accept the difficult task that the party, the guerrilla forces, the front lines have set before me, in the execution of which I can lose not only my precious time but all the time that I had imagined was remaining to me? Do I write sonnets or devote myself to studying peasant revolutions? In other words: we don't want to say that a writer is good for the Revolution only if he goes into hiding in the wilderness or kills the police chief, but we believe that a good writer, when he's in a guerrilla unit, is closest to all that the fight for the future, the advent of hope, etc., means; that is, to the raw, positive content that all the theoretical meanderings have hidden for so long. . . .

As I see it, anyone who consciously and responsibly affirms that Che Guevara is his ideal cannot then go on telling petty little lies without ending up a shameless man, a *sinvergüenza*."

It was characteristic of Roque to speak of theory as if it were truth and not the opposite. To be like Che is to die like Che, and Roque was not about to be a *sinvergüenza*—a shit-eater. The flaw that marred his poetry also cut short his life: he took the meaning of each word too literally.

The way he dealt with his country, the familiarity that allowed him to tell stories about the dictator Martínez's invisible doctors as if they were old family stories—as indeed they were—perhaps helps explain that sudden boom in revolutions that took place in the "narrow waist of America"—El Salvador, Guatemala, and Nicaragua—against the tyrants in that small region. Roque's knowledge was completely different from the rhetorical expositions I heard from the lips of Eduardo the guerrilla and his successors, who were trying to overturn immensely more powerful regimes in vastly larger nations. In the lessons they delivered everything was there except the exalted light of afternoon, the smell of rot in the marketplaces, the bawdy jokes and tasty peasant food of the homeland they were trying to redeem. Perhaps it wasn't their fault; it was just fate that Roque happened to be born in a country the size of a handkerchief, with three million inhabitants, which therefore he could feasibly embrace, know, and live on intimate terms with. That small, compelling, and absurd country makes its presence felt in all his final poems.

YA TE AVISO . . .

Patria idéntica a vos misma
pasan los años y no rejuveneces
deberían de dar premios de resistencia por ser salvadoreño
Beethoven era sifilítico y sordo pero ahí está la Novena Sinfonía
en cambio tu ceguera es de fuego
y tu mudez de gritería

Yo volveré, yo volveré
no a llevarte la paz sino el ojo del lince
el olfato del podenco

amor mío con himno nacional
voraz
ya le comiste el cadáver de don Francisco Morazán
a Honduras
y hoy te querés comer
a Honduras
necesitás bofetones
electro-shocks
psicoanálisis
para que despertés a tu verdadera personalidad
vos no sos don Rafael Meza Ayau ni el coronel Medrano
habrá que meterte en la cama
a pan de dinámita y agua,
lavativas de coctel Molotov cada quince minutos
y luego nos iremos a la guerra de verdad
todos juntos
para ver si así como roncas duermes
como decía Pedro Infante
novia encarnizada
mamá que parás el pelo.

I'M WARNING YOU

My country, identical to yourself
the years go by and you're not getting any younger
they should give out endurance awards for being
Salvadoran
Beethoven was deaf and syphilitic
but the Ninth Symphony exists
your blindness, though, is fire
and your muteness clamor.

I'll be back, I'll be back
and I won't bring peace, but the lynx's eye
the hound's nose
my love has a national anthem
voracious
you've eaten the body of Don Francisco Morazán
in Honduras

and now you want to eat Honduras
you need a good thrashing
electroshocks
psychoanalysis
to awaken you to your true personality
you're not Don Rafael Meza Ayau or Colonel Medrano
you'll have to be kept in bed
on a diet of dynamite and water
a Molotov enema every fifteen minutes
and then we'll go off to war in earnest
all together
to see if your snoring means you're really asleep
as Pedro Infante used to say
bloodthirsty bride
hair-raising momma.

It's interesting to note, before jumping to May 10, 1975, that during the dialogue in *Casa,* Roque's pleas for coherence between consciousness and practice are entirely ignored by the other participants.

At the beginning of the 1970s Roque began publishing fewer and fewer articles in *Casa,* and his name disappeared from the editorial board's roster. His clandestine forays into El Salvador appear to have become more frequent, and it was probably around that time that he made common cause with other young dissidents from the fossilized Partido Comunista de El Salvador, to propel the path of armed struggle toward Communism, as the phrase went. The new grouping called itself the Ejército Revolucionario del Pueblo, or ERP. A Communist Party militant since his adolescence, several times jailed and exiled, and also a published and celebrated poet, Roque must have had a very hard time hiding, especially in a small, inbred city like San Salvador. (I have no information on this point, but it seems unlikely that the ERP initially followed Che's guidelines and tried to survive in the jungle, because there's no jungle left to speak of in El Salvador.)

Whatever the conditions were, Roque's life in hiding must have been stifling and claustrophobic in the extreme. In any group that, by the very act of taking up arms, has eradicated all notion of tolerance, it's not surprising that deadly rivalries burgeon. When, in mid-May 1975, his companions-in-arms announced to the world that they had put Roque Dalton to death, alleging as their motive the poet's secret ideological alliance with the CIA, the charge was so absurd that even Fidel grew indignant. Years later some friends of mine, the members of a dissident branch of the ERP that was founded in the wake of Roque's assassination, offered another explanation. According to them, Roque, ever the skirt-chaser, had gone after the girlfriend of one of his comrades, perhaps that of Joaquín Villalobos, the sharp-eyed military leader of the incipient organization. I don't know why I feel that Roque would have preferred this version of the cause of his death. I see him and don't want to see him, curled up on the cot in the rooftop garret where he was being held prisoner. I see and don't want to know whether they shot him in the back while he was asleep or put him in front of a firing squad and he himself gave the order to fire; whether it was his own friend Villalobos who shot him or if someone else was assigned the task. Roque, who had escaped from so many jails, so many of destiny's ambushes, died, pissed off and all alone. His body was never found.

The month of September is almost over now, and there's not much time left before I leave Cuba forever and this story ends. Only a few weeks from now Adrian will call to announce that he's found an apartment for the two of us, and I'll say, "That's wonderful!" and write another letter to Jorge. I'll see Roque one last time, walking down Rampa one afternoon with the sun behind him, and he'll open his arms wide and shout, "*¡Mamita linda!* Why so alone?" and scold me for not stopping by the house and invite me to the beach again. Soon I'll say good-bye to my students, but before that I have to tell the story of their school. For it wasn't until thirty years later that I finally came to understand why we at the Escuelas Nacionales de Arte breathed an air of abandonment and mortal solitude, as in the mansion of Miss Havisham, the spinster in Dickens's *Great Expectations* who keeps her parlor, her cake, and her bridal gown just as they were at the moment she learns that her fiancé has jilted her.

I found the reason in a book about the ENA, *Revolution of Forms: Cuba's Forgotten Art Schools,* written by the U.S. architect John Loomis, and it was simple: in 1970 even the teachers at the school of architecture in the Universidad Nacional were discouraged from taking their students to the art schools. I didn't learn this at the time because the disgrace into which the ENA had fallen was not talked about. Or perhaps visiting the school wasn't exactly forbidden (I know people who were boarded at the school during one convention or another in the mid-1970s), and talking about it was allowed, strictly speaking, but Elfrida, Lorna, Hilda, and Tere unconsciously tried to avoid any problems with the state by keeping silent, a strategy that, at the same time, allowed them to avoid some disheartening reflections on the complex role the Revolution played in their own lives and art.

Completely unaware that I was inhabiting a poisoned, almost radioactive complex that the Revolution had declared to be contaminated from its origins, I spent many afternoons strolling through the startling village that housed the Escuela Nacional de Artes Plásticas. On its long meander the main pathway curved like a riverbed past the circular structures that housed the workshops and classrooms, and every time I walked along it, I thought pityingly of the poverty of this government, which didn't even have the resources to repair the lovely fountain that adorned the tranquil plaza at the center of the complex.

It wasn't always that way. In January 1961 the architect Ricardo Porro, recently returned from a long exile in Venezuela to join the Revolution, was visited by an old friend, a pretty, high-spirited woman who unexpectedly dropped in on the cocktail party Porro happened to be giving that evening. "Listen to what's just happened to me," she told Porro. "I was walking along the street when this big fancy car pulls up next to me, the door opens, and I see Fidel waving me in."

Fidel gets right to the point. "We've decided to use the facilities of the former Country Club to create a great school of all the arts," he tells her. "This project is urgent. We need to have a master plan within four months. Do you know of anyone who can develop it?" Porro's friend hadn't been able to think of any candidate but him.

Fidel hoped to inaugurate the schools at the end of that same year, so construction would have to begin as soon as possible. Moreover, the budget would be absolutely rudimentary. It was an impossible project, and therefore Porro accepted it with joy. This, he thought with deep emotion, would be his opportunity to use materials like brick and the simplest and most economical construction techniques in order to found an authentically Cuban architecture.

Miraculously, Porro and the two Italian architects he recruited for the project, Vittorio Garatti and Roberto Gottardi, delivered their plan for the schools almost on time. It was truly revolutionary, and its conceptual beauty was astonishing. Five schools built out of brick and surrounded by jungle, conceived as an explosion of fragments—seen from the air, the design of each school was a variation on the form of a spiral at the moment it explodes—and at the same time as an African village—seen from within, each school was a complex of curving buildings, protectively circling a series of little plazas. The architecture of the School of Plastic Arts in particular alluded to Cuba's joyous sexuality: each classroom—a cupola crowned by a small pointed skylight—had the unmistakable shape of a breast. At the center of the main plaza, water gushed from a fountain that evoked the form of a conch or papaya—the latter word so closely associated with the female pudenda in Cuba that it cannot be uttered in polite company.

Construction started just before the invasion of Playa Girón and ended just after the missile crisis, and the schools enjoyed Fidel's support and praise throughout those months, Loomis writes. Roberto Gottardi was in charge of the design of the School of Dramatic Arts. Though Vittorio Garatti didn't manage to finish building his School of Music, he collaborated with Alicia Alonso on the design of the School of Ballet, built to her specifications, and this school was completed (though on the day the director of the Ballet Nacional went to see her school, which was now almost ready for its first class, she reportedly said, "I don't like it," and walked away, never to return). Porro himself designed the School of Plastic Arts, the most beautiful of them all, and also the School of Dance.

Brick vaults immediately became the unmistakable leitmotif of the ENA: they revalidated both craftsmanship and what Cubans call *cubanidad,* while at the same time helping to define an absolutely original space.

That, in fact, was precisely the accusation put forward by the enemies of Porro, Garatti, and Gottardi as they plotted their fall from grace. The Escuelas Nacionales de Arte revalidated individualistic and skill-based craftsmanship, they accused; the schools were built of brick and not prefabricated modules, they promoted sensuality and alluded to ideas of *cubanidad* and Africanness that were unacceptable to the Revolution, which was proletarian, committedly internationalist, and resolutely opposed to any and all manifestations of decadence. Low mutterings against the schools were already audible when their construction began. They rose in volume in 1963. The Ministry of Construction, which was in charge of the building process, gradually began withdrawing its support. The minister was a twenty-six-year-old ex-guerrilla named Osmany Cienfuegos, who had fought alongside Ernesto Guevara. When Che confronted a problem for which he found himself completely unprepared, his instinct was always to seize the most radical option. However, in general the cadres of the Cuban Revolution had the same inclination as the rest of us: when facing an unfamiliar situation, they opted for the conservative route. Thus, as the controversy surrounding the schools grew (quite possibly stirred up by the many architects who had never managed to get their hands on such a juicy project, given the state's very scant plans for new construction), Cienfuegos began withdrawing his support.

In 1965, Loomis relates, Fidel himself joined the attack on the school, in a speech that criticized the individualistic or "egocentric" criteria of certain architects, then lauded the Soviet model of standardized construction. (A few years earlier Khrushchev had vehemently denounced "antiproletarian architecture," referring to buildings not constructed out of prefabricated modules.) An initial measure extinguished the scandalous papaya fountain. Then the budget shrank, and finally the inaugural ceremonies were canceled. In July 1965 the classrooms of the Schools of Dance, Music, and Plastic Arts were used for the first time, without festivities of any kind, Loomis writes. Under increasingly insistent pressure from the architects' union, and fearing even more serious consequences, Porro tried to speak to Fidel to ask that he be allowed to leave Cuba on good terms. In 1966, Celia Sánchez herself notified him that the plane tickets that would take him and his wife into exile in Paris had been authorized. Garatti was jailed, then expelled from Cuba eight years later. Only Roberto Gottardi still lives in Cuba today.

In his Paris studio, over a dinner cooked by Ricardo Porro himself and his wife, Elena, with modest ingredients and splendid results, the maestro told me about the debacle of the Escuelas Nacionales de Arte. Tall, bald, extremely cultured, immensely large, witty, and with a strange, sweet innocence, Porro lives in peace, teaching classes at the university, keeping busy in his studio with the surrealist sculptures that obsess him, and creating public buildings as singularly beautiful as the ENA, which the Paris mayor's office has commissioned from him.

I asked why he had been commissioned to build a School of Dance when in fact no great tradition of modern dance existed in Cuba. "Among other reasons, because it was considered prudent to support a form of dance that was less effeminate than ballet, so the boys who wanted to dance would run less of a risk," he answered. "In fact, an entire series of decisions was made on the basis of that fear. Alicia Alonso herself, who had so much support from the government, began recruiting students among the *guajiros* in the countryside, or in orphanages, doing her best to ensure that they were uncontaminated by the virus of homosexuality. For that reason too it was decided that a separate dining room would be built in each school. I thought it was ridiculous. The logical thing was for the Escuelas de Arte to function as a single vast center of communal life and artistic interchange, but no: it was best that each school have its own separate dining room, so that the boys from the dance schools wouldn't endanger those from the other schools. Of course, with all the economic hardships, that turned out to be impossible, and the dining room of the old administrative building had to be used."

I asked him why the Escuela Nacional de Danza had no mirrors. "Because there wasn't any money left," he answered. "I knew it was going to be like that. I told my *compañeros* and the construction supervisors, 'Let's do everything as fast as we can; this whole thing is going to be over very soon.'"

"Come on, dummies! When you start your leap, it's the *front* leg that gives you the momentum to start turning. And it's the *back* leg that helps you end the turn, but you have to pull it in underneath you inmediately! Don't leave them both dangling in the air! There you go! Use your abdomen! Pull everything in to your center! If you don't, you're going to fall!"

I was running and shouting after Orlando, Manolo, José, and Humberto, a student who had great élan and very stiff legs, cheering them on and prodding their legs so they'd remember to bend them in time. "That's it! That's it! Just the way Humberto is . . . falling," I concluded, watching him go down for the third or fourth time.

The four boys I had chosen to rehearse with me all wore the alert, satisfied look, *Use me, use me,* that gives wings to dancers when the work is going well. We were all sweating, and they would fall or lose the tempo, then rub the sore ankle or knee and go back to their places with eyes full of hope and gratitude. I wasn't sure I was giving them the type of choreography they needed in order to grow: Was I doing all right? Was this better than what Elfrida gave them? Would I manage to come up with a new phrase by tomorrow? But I was happy. The same passage of *Tales from the Vienna Woods* crackled out again and again from the little tape player, and each time we returned to our task. "This music is a river, not a street full of potholes," I insisted. "You don't pull the waltz, the waltz pulls you. Especially during the *glissade en plié.* Look: use your stomach muscles, keep your torsos still, and slide along as if you were sucking up the floor with the soles of your feet. Nice and flat, nice and smooth, nice and gentle. Got it? Good, let's try it again. No bouncing! Slide along on the music! TAM-taram-tam-tam!"

Twyla couldn't possibly have taken this long with the business of composition: I'd spent the whole of the previous afternoon putting together three phrases that added up to thirty seconds, and it had taken a full hour to set them on the four boys' bodies. We'd spent days on the same phrases. Could it be that we'd learned this slowly in Twyla's rehearsals, too? What did she do to keep from despairing of us? And what would happen when it was time for me to include the girls? But don't complain, *chica*— *Que esta tiñosa te la has parqueado tú,* I told myself; it was a Cuban expression meaning, more or less, "You parked this jalopy and now it's yours." Until then the Cuban accent and the local sayings had not struck me as particularly delightful, but in recent days, for the first time, I was beginning to imitate them. Should I let Adrian know I was going to be staying just a few weeks more, at least until we'd completed five minutes of a dance that the kids could present for the end of the school year?

The rehearsal concluded, and I noticed that instead of approaching me as they usually did, with questions about technical details or to ask me to have just one more look at their turning leap, José and Manolo stayed in a corner, whispering to each other.

"Alma, we need to talk something over with you," said José, who always took the initiative. And he suggested something that, out of fear, he had refused to do almost two months earlier: "Can we visit you in your hotel this afternoon?"

Three students arrived that afternoon, but they told me they were a delegation. They looked pale and worried and had a slightly heroic air. They did not want any lemonade. "We're going on strike," José immediately blurted.

"What? But *muchachos,* you can't—that's absolutely forbidden. Why?"

"So that conditions at the school will change."

"Yes," said Antonia.

"That's why," said Roberto.

"But you won't achieve anything that way," said I, the revolutionary. "You're out of your minds! Don't you see that things are getting better since the meeting with Mario Hidalgo? Elfrida's being more reasonable, we're looking into restructuring the program, especially for the younger pupils, and we're rehearsing the waltz."

"But you're leaving."

"I don't think I'll be leaving all that soon. If it will help, I can stay through the end of December."

All three shook their heads. No. Fundamental change was needed, and all the fourth- and fifth-year students were now in agreement.

"Have you thought about the kind of hot water you're going to get Orlando into? It's not as if he needs any more problems, after that meeting."

"We haven't even told him. Anyway, he's in the same situation we are—he has nothing to lose. But we need to know something," said Roberto, addressing me more seriously than anyone ever had before in my life. "We're going to ask that Elfrida be removed as the director, and we want to know if you're prepared to stay on in her place."

I explained that in my opinion all a walkout could do was make conditions even harder for the younger students and leave a black mark on their own records before graduation. I told them I had no administrative talent even with regard to my own life and categorically rejected the possibility of taking charge of the school should the strike succeed, but I doubt that they believed me. I spent the days between the students' visit and the strike on tenterhooks.

No strike was ever more touching or more absurd. For a long time, moreover, I believed that there simply had never been any other strike in all the years that Fidel had been in power. That's how the official history would have it, but I'm now convinced that hundreds or thousands of small strikes like the one by the ENA's dance students must have broken out, small uprisings that lasted a morning or a day and then were squelched by force—or more probably, as in the case of the dance school, by secretly negotiating a few minimal concessions in order to resolve the conflict right away and protect the authorities from embarrassment.

Having refused to support my subversive students, I didn't learn much about the movement. In fact, I don't even remember the date of the strike, but I do know that by then it was no longer raining every afternoon, and a constant, cool breeze blew a carpet of dry leaves down the path to the school. One morning I found Tere at the foot of that little path, arms crossed and brow furrowed. She didn't even smile when she gave me the bad news. "Go home," she said. "I think it's for the best. You do know what those crazy kids are up to, don't you?"

I went back to the hotel, reviewing my own conduct along the way. I had treated Elfrida arrogantly, I had generated dissatisfaction among the students, heedless of the fact that they had no alternatives, and I had begun to take pride in their idealized image of me and had even promoted it. And yet we'd been happy together, and I believed with all my soul in their right to free themselves from Elfrida's incompetent tutelage—and, in the bargain, from that little smile of hers that was like a pair of scissors, and her way of saying *"ssomos . . . rrevolussionariossss"* at the drop of a hat. Yet again—and how many times had this happened since I came to Cuba?—I was confronting a paradox that was impossible to resolve: I knew I'd been a determining factor in the strike movement—or to put it another way, if I'd never come to the school, the students would never have thought of staging this protest—but I didn't know what role I could play in it. I felt useless.

I didn't have to live in perplexity for very long. The strike was resolved that very afternoon or the next day. I think the students expressed their demands and their dissatisfaction directly to Elfrida, because she was not a woman to abandon ship in an adverse situation, but I seem to recall that much of the diplomatic work also fell to Tere, Hilda, and Osvaldo, the teacher in the academic area. I think they must have been very careful not to involve Orlando. In theory, everything went back to normal, and the classes and my rehearsals went on as usual. I don't remember if, in the end, it was only the older students who refused to show up for classes or if they had managed to extend the rebellion to the students in the lower grades as well. I believe the strike was so short because everything in life takes practice, and my students didn't know anything about how to rebel; they had no reference points. Nevertheless, things didn't come out as badly as I'd feared: after the strike their situation improved. There were changes in their diet, I think the fifth-year students were granted permission to take classes with the Conjunto, the modern dance company, and neither José nor the other leaders of the movement were expelled.

I never learned what Orlando's attitude was toward the rebellion, or how the students themselves saw their brief attempt at insurrection. And I'm aware that this account of the most important event that took place during the six months I spent in Cubanacán is worse than meager. But that's because I had to pay a price: the students did not bring up the subject with me again. Not that subject or any other, except the things that can be talked about in a dance studio during a class.

In any case, it seems unlikely that they went so far as to request the removal of the director of the dance school in so many words, though I suspect that my name did come up somewhere in their list of demands. I say this because when I went to see Elfrida a few days later to talk about the possibility of prolonging my stay until the end of December, given the students' interest in making as much progress as possible with the little piece of choreography we were rehearsing, she answered, with lips pressed together very tightly and eyes blazing, that, on the contrary, she had recommended to the administration of the ENA that my work conclude at the end of that very month.

I was relieved.

Adrian called to let me know he'd found an apartment for us. I could hear his smile over the telephone wire when I told him I would be in New York in less than two weeks. "I'd better hurry up, then: I'm going to paint the walls. And I have to find a bed." I heard him smile again. "I don't imagine you'll want to sleep on the floor." It wasn't a joke but a declaration: he was going to find a bed because he was prepared to accept me as I was, love of luxury and all.

I fought against the idea, which was gaining ground within me, that living with Adrian might be even more arduous than living in Cuba. I sensed that I wasn't reacting with the appropriate enthusiasm.

"What's the apartment like?"

"It's big, it has wood floors. And the rent is very cheap: a hundred and three dollars."

"Does it get any sun?"

"One of the bedrooms gets some sun. I'm going to turn that into my study, but you can come visit me in there whenever you want."

"What street is it on?"

"One Hundred Eighty-seventh."

"Harlem?"

"What's wrong with that?"

I made a useless effort not to let my voice falter. In those years that section of Harlem was dangerous, and Adrian, once again, seemed to have no interest in protecting me. "Are there any trees on that block, maybe?"

"I'll check. I don't think there are too many trees anywhere in Manhattan."

It's hard to reconstruct those final weeks in Cuba: after the strike and my meeting with Elfrida, the days flew. Initially I'd thought about leaving, then I thought about staying, and then it turned out that I was leaving even before I'd planned to. Knowing I wouldn't have time to finish it, I stopped rehearsing the waltz and gave some rather boring classes in which I tried to explain all the theoretical points I hadn't previously brought up, as if the students were likely to remember words more easily than what they had already succeeded in assimilating with their bodies. I went to the theater every chance I got. The weather grew colder. I wore the sweater my mother had sent. Through Galo I donated the little tape player to the Teatro Estudio and distributed at the school most of what I'd brought with me to Cuba. Carmen, whose feet were the same size as mine, kept all the shoes. Tere spent an entire afternoon at the Nacional helping me pack, and when she left, she was decked out like a shrine, wearing my necklaces and taking home the bottle of French perfume. She smoothed a little meringue of it onto her wrist and shook her head in wonder. "With this on, Mariano's going to want to stick his *pinga* in me all day long." She blushed. "*Peddona*. It's just that, you know, that's how Mariano says make love."

I went to the foreigners' shop five afternoons in a row, and on each trip I bought the pack of cigarettes, pouch of sweets, and box of chocolates to which my still-valid ID entitled me. It was then that the students made their vow to retain an eternal memory of me by never eating any of the chocolates—a vow that they broke joyfully that very evening.

The next morning we said good-bye. There was no reason to hold class, but I tried. By common consent we stopped halfway through and sat down on the floor to chat. ("Alma, tell us about how cold it is in New York. Is it true that there are people so poor that they don't even have a place to live, and they die in the street?")

In general we maintained our composure; the only ones who attempted any tears were Carmen and Nieves, a small, extraordinarily timid mulatta who always gazed at me with bright sparkling eyes and danced with the dramatic projection of a giant. I thought sorrowfully of all the work I hadn't done with her. Sitting there on the floor, we went over our favorite subjects for the last time. ("Alma, tell us again what that piece by Martha is like, *Clytemnestra?*") I made my last suggestions and tried unsuccessfully to find some final, or memorable, or at least funny thing to say. When Elfrida and Lorna interrupted us, I was almost grateful.

They didn't take up much time, either. "We want to thank Alma for the effort and sincerity of her work," Elfrida must have said, without including the word *compañera*. "And we wish her all the best in whatever she decides to undertake after returning to New York." While Lorna was giving me a hug, Elfrida left the studio. Instantly, as if her departure had been the signal, the students began to shout out a Cuban stadium cheer, accompanied by contrapuntal clapping. "*Bombo chía chía chía, bombo chía chía che,*" they choroused, and when it was over, Yasmina went running to the dressing room and came back with a little white box, which looked as if it should contain a rosary, in which the students had placed the little doll made out of thread and the foil that the chocolates they'd eaten the night before had been wrapped in.

"We have some presents, too," said Tere, smiling. She, Osvaldo, and Hilda had been sitting on one of the steps at the entrance to the studio for quite a while. Tere gave me a Santería necklace that stayed with me until I took it to be repaired in Cuba a few years ago and lost it. She had had it made "by someone who specializes in that area," said Tere, in order not to say *babalao*, or Santería priest. It was a very unusual object, she explained, because in general a Santería necklace is made out of beads in colors that represent a single *oricha*, or saint. Under very particular circumstances, however, necklaces that are "very strong, with lots of protection," can be made. The one I was taking with me to New York had the powers of Ochún, goddess of the rivers, Changó, god of thunder and war, Oggún, god of the forest and of metals, and Elegguá, the being who opens and closes all roads, including those of life and death.

"And Osvaldo and I wanted to give you this, from the whole dance school," said Hilda, the school secretary and party delegate. She handed me the little mahogany box with embedded silver thread and the word *vuelve*—come back—clumsily scratched inside it. "And this, which for us is very precious." From a large manila envelope, which was beginning to come open along the edges from so much use, she pulled a smeary photocopy of a book that had just been published. It was the biography of Tania the Guerrilla, the young German-Argentine who died in Bolivia fighting alongside Che. "She is the best example we have of the authentic revolutionary woman; she is the best you can take with you from here. We give it to you with all our hearts."

The students wanted to walk with Tere and me to the bus stop, but I asked them to stay behind in the studio.

For our farewell dinner Carlos stood in line at the 1830 restaurant for an entire day and night. Finally, as Galo had promised, we would dine together in a luxurious restaurant with fine crystal and white tablecloths. I regret not remembering a single

one of the dishes we were served, because the effort Carlos made
in order for us to sit down around that table was great. All the
rest is still clear in my mind. Galo brought a thick sheet of paper,
rolled up, which turned out to be an ink drawing by the painter
René Portocarrero. We talked about Fidel and culture and the
position of the intellectual vis-à-vis the Revolution, about our
friends in Mexico, and Christmas in New York. Somehow the
most recent solar eclipse came up.

"I saw it," I exclaimed. "I saw that eclipse in New York, and
you saw it here, and then we met. How incredible!" Galo gazed
at me in amusement. "But I still don't understand how something as small as the moon can completely cover up the sun."

"Verily, little girl, I say unto you," Galo sighed, "I have never
seen anyone as ignorant as you are. But yours is a very strange
ignorance: you recite Baudelaire"—"That's because Jorge sent
me a poem," I interrupted in shame, but Galo ignored me—"yet
you have a concept of the solar system that not even the blackest
child in the streets of the port of Havana . . . I'm starting to
believe you when you say you never went to school."

"It's not completely true," I clarified, embarrassed by my own
lies and exaggerations. "I did go to elementary school when I was
living with my mother in Los Angeles, though they made me
skip third and fifth grade because it was a pretty bad school, and
since I was reading all my mother's books at home, I was learning faster than the other students. In Los Angeles I learned
English." I was determined to keep at this tally until I had clarified everything. "Then when we went back to Mexico, I spent all
my time in the Ballet Nacional, which strangely enough was a
modern dance company, not a ballet company, as you know, and
it's true that I didn't want to go to junior high or high school.
What's more, I was very young but very tall, so I didn't fit in
anywhere. But the director of the Ballet Nacional, Guillermina
Bravo, hired a teacher to teach the company members Nahuatl,
the Aztec language. That was very interesting. Then I went to
live with my mother in New York, but by then I was already sixteen and wasn't required to go to school, and since I didn't have
an elementary school certificate or junior high school or any-

thing, the public school system didn't know what to do with me. A friend of my mother's helped me get a scholarship in an experimental alternative high school, and I spent two years there and finally graduated. It was fun: they didn't make me study math, but I did do biology, and if you want, I can explain perfectly how deoxyribonucleic acid works and the inner structure of an egg. And I learned French there. So I have been to school, but I never learned anything about the planets."

"Nor about many other things, you ignorant child," Galo concluded. "But now I understand—you grew up the way homosexuals do: weird."

"And your parents never worried about it or tried to get you to go to school?" Pablo wanted to know.

"Why would they worry about her education!" Galo exclaimed. "They were worried because they had such a weird daughter and didn't know what to do with her, weren't they?"

"Leave her in peace, Galo," Carlos warned.

Galo did not like good-byes. When we left the restaurant, he handed me the drawing, ruffled my hair, and gave me a quick kiss on the forehead. Pablo and I had a long hug, and Carlos, Boris, and I walked to the beach, where the moon was tracing a blue path across the sand.

"Carlos wants to give you something, too," said Boris. Carlos extended a clenched fist. "Take it, *chica*," he said. "But I want you to understand what it is." I took the dark velvet pouch, tied shut with a cord. "I know life in New York is hard, and we want to help make it a little easier. What you have there once belonged to my mother, but she can't use it anymore, and neither can we. It's no good to anyone here in Cuba. It's not much, but at least you can sell it and use the money to pay for classes or buy a coat or pay the rent—whatever you want."

In the moonlight I saw a pair of tear-shaped art nouveau earrings. The setting (was it platinum?) framed an elongated piece of transparent quartz, with a sparkling emerald chip in the center.

"I can't," I said.

"They're yours."

"I can't, I can't," I repeated, my face drenched and a terrible turmoil rising from my chest to my throat. "I'm going to start coughing like Marguerite Gautier again. *¡Coño!* I can't stand it anymore."

"Both of you really do understand how eclipses work?" I asked, a few paces farther along.

"But we already explained that to you in the restaurant!" Carlos protested.

"You know, Galo's right: this creature understands everything except what she doesn't understand in the least," laughed Boris, and adopted a certain efficient manner that he had—like a symphony conductor, I always thought, with his slim little body that would have looked so good in white tie and tails. "All right, we're going to explain it so that you understand it as a dancer. Carlos, get in the middle. He's the sun, and he turns very slowly," Boris instructed me.

"Now, you're the earth, and you have to turn more quickly because you weigh less than the sun." I dried off my face, blew my nose with the handkerchief Boris held out to me, and started to turn.

"And I'm the moon, the quickest of the three. And now I'm going to run rings around you, while still spinning myself, while you spin and run rings around the sun. And we'll keep doing it until the eclipse occurs."

And we laughed and spun and laughed and spun, until the eclipse occurred.

Epilogue

I lasted only a few weeks in the apartment Adrian found. Neither one of us was much good at meeting the other's needs. Two years later Jorge wrote to me in New York announcing that he wanted our relationship to end, thus precipitating the collapse I'd been heading for since I decided to go to Cuba to teach dance. Before that breakup, and after I stopped living with Adrian, I took refuge with a dancer friend who soon found me an apartment in the same building she lived in. In that secret niche, a fifth-floor walk-up full of light with the tub in the kitchen and the toilet down the hall but with a window that overlooked a garden full of trees, I began my life in New York all over again.

In the early months of my return I lost a good number of my dance-world friends, who couldn't understand the new vocabulary I'd brought back from Havana or my reproaches for their lack of solidarity with the world's sufferings. I made new friends who shared my concerns. I protested against the Vietnam War in New York and in Washington, and I dedicated long hours of work to Latin America's struggles for liberation. I stopped dancing. In all the rest of my life no other activity would ever be even remotely as difficult, exhausting, or demanding, or grant me as much joy. The Chilean military coup against the government of Salvador Allende was a black moment for all of us who considered ourselves leftists. For several years afterward I lived in a state of absolute indifference, unable to recover from the triple loss of dance, the hope Chile had represented, and the man who always refused to explain why he no longer wanted to be with me. More or less by accident I found myself in Nicaragua during the days of the Sandinista revolt against the dictator Anastasio Somoza and started working as a reporter. The euphoria of that just cause awoke some sort of interest in life within me once more, and over the years I slowly came to terms with myself, no longer as an ex-dancer but as a reporter, and then as a writer. During the time I spent in El Salvador, in the early years of figuring out how to put words together, I thought a great deal about Roque Dalton.

As I said at the beginning, most of the mementos my friends and students gave me when I left Cuba were lost. The ink drawing by Portocarrero disappeared, perhaps in Central America when the house I was renting in Managua was robbed, or perhaps in Mexico, when a trunk in which I kept it and other talismans was ransacked. I still have Hilda's wooden box, and the lower part of the little cardboard box from the students—and I also have a letter I've forgotten to mention, a letter I received in New York not long after I left Adrian. It still has the damp smell that permeated even the paper in Cubanacán. The letter is signed by a stranger who identifies himself as the recently appointed new director of the School of Dance. Without mentioning Elfrida's dismissal or my conflicts with her, he invites me to return to the ENA and help him restructure the dance program.

I never once thought about accepting. My life was in turmoil; I lived in such intense pain that sometimes I had to stand paralyzed in the middle of a busy street, unable to draw breath, and the idea of going back to Cuba offered no relief. But above all I believed myself incapable of living up to the hopes the students had placed in me. I was twenty-one years old and didn't have the slightest talent for management or for commitment. It occurs to me now that the news must have come as a blow to the students, since they had no way of knowing that I was right.

When I finally did go back to Cuba in 1979, it was a last-minute trip out of Managua, aboard an aged Tupolev cargo jet. The photographer Susan Meiselas and I managed to squeeze in alongside a delegation of twenty-six Nicaraguan guerrillas who'd been invited as very special guests to the commemoration of the attack on the Moncada barracks. (The number of delegates was symbolic, since, as you'll recall, the attack took place on July 26.) It had been barely a week since the Frente Sandinista de Liberación Nacional had ousted Somoza, and I was able to witness the first encounter between this band of hungry, ragged guerrillas, most of them campesinos, and the Revolution that had given meaning and hope to their struggle. It may have been the first time I understood the lasting strength of Fidel Castro's image throughout Latin America; I saw the Sandinistas blissfully contemplating a row of red tractors that, the guide informed them, were the property of the people. "And all of them brand-new, *hermano*!" one guerrilla sighed.

That trip went by in a flash. The July 26 commemoration was held in Camagüey, and we spent only a few hours confined in a safe house in Havana before heading back to Managua. I returned to Cuba again four years later, during the days of the Reagan administration's invasion of Grenada, when the Cuban people were expecting a parallel invasion of their own island at any minute. Three years had passed already since Galo—and his friends as well, I imagine—left the port city of Mariel on a motorboat headed for Key West, in Florida.

Tere was now the assistant director of the Conjunto Folk-lórico. Elfrida was no longer at Cubanacán, and neither was Lorna. Following her departure from the dance school, Elfrida had gotten herself transferred to Guantánamo, where she founded a dance group, choreographed many dances, and died surrounded by the love of her disciples in 1998, according to a recent article in *The New York Times.* I found out none of this at the time. I could claim that my work reporting on the Grenada crisis was so intense I didn't have time to look up my old colleagues, but that's not true.

I didn't seek out Tere or go to Cubanacán because I didn't want to revisit the morass of painful and conflicting feelings that was the aftermath of my stay in Cuba. I did learn, sometime later, that the student most resembling the one I've called "José" had earned a degree in anthropology, or perhaps ethnography, and was working outside Cuba, but without renouncing the Revolution; that "Antonia" had founded an avant-garde dance group that toured successfully abroad; and that "Roberto" was the director of a dance group in either Santiago or Matanzas. I'm fairly sure that it was "Pilar," the chubby girl with hair as black as ink, who turned up in the pages of a book I saw one day, in a photograph with a caption that described her as the great interpreter of Yemayá, Santería goddess of the seas.

Not much is left in Cuba of the Revolution I knew. The complex of buildings that make up the Escuelas Nacionales de Arte, now considered one of the forerunners of postmodernism and a masterpiece—the only masterpiece—of Cuban revolutionary architecture, is falling apart, transformed by permeating dampness and rampant jungle into what has been called "postmodernity's first ruins." An international group of architects tried to gain formal recognition of the complex's importance from UNESCO, but the Cuban government refused to support the initiative.

The 1950s with their rumba and *rompe y rasga* were an unacknowledged nostalgia in 1970, but today everyone admits that the Batista era was the golden age of Afro-Cuban music. The elderly performers who survived official indifference and prejudice during the harshest years of the Revolution now travel the world and perform before huge crowds.

The Soviet Union no longer exists. The outlaw dollar is now virtually the official currency of Cuba. The Habana Libre was bought by an international hotel chain. Tourism flourishes and along with it prostitution, whose abolition was one of the regime's most legitimate sources of pride. The wormlike former *gusanos* metamorphosed, according to a popular saying, into *mariposas,* or butterflies, and the dollars they send are the nation's primary source of income.

There have been other transformations. Some of the most fervent supporters of the Revolution have announced their disenchantment in recent weeks, driven to this step by a series of summary trials and executions, and by the infiltration and persecution of organizations in Havana that have struggled to establish a free press and a more flexible political system. The most recent crackdown was not markedly different from previous ones, but it did serve to underscore that, after all these decades, Fidel's revolution has failed tragically at its stated goals—greater social equality and better living conditions for all—while remaining hostile to the range of civil and individual rights even its sympathizers now demand.

The handsome Comandante en Jefe ages as the world looks on. And what some Cubans feel today is nostalgia for the hard years, when life was sometimes unbearably difficult and had meaning. There are many Cubans who believe, or fear, that when the Comandante en Jefe dies, even the memory of those times will disappear, but to me what seems most bizarre about the Cuba that Fidel will leave behind is its current status as a curio. The revolution that was supposed to modernize the world is now treasured as a timeless relic by tourists from a world all too horrifyingly modern.

I was forgetting to say that I still have Carlos's mother's earrings. I've never worn them, but every once in a while I take them out of their velvet pouch to admire them and remember the days I spent in Havana.

Acknowledgments

Many dear friends helped me throughout the process of giving a handful of fragile memories the shape of the present book. Above all, I wish to thank two people: my editor in shining armor, Robert Gottlieb, who patiently needled and coaxed me to write, and then agreed to my proposal that I write the original text in a language he could not read; and my translator, Esther Allen, who encouraged this mad idea from the first and then turned my stammering Spanish-language manuscript into an English text far more beautiful and assured than I could have written.

Without Marcela Fuentes-Berain's joyful stratagems, I could never have written the terrifying first sentence or, indeed, the first chapters. My assistant, Emilio Sánchez, excavated in libraries, turned up documents, wore out photocopying machines, and throughout remained his sunny-natured, loyal, and generous self. Words cannot express my gratitude to Gloria Loomis, friend first and always, agent only when required, who has put up with my kvetching for what must seem to her like an eternity by now. I cannot imagine writing anything at all without the invaluable commentary and support that Bob Silvers and John Bennet always provide.

At *The New Yorker,* my longtime home, David Remnick welcomed the idea of publishing much of the first chapter even though it was not, at first reading, an easy fit. John Bennet edited the text with his usual magic, Nandi Rodrigo kept it accurate, and Anne Goldstein made it shine.

Ginger Thompson, Gladys Boladeras, and Joe Lelyveld helped me find shelter in Mexico City. Once again, the Espinosa family and Percy and Nancy Woods did the same in San Cristóbal de las Casas. Arnoldo Kraus kept me healthy. Phil Bennett, Damian

Fraser, Pablo Ortiz Monasterio, and Luis Miguel Aguilar read a first version in Spanish, pointing out gaps and helping me firm up the text without drawing any blood at all. Iván Arango unfailingly came to my rescue. Carlos Tejeda, James David, Jorge Cavillo, and Walter González made me feel, at last, at home, giving me a place to set out from.

At Pantheon, I treasure the generous encouragement of Dan Frank and Janice Goldklang, and the wise support of Altie Karper. My gratitude goes also to Janet Biehl for her lovely craftsmanship. The MacArthur Foundation offered the dazzling support that first allowed me to start imagining this book.

I wish especially to thank the journalist Roberto Céspedes and two other Cubans whose friendship I now cherish—Ricardo Porro, master architect of the National Schools of Art, and the novelist José Manuel Prieto. Roberto read the manuscript for factual errors and then delved into further fact-checking and suggestions with a generosity that humbled me, and so, at a later stage, did José Manuel and maestro Porro. No personal commitment or prior obligation required them to do so—it's just that some Cubans are like that.